Parental School Choice in First Nations Communities

Evelyn Steinhauer

Parental School Choice in First Nations Communities

Is There Really a Choice?

VDM Verlag Dr. Müller

Imprint

Bibliographic information by the German National Library: The German National Library lists this publication at the German National Bibliography; detailed bibliographic information is available on the Internet at http://dnb.d-nb.de.
 Any brand names and product names mentioned in this book are subject to trademark, brand or patent protection and are trademarks or registered trademarks of their respective holders. The use of brand names, product names, common names, trade names, product descriptions etc. even without a particular marking in this works is in no way to be construed to mean that such names may be regarded as unrestricted in respect of trademark and brand protection legislation and could thus be used by anyone.

Cover image: www.purestockx.com

Publisher:
VDM Verlag Dr. Müller Aktiengesellschaft & Co. KG , Dudweiler Landstr. 125 a, 66123 Saarbrücken, Germany,
Phone +49 681 9100-698, Fax +49 681 9100-988,
Email: info@vdm-verlag.de

Zugl.: Edmonton, University of Alberta, Diss., 2007

Copyright © 2008 VDM Verlag Dr. Müller Aktiengesellschaft & Co. KG and licensors
All rights reserved. Saarbrücken 2008

Produced in USA and UK by:
Lightning Source Inc., La Vergne, Tennessee, USA
Lightning Source UK Ltd., Milton Keynes, UK
BookSurge LLC, 5341 Dorchester Road, Suite 16, North Charleston, SC 29418, USA

ISBN: 978-3-639-00484-7

Table of Contents

CHAPTER 1: INTRODUCTION TO THE STUDY 1
   Location of the Researcher 2
      Personal Introduction...2
      Family History..3
      Educational History 5
   Context, Purpose, and Significance of Study 10
      Context 10
      Purpose 11
      Significance 13
   Summary/Organization of the Chapters 14
   Definitional Aspects of the Work 15
      Delimitations and Limitations of the Study...15
      Definition of Terms 15

CHAPTER 2: LITERATURE REVIEW 17
   History of First Nations in Canada 17
      Legislation 18
      Royal Proclamation 18
      Indian Act 19
   Phases of First Nations Education in Canada 20
      Traditional Education 20
      Education by Missionaries 23
      Residential Schools 23
      Integrated Education..25
      Indian Control of Indian Education...26
   First Nations Schooling Today 27
   Parental School Choice in First Nations Communities 29
   Parental School Choice Within non–First Nations Communities 30
   Overview of the Literature...32

CHAPTER 3: INDIGENOUS RESEARCH METHODOLOGY 33
   Accepting the Responsibility of Conducting Research 35
   Indigenous Knowledge in Indigenous Research..37
   Indigenous Worldview...40
   Data-Collection Process...43
      Choosing a Method..43
      Interviews 44
      Storytelling 45
   Community Selection 46
      Saddle Lake Cree Nation...47
      Whitefish Lake (Goodfish Lake) First Nation...48
   Participant Selection 49
   Cultural Protocol..51
   Ethical Behavior 52

Trustworthiness 52
Analysis of the Data..53
Reporting the Findings 54
Presenting the Findings...54

CHAPTER 4: THE OFF-RESERVE SCHOOLING EXPERIENCE: FINDINGS....................55
Introduction..55
Unfair Treatment 58
    The Special-Needs Categorization 58
    The Blame-the-Native-Student Syndrome 61
    Time Spent in Detention...64
    Streaming Native Students...65
Low Teacher Expectations 68
Racism 72
    Internalized Racism..73
    Racism and Its Effect on Self-Esteem and Identity Development 76
Loss of Opportunity for Cultural Learnings 83
Concluding Reflections 85

CHAPTER 5: THE ON-RESERVE SCHOOLING EXPERIENCE: FINDINGS 88
The Challenges of Attending an On-Reserve School 89
    Curriculum and Teaching Concerns (Low Teacher Expectations) 89
    Safety and Discipline..95
The Positives of Attending an On-Reserve School 100
    Comfort and Familiarity 101
    Culture 103
    Language 105
    Prayer...106
Summary Statements 110

CHAPTER 6: THE SIGNIFICANCE OF RELATIONALITY, PARENTAL INVOLVEMENT,
AND NATIVE TEACHERS 112
Relationality..112
    Student-Teacher Relationships...113
    Peer Relationships 114
    Family Relationships 116
    Relationships to Place..117
Parental Involvement 120
    Defining Parental Involvement..122
    Challenges to Parental Involvement..125
    Differing Expectations Between Parents and Schools for School Involvement 128
    Educational Attainment Levels and the Impact on Parental Involvement 129
    Negative Schooling Experiences and Parental Involvement...................................130
    Social and Familial Issues and Parental Involvement 131
Native Teachers for Native Students 135
Retention of Aboriginal Teachers...136
Concluding Reflections 140

CHAPTER 7: DISCUSSION, SUMMARY, AND CONCLUSION 141
    Discussion of Findings 141
    School Choice Decisions and the Ideal School 141
    Characteristics of the Ideal School for Aboriginal Children 145
        Strong Leadership 145
        Unity of Purpose 146
        A Caring, Nurturing, and Safe Environment 147
        A Raised Bar 148
        A Native Teaching Staff 149
        A Curriculum That Embraces a Native Epistemology 150
    Conclusion 154

REFERENCES 157

APPENDIX: PARTICIPANTS' RECOMMENDATIONS FOR THE IDEAL SCHOOL 165

CHAPTER 1:
INTRODUCTION TO THE STUDY

Many students fail not because they do not have the ability to learn, but because the system has failed to teach them. (Watt-Cloutier, 2000, p. 123)

Like Watt-Cloutier (2000), I believe that Native children have the ability to learn within the current education system, and the fact that many do succeed in graduating from high school is evidence of that. However, many more Native students do not graduate from the schooling system. Although some slight increases in graduation rates have been noted over the past few years, "Native education has still not reached parity with non-Native education in Canada" (Tessier, 2003, p. 1), and predictions are that this will not happen anytime soon. This projection appears to be true in situations of schooling for First Nations children, whether these children are schooled on- or off-reserve. This work addresses the topic of parental school choice on First Nations reserves and looks at the factors that guide First Nations parents in their decisions to send their children to off- or on-reserve schools. For those parents who have a choice, what is the basis for their decision?

Watt-Cloutier (2000) held the system responsible for the disparity in graduation rates between non-Native and Native students. She looked back in history and concluded that, initially, and perhaps unintentionally, "assimilation attempts of the governments . . . did instill into us, some confidence that we could actually learn as well as the next person" (p. 115), but within the school systems today, this is no longer the case. Watt-Cloutier suggested that educators do not have much faith in Native students' success because they "challenge our youth so little that it undermines their intelligence" (p. 115). She explained her position:

> Academic standards and rigour have been lowered in the name of respect for the "different learning styles" of Aboriginal peoples. Certainly there are cultural differences and value systems that must be respected at every level. However, these kinds of generalizations must be used with caution. What follows the lowering of standards is the lowering of expectations of all involved . . . The low self-esteem we are living with today did not occur overnight, and we must work to rectify it in every possible way. I caution academics about being too quick to make assessments and generalizations in an area in which very few Aboriginal people have participated in the basic research about the learning styles of our people. (pp. 115-116)

Failure can mean different things to different people. Although I personally was fortunate in successfully 'making' it through the system and graduating with my peers, I believe that the schooling system failed me in a very significant area of my development as a human being: the area of cultural identity development. In looking back, I see a situation in which I was struggling to fit in when I should have been spending time learning within a comfortable and safe social environment. I remember the pervasive negative stereotypes that my non-Native student peers projected onto me and the ongoing psychological adjustments that I felt compelled to make in the way that I saw and felt about myself as a First Nations student in a school where Native children were in the minority. I lived in consistent and constant conflict between my own cultural values and those that prevailed in the schooling environment. As a six-year-old child, it was difficult for me to make sense of my own identity as a Cree person, a non-White person, especially when the messages I was receiving were "White is right," "White is superior," "White is the standard." From my perspective today, I see that these racially motivated descriptions of reality and identity became internalized within my psyche as a child, resulting in many years of personal struggle as a young adult to overcome feelings of self-loathing.

Location of the Researcher

Personal Introduction

I want to share my own story as an introduction to the research topic of this study because I believe that it will help the reader to understand the necessary connections between my own life and experiences, the lives and experiences of my family, and this particular research focus or topic. The notion that research by Indigenous researchers is motivated to a very large degree by the needs of their own communities and extended families is not new; it is evident both in traditional teachings and in the recent writings of Indigenous scholars (Absolon & Willett, 2005; Kovach, 2005; Potts & Brown, 2005; Strega, 2005), and my own decision to conduct this study certainly falls within this description. Within this work generally, I will share stories from the participants whom I interviewed as well as my own stories, and the literature and other references will be woven throughout the content of these stories in ways that will exemplify and enhance the teachings that are intended to flow through them.

As a personal introduction to this work, I will share a story about a little girl who is leaving her home on a First Nations reserve and heading off to her first day of school, off the reserve. Although not likely to be obvious on first reading, this story contains most, if not all, of the elements that the research participants brought forward and/or highlighted in their discussions of parental choice for First Nations parents on First Nations reserves.

Once upon a time . . . *"I can't wait!" "I can't wait!" This was all her mother heard for several days before school started, and then it was finally here—the first day of school! Ever since her brother started going two years ago, she longed for this experience. She wanted to be a big girl going to the big school. She spent much time daydreaming about the fun she would have and thinking about the numerous friends she would make. She would learn to read and write, and as soon as she could do that, she was going to read bedtime stories to her sister and baby brother!*

Today she awoke very early, unable to sleep another wink. She had carefully laid out her new clothes by her bedside the night before and thought about how beautiful her new outfit would look on her. At the crack of daylight she jumped out of bed and into her new clothes, admiring herself in the tiny mirror that hung over the dresser. She was beautiful, and she was sure that her new friends would think so too. They would probably ask her where she bought her nice black shoes, and she would tell them.

By the time her mom awoke, she was already dressed, washed, and ready go. She nibbled on her cereal and watched the clock in anticipation. Finally, it was time for her and her brother to leave. She giggled as the big yellow bus approached. "This is going to be the best day of my life," she thought as she climbed aboard.

The school doors looked so huge, but she was not scared because she was a big girl now, and today she was going to make some new friends—little girls who would become her best friends. Immediately, her eyes set in on two pretty little girls with beautiful bows in their hair. The girls seemed to be having such a good time. They were smiling and obviously enjoying each other's company. She walked up to them slowly, smiled her biggest smile, but they didn't smile back.

All of the children who moments ago were having such a good time dropped whatever they were doing and fell silent. They stood very still, and they just watched as the children from her bus walked by. There was not a sound, not a smile, not a nod; there was nothing. . . . And then it started—roars of laughter, followed by some ugly words. These words hurt, and she could feel them settling in the pit of her stomach. Tears blurred her eyes, but she was not going to cry.

Why are they laughing? What are they saying? Are they laughing at us? Are they laughing at me? How can they be laughing at me? Look at me, look at how nice I look, look at my nice new shiny shoes! Are they laughing at me?

This is the story of my first day in school, and, in the context of this work, I hope that it will clarify for the reader where I am situated as the researcher in terms of personal history and social context. Within the Cree culture in which I grew up, I expect to provide or be asked for certain and specific types of information when I am introduced to someone whom I have not met before and with whom I am likely to have further connections. The first thing they want to know about me is where I am from: What community are you from? Who are your parents, grandparents, relatives? Knowing this information, new acquaintances are usually able to connect me with family and relatives. Although not often explicitly mentioned, they may make further connections of a political, cultural, and/or social nature. These exchanges of personal histories and information are statements and guides of commitment towards the establishment of a new relationship, and both parties interpret and act upon them as such. Wilson (2003) talked about this sharing of information in terms of "strengthening new relationship":

> One thing that I have noticed of Indigenous people everywhere . . . is that they ask a new acquaintance where they are from. From this information, an exchange takes place of "do you know . . . ?" or "are you related to . . . ?" or "do you know where . . . is?" Or "I was . . . there three years ago." The person is put into relationships through mutual friends, or even through certain landmarks, places or events. Shared relationships allow for a strengthening of the new relationships. This allows you to become familiar or comfortable with the person. Getting to know their relationships to other people or space is an appropriate way of finding out about them. (p. 163)

Because of the significance of this practice in expressing mutual respect, I have decided to include my family history as a part of my personal introduction as the researcher in this work. My lived experiences and my ongoing relationships with family, ancestors, community, place, space, and territory have shaped my identity. My past is important because it reinforces and contributes to the person I am and will continue to become.

Family History

My name is Evelyn Louise Steinhauer, and I am a member of the Saddle Lake Cree Nation. My parents are the late Archie Steinhauer and Nancy Steinhauer (née Whitford). Legally, I am recognized as a Cree person, but my ancestry is mixed because my mother is Métis. My maternal grandmother, the late Alice Whitford (née Bull), is Cree; and my maternal grandfather,

Steve Whitford (Koroluk), is Ukrainian. My paternal grandparents were the late Augustine Steinhauer and the late Sarah Steinhauer (née Pruden). My maternal grandfather, who celebrated his 100th birthday on August 10, 2007, is my last surviving grandparent.

On my father's side, my ancestry can be traced back to Henry Bird Steinhauer, a Methodist minister, school teacher, and Native leader. Henry Bird Steinhauer, or Shahwahnegezhik Kachenooting, as he was originally named, was born in 1818 to Bigwind and Mary Kachenooting. An American benefactor from Philadelphia took interest in Shahwahnegezhik when he was still a very young man and offered his family an opportunity to have their son educated in the "White way." In exchange for this education and financial support for their son, Shahwahnegezhik Kachenooting's parents agreed that their son would assume the Steinhauer name, and he thus became Henry Bird Steinhauer.

Steinhauer attended a number of schools, including the prestigious Upper Canada Academy from which he graduated at the head of his class in 1839. His education was interrupted a couple of times by teaching jobs, but eventually he completed his theological studies and began missionary work in 1840. He met Jessie Joyful (Seeseeb Mamanuwartum), and they were married on August 5, 1846. Together they had five daughters and five sons. In 1854 Henry Bird Steinhauer went to England with Egerton Ryerson[1] (Britannica Online, 2007) to raise awareness of Western missionary work. He returned the following year to begin his missionary work at Lac La Biche, Alberta, and later at Whitefish Lake, Alberta, where he lived until his death in 1884 (Steinhauer, 2003).

On my mother's side I have been able to trace my ancestry back to only my grandfather, Steve Whitford, born Steve Koroluk in 1907. His story has been recorded in Balan's[2] (1984) *Salt and Braided Bread: Ukrainian Life in Canada* and is as follows:

> *The unusual story of one Alberta pioneer family reveals how misfortune could change the people's lives in the most dramatic and unforeseen ways. . . . A Ukrainian farmer near Andrew lost his wife when she was giving birth to their sixth child, a baby boy. The blow was especially severe because the winter had been long and difficult, and the family was reduced to eating a thin gruel made of wheat. A week after the woman's death, the husband was working outside . . . when he heard a gunshot from a remote corner of the land. Investigating, he came across a hunting party of Cree Indians, one of whom spoke Ukrainian. The two men began talking, and the farmer explained the unfortunate situation that he and his children found themselves in. When the Indian asked why he did not hunt to supplement their meager diet, since game was plentiful in the area, the farmer replied that he was so poor he did not even own a gun. They continued talking, and after a while the farmer made a desperate proposition. Realizing that the newborn would probably die without a mother, he suggested that the Indians take the baby with them in exchange for one of their guns. The oldest children would remain with their father, as they could look after each other and also be of help to him.*
>
> *Sympathetic to the man's plight, the hunters agreed and took the week-old child with them to be raised by the women of the Goodfish Lake Reserve northeast of Vilna. By*

---

[1] Egerton Ryerson (1803-1882) was a Canadian provincial educator and Methodist church leader who founded the public education system of what is now the province of Ontario (Britannica Online, 2007).

[2] Jars Balan is widely known as an author and editor. In addition to the abovementioned book, he has edited numerous books and periodicals dealing with Ukrainian Canadian themes and produced scholarly and popular articles on a broad range of Ukrainian Canadian topics over the years (Balan, 1984).

> *the time the father tried to persuade him to rejoin the family near Andrew, the boy—now named Steve Whitford—had become so accustomed to his adopted lifestyle and people that he refused to go, and answered in Cree, "I'm an Indian." Whitford eventually became one of the most respected members of the Goodfish Lake community in which he married, living outside the perimeter of the reserve (since he was never legally recognized as an Indian).* (p. 116)

A cornerstone of Cree culture can be summed up in the words *family, kinship,* and *place*: "Family is the backbone, the foundation of our culture. We are given substance, nurtured, and sustained by family. Kinship goes beyond family and is the connection we feel to the world at large and everything in it" (Marshall, 2001, p. 210). Within this same worldview or knowledge framework lie the responses that each of the participants in this study has shared. The stories and the thinking that is reflected in each story must be interpreted within this context while at the same time understood in relation to contemporary notions of schooling and education.

Educational History

Although I have lived all of my life on a First Nations reserve, I received all of my formal schooling within a public (provincial) school system located off-reserve. It is this schooling experience that has contributed in significant ways to shaping the person I am today. I have always struggled with different aspects of my identity, and I think that it would be accurate to say that, until recently, I have never been totally comfortable "in my own skin."

From that very first day when I set foot in the public school, I knew that I was different. At first I did not quite know why, but over the years it became very clear to me that being born an "Indian" was a curse. Textbooks affirmed that Indian people were mere hindrances in the development of Canada. Sometimes I would read about the "noble savages" who helped the pioneers set up homelands in the vast, empty wilderness, and at those times I would feel grateful that there were a few good Indians. But most of the time I was reading about the uncivilized, backward Indians who really had no place in this "new" world. In those books I was introduced to the "hostile savages" who needed to be subdued, the childlike creatures who needed constant direction and protection, and the ungrateful beings who never showed gratitude for being rescued.

In the news and media I saw drunken, violent, disheveled Indians who deserved to be treated like animals. I lived in constant embarrassment, and during the times that we were learning about the history of Canada, if we happened to come across stories about Indians, I would hold my head down and avert any eye contact with my peers or the teacher. I would sit in humiliation, hoping that I would not be singled out. I knew that if I was called upon to speak, it would only confirm what they already knew—that Indians were dumb, lazy, uncivilized, senseless people who were incapable of learning (Binda & Calliou, 2001; Bruno, 2003; Calliou, 1995; Mackay & Myles, 1995).

It was through this process of invalidation and debasement, of wiping out my presence in the textbooks and in the classroom, of making me invisible that the system failed me. Without any validation or positive recognition of my individual being, all other aspects of my schooling were affected. I did not do as well as my peers, and I realize now that much of this might have been due to my own lack of participation. But how could I participate when I believed that I had nothing to offer? How could I be part of a group when I was so different, when my English was weak and my vocabulary was limited, and when everything that came out of my mouth sounded so stupid?

I believe that this lack of participation in class limited me even further. I was always the last person to be picked for any of the teams, and I was never (not even once) invited to any of the birthday parties. Being ostracized for most of my elementary years meant that any good feelings that I had had about myself before I started school were almost totally diminished during those years; my spirit was crushed. School was something that I had to endure; it was not a place I wanted to be. My parents wanted me to be there, and I knew I had to please them. Growing up with traditional Cree values, I was taught that I must obey and respect my parents, that I should never talk back, and, most important, that I should not bring shame to my family. If I failed in school, I knew that I would be defying everything that I had been taught at home, so I did everything in my power to forge ahead in/through a system that caused me so much pain.

A few of the participants in Breen's (2003) research suggested that "some students may find school to be their 'refuge,' their lifeline for survival, and the only hope for their future" (p. 138). One participant in my study seemed to concur with those in Breen's research: "A lot of kids depend on our hot lunch program here. They eat, because they get breakfast and lunch." Some of these children, she indicated further, are hungry not only for food, but also for structure and maybe "normalcy, if you can call it that." She indicated that these children view school as a safe haven and perhaps even see school as a way of "escaping the woundedness that exists in their families."

I am certainly aware from my own observations and experiences that some children do find a form of refuge within the school environment. However, in my case, school was something that I had to endure because I knew that obtaining an education was important to my father. Home was my refuge. This was where I could just be me, where I could wear my hair in braids and run around barefoot. It was where I did not have to worry about sounding too "Indian," and it was a place where I was free to laugh out loud. To survive in both worlds of home and school, I quickly learned to become two different people—a carefree little Indian girl at home and a "brown skinned, wanna-be White kid at school." I was confused about my cultural identity.[3] I carried questions of deep anguish and despair for a young child; there was no one to whom I could turn for answers: Why did I have to be born an Indian? Why did I have to be so ashamed of my heritage when my father and other community members seemed to embrace theirs? Breen (2003) explained that a "consolidated cultural identity exists when there is consistency among the components; a confused identity is present when there is inconsistency or uncertainty" (p. 6). It was unfortunate that I had to endure such inconsistencies and that my true self had to be turned off when I walked through the front doors of the school, but this was my reality at that time.

Looking back now, I recognize the fact that it was a point of survival when I graduated from my primary and secondary school experiences. Racism and discrimination were prevalent in the school, but no one, to my knowledge, ever acknowledged that the phenomena existed. In fact, racism and discrimination were denied. It was not uncommon for my peers, the other students, to snicker and call me "squaw" as I walked past them in the hallway. Their words were piercing and left me feeling dirty and ashamed. On a few occasions when I reported these incidents to the teachers and administrators, their responses would be simply, "Oh, that's okay;

---

[3] *Cultural identity* is "is the (feeling of) identity of a group or culture, or of an individual as far as he is influenced by his belonging to a group or culture" (Wikipedia, 2007, ¶ 1).

they didn't really mean it"; and this only served to reinforce the feelings of shame that I already carried deep within my heart.

Remarks such as these, especially made by a person in a position of authority and whom we trust for protection and safety, only help to inculcate in Native children the "idea that they are out of step with the rest of the world that they have no friends; and that their feelings of resentment and resistance are foolish and, far from being justified, simply prove just how savage and ignorant they must be" (Daes, 2000, p. 7). Racism does exist within school systems, and there is substantial research that points to the fact that many minority students are subjected to different forms of it on a daily and consistent basis (Calliou, 1995; Makokis, 2000; St. Denis & Hampton, 2002; Steinhauer, 1999). Whoever coined the phrase "Sticks and stones can break my bones, but words can never harm me" obviously never had to endure the racism that most Aboriginal students have. I learned that if I were to survive in the world that existed outside of my home, I would just have to accept racism, rejection, discrimination, and unfair treatment as a part of life. This learning was part of my survival tool.

The feelings that I had as a child in school led me to judge myself very harshly and negatively and to believe that I would never be as good as my non-Native peers. Breen (2003), referring to the work of Delgado (1997), said that feelings such as these lead Native youth to "conscious and subconscious beliefs of powerlessness and oppression" (p. 137). Daes (2000) pointed out, "The experience of oppression is spiritual death" (p. 5), and other researchers (Calliou, 1995; Daes, 2000; Makokis, 2000; St. Denis & Hampton, 2002; Steinhauer, 1999) have taken this further by suggesting that many Native children have learned to survive in this way because they feel helpless and powerless. Calliou saw it as a reality, but it should not have to be so because racism can be "physically, emotionally, psychologically, and spiritually draining to both sender and receiver" (p. 57). She added:

> Racism must be named, and teachers must know that in so doing emotions will emerge from the underground of denial within individuals, lunch rooms, classrooms, textbooks, media, or schoolgrounds. These events can provide the occasion for lessons to unlock the cycle of denial and begin the dialogue to generate awareness. (p. 58)

My own feelings of powerlessness as a student in school followed me through to adulthood, and if I were to pinpoint a time when I started to feel more confident, I would have to say it was during my first year in graduate studies at the University of Alberta. It was at this time that I began to reevaluate and reflect on all of my earlier life experiences. It was the beginning of my healing journey. It was then that I began to embrace my "Indianness." It was a humbling experience to learn that the people who were in the First Nations education graduate specialization, both students and professors, were embracing Indigenous knowledge and Indigenous ways of knowing. For the first time in my life I began to feel comfortable "in my own skin." I understood fully the words of Daes (2000): "The experience [was] like stepping into the sunshine after years of sitting in a darkened room. . . . The sunshine wipes away the dark loneliness" (p. 8).

I had always known that our Cree ways of knowing and being were useful to Native people, but because of my earlier schooling experiences, I had never considered that this knowledge might be useful in a formal educational setting. During my master's program I came to realize the significance and possibilities of Indigenous people like myself engaging in dialogue at higher levels of study at universities, creating our own "intellectual, theoretical, and epistemological spaces" (Cohen, 2001, p. 140; Battiste, 2002; Cajete, 2000a; Ermine, 1995;

Meyer, 1998). I had come to believe that there was no place in academia to be "Indian," but my experiences in graduate studies were proving this perception to be wrong. In the First Nations education specialization, I was encouraged to embrace my Aboriginal Cree knowledge and to turn to and rely upon my own traditional teachers. I came to realize that the traditional teachings with which I had grown up, including the empirical knowledge that I had gained over the years, the revelations, dreams, and intuitions that had always guided my actions, were in fact the primary and valid ways of my own knowing, doing, and being; the validation of this knowledge that I already knew was elating and freeing for me. Finally, it was acceptable to say, "There are other valid ways of 'seeing' and understanding the world beside those of the dominant West" (Sefa Dei, Hall, & Goldin Rosenberg, 2000, p. 16). Steinhauer (2001) summed up my feelings well when, during her candidacy exam, she exclaimed, "I never thought I was coming here to learn to be Indian. My Indianness is now solidified with complete confidence" (p. 2).

Acknowledging my "Indianness" was so exhilarating that I wondered why my parents had never encouraged me to be an Indian before. They must have known that I was ashamed of being an Indian, but they never said anything. As a child, I often wondered why my parents chose to send my siblings and me off-reserve for our schooling, but I never asked why. This question continued to plague me, and although I did ask my mother one day, she could not provide an answer. All she could say was that this is what my father wanted. My father, who was adamant about his children receiving an education, passed away when I was only 12 years old, and I never did have the chance to ask him that question. At times over the years I would be angry with him, and I would ask, "Dad, if you loved me so much, why did you put me through all this pain? Why did you allow them to treat me so badly?" Of course, he could not answer me; I knew that. But I had hoped that I would receive some kind of sign that he had heard me or that he would come to me in a dream. Then one day an answer did come—in August 2006 at our annual Indigenous Peoples Education program retreat. My journal entry of that day reads as follows:

> *It was a very good day today, but emotionally, I am exhausted. The whole group was sitting in a talking circle[4] when the male Elder looked at me and said, "In the mid-1960s, your father used to talk about the concerns he had about the curriculum and the schooling system of those days, and he worried that the needs of the Native children were not being met." His words caught me off guard. I did not know this about my father! This was all news to me! He had been gone since 1972, and people had long since stopped talking about him, but today I learned something new about him. I realized that his passion about education stretched beyond his own family and into the community. I felt a sense of pride, and I listened to the Elder speak about him. I left the circle thinking about my father. "I wish I would have known more about my father. I wonder what our lives would have been like had he not passed away. What would he have done to address his concerns about First Nations education?" These and many more questions played over and over again in my mind, and then the answer came to me; not in a dream as I expected, but the answer merely just popped in my head. It was like someone was talking*

---

[4] A *talking circle* is a method used by a group to discuss a topic (or various topics) in an egalitarian and nonconfrontational manner. The group members sit in a circle and comment on the topic of discussion. Each person in the circle is given the opportunity to speak in turn. Normally, the speaker holds a talking stick, stone, or other object as he/she speaks and passes it to the next person when he/she is finished speaking. Unlike standard meeting formats, in an effective talking circle other participants do not interrupt speakers under any circumstances.

to me, and I heard, "You needed to travel down the path you did. You needed to have the experiences that you did, so that you could finish your father's work. Your father didn't know you would do this, but long before you were born, the plan was already made."

I realized then that this was why I had gone to graduate school. By having the experiences that I did in school, it would build in me the desire to learn and understand more, thus leading me down the path of academia. When I realized this, the tears would not stop. I cried and cried, and I finally understood what my grandmother meant when she would tell us in Cree, "God has a plan for each one of us." This was God's plan for me, and my father was instrumental in moving that plan forward. What an exciting revelation! I wish I would have known this before I had my own children, but I guess it was not supposed to be.

As an adult with my own children, I made the same decision that my father did in sending my children off-reserve for their schooling, and they were schooled in the same school that I had been. As I recall now, however, I do not think I gave the decision much thought. This was the school that my siblings and I had attended, and this was where my children would go as well. As I reflect back, I wonder if, subconsciously, there was more to my thinking than that. Perhaps, like so many other Native parents, I had thought that my children would receive a better education in the provincial school system. Was this thinking a prime example of my own internalized racism? Was my decision an outcome of an ingrained notion that "White is better"? These questions point to an issue that needs lengthy and careful reflection, one that I am committed to continue exploring.

Today, at rates even higher than ever before, First Nations parents who are living on reserves are making the decision to send their children off-reserve to nearby provincial schools. In his study, Breen (2003) found that many parents in the communities in which he worked were making this decision because they honestly believed that the off-reserve schools were better for their children. One of his respondent's comments clearly suggested this:

> I don't think that the parents have much faith in the school system here [on-reserve school], and I think some of them want their children to have a better education, and they feel they can get it in a more urban centre. (p. 72)

Another of his participants, in talking about the provincial school system, asked, "Which system is going to get them to university? How many kids do you see in the last ten years going to university from this [on-reserve school] system?" (p. 72).

It would be difficult, and perhaps unfair, to lay blame on any one person or group for the low self-esteem and the feelings of powerlessness that I endured during my primary and secondary school years. Certainly a common argument to explain such circumstances and behavior is that all parties involved were doing the best that they could with what they knew. This does not negate or address the negative or destructive effects of such practices and beliefs on Native students.

Historically, and probably until the mid-20th century, Native parents had no choice about whether and/or where their children would be schooled. However, today First Nations parents do have some choice, at least in relation to where their children will be schooled. In this introduction to the study, I have shared some of my personal background as a way of situating myself within the context of this research effort to produce a deeper understanding of parental school choice for First Nations parents who are living on reserves.

Context, Purpose, and Significance of Study

Context

"Indian education in Canada is a very complex and intriguing subject" (Diamond, 1989, p. 86) and has been a topic of discussion since the time of Europeans' arrival on the shores of Turtle Island. Many practices and policies have been implemented, first by the early settler societies, and later by the European-patterned forms of Canadian governments in an effort to civilize or assimilate the Indians through improved Indian education. Through this history and into the present, the attrition rate for Aboriginal students has remained very high for all types and at all levels of education (Breen, 2003; Curwen Doige, 2003; Kirkness, 1999). Today, Aboriginal students continue to leave school before high school graduation at a higher rate than that of non-Aboriginal youth (Brady, 1995; Royal Commission on Aboriginal Peoples [RCAP], 1996), and the "reality is that fewer than 40% (at best) of all First Nations students are graduating from school anywhere in Canada" (Breaker & Kawaguchi, 2002, (p. 14). Of these graduates, only about 9% will enter university and only 3% will complete their university programs compared to 14% of other Canadians (Alberta Learning, 2002).

Many initiatives have been undertaken in Alberta and throughout Canada to improve these statistics. Some of these Native education efforts of school systems, higher education institutions, and government have included specific organizational objectives aimed at hiring Aboriginal teachers and "paraprofessional" Native liaison officers, the development and promotion of Indian teacher education programs, and formal reviews and recommendations related to existing Native education policies. Wotherspoon and Satzewich (2000) spoke to the impact of these efforts: "Regardless of positive efforts taken . . . to meet Native students' needs and to attract and retain teachers of Aboriginal origin, there remains within the structure . . . serious inadequacies for Aboriginal children" (p. 137). Although some types of improvements have been recorded in Aboriginal education since the introduction of the Indian Control of Indian Education policy (National Indian Brotherhood [NIB], 1972), the schooling success of Aboriginal learners remains low. The federal government continues to dictate, both directly and indirectly, most aspects of Native education for First Nations communities engaged in on-reserve schooling. This firm control is maintained through budget and financial regulations and limitations and formally structured program and curriculum policies that tie First Nations schooling directly to provincially controlled and administered forms of educational programming. The opportunities for First Nations to actually develop their own systems and forms of education for their own people is not a reality, even for those communities (reserves) that are offering on-reserve schooling. These concerns are reflected in many of the comments of the participants because they are foundational, albeit often invisible, elements in the determination of the school choices of First Nations parents who are living on reserves. Researchers and educators in the field of Aboriginal education have been saying that Aboriginal people need to take control of their children's education and that government control of these efforts has to stop (Chisan, 2001; Jules, 1999; Makokis, 2000; Wotherspoon & Satzewich, 2000).

Earlier studies by Aboriginal researchers such as Kirkness (1999) indicate that First Nations peoples need to evaluate the education that they are providing to their communities. She felt that "high-powered, high-priced consultants who know nothing about our communities" should be kept out of this process because, in the past, "what was recommended did not resemble anything that was said, . . . and the evaluators had a blueprint solution for Aboriginal education that was not necessarily valid for all communities" (p. 27). Kirkness's points continue to be relevant in today's context. For example, the "positive efforts" that Wotherspoon and Satzewich (2000) described may not, in fact, be so described from the perspectives of Aboriginal parents, educators, community leaders, and/or traditional teachers and Elders. Then again, those perspectives may depend upon location and other circumstances such as availability of financial and human resources. Whichever way these statements may be viewed, it is commonly accepted in Aboriginal communities such as those represented in this study that the views of most of these direct beneficiaries of such "positive efforts" in Aboriginal education are rarely, if ever, made known in the formal arena of contemporary education. Despite the fact that at least two formal reviews of Native or Aboriginal education in Alberta over the past decade have quoted Aboriginal people's recommendations, educational practices and policies and statistics of success for Aboriginal students continue to carry forward the same story, denying the same charges, reframing the same challenges, and promising the same ends. The narratives and commentaries in the later chapters of this work support this claim.

Aboriginal educators have stated clearly that joint collaboration amongst their own people (mothers, fathers, grandparents, high school and postsecondary students, members of school boards, and band councils) has to occur if Aboriginal people are to find ways of improving high school graduation rates for their children (Alfred, 1999; Battiste, 2000; Kirkness, 1999). Decisions about the kind of education that we want for our children should be based on our own "community's philosophy, goals, and objectives" (Kirkness, 1999, p. 28), because no two communities are exactly alike in this respect. Kirkness contended that Aboriginal scholars need to become more involved and community members need to start taking an active role in required educational research that, until now, has been carried out primarily by "outsiders" to the communities. Along with many other Aboriginal researchers and educators, she emphasized that it is through the means of our own pedagogical, methodological, and theoretical frameworks that answers to our issues need to be sought.

In going to the root of our issues as Aboriginal peoples, we will be forced to look at concerns such as racism and oppression. These are topics often skirted or totally omitted in mainstream education research and literature because they are unpleasant to speak about and can easily cause hurt and discomfort. Native people often speak about the importance of meeting the mental, spiritual, emotional, and physical needs of our children and assert that our children are our future. When racism and oppression are a part of the daily experiences of our children, we cannot avoid addressing them. When we face the suffering of our own children because of racism, we will be better able to deal with the discomfort of the educator and the administrator who chooses to deny such racism and oppression within the social environment that he or she manages. These are hard tasks and responsibilities that Aboriginal parents themselves will often avoid or not be aware of for a multitude of reasons, historical, social, political, and psychological. In general and too often, the talk that addresses these issues does not get acted upon (Battiste, 2002; Goddard, 2002; Makokis, 2000).

Purpose

I conducted this study in an effort to contextualize the multiple and complex issues that shape the schooling experiences of First Nations children. By focusing on one prevalent and foundational aspect of First Nations schooling in Canada—parental school choice—I hoped that many of these issues would be revealed. While I was carrying out the work, they were revealed, and in the following chapters I will discuss these issues in some detail.

In this study I worked primarily with two First Nations communities in an attempt to identify the factors that parents from these communities consider when they are making school choices for their children. The choices available to the parents in this particular study are basically between the off-reserve public school, the provincially funded school, and the on-reserve Indian Affairs federally funded school. All of the parents interviewed had these options in school choices open to them because both communities have on-reserve schools within their communities as well. This is not always the case for First Nations communities.

As background for this study and these communities, the Director of Education and a school board member estimated that approximately 75%-80% of all school age children from these two communities attend schools off-reserve. As little as 20 years ago, approximately 50% of all on-reserve school-age children from within these communities attended the band-operated First Nations schools, but there has been a steady decline in these numbers. With millions of dollars being spent on the operation of First Nations band-operated schools, and with numbers declining at such a rapid rate, community leaders and federal government officials are beginning to question the feasibility of keeping these schools open in some locations.

At a band[5] meeting on March 8, 2005, in one of the communities that I studied, a leader asked, "What will it take to bring our children home?" Communities want answers, and Jules (1999) suggested that "Native people must provide the answers" (p. 42). He added, "The answers must come from we who understand the problem best, we who have been there" (p. 42). But before implementing any changes (possibly forced changes), the leadership needs to know why First Nations parents are making the choices that they do. It is my intention that this study will provide some of the answers that our communities are seeking and serve as a resource as First Nations leadership plans for the future education of First Nations children.

By interviewing two sets of parents—those who send their children to off-reserve schools and those who send their children to on-reserve schools—about their school choices, I am able to present a clearer picture about the bases for these decisions. I have a much clearer picture of parents' expectations and desires for the education of their children and a better understanding of what they believe is the significance of schooling and education in general. The interviews revealed that school choice decisions should not be taken lightly and that parents are generally aware of the consequences of their decisions.

I hoped that this study would result in more dialogue in my community, and it has. Wherever I go, whenever I talk about school choice in First Nations communities, interest is sparked. Everyone wants to talk about the rationale and implications of these choices, and they are always eager to share their own experiences. Everyone recognizes that the current educational system, whether on-reserve or off-reserve, is not meeting the needs of our children, and they all have their own ideas about what an ideal school system should look like. Those who participated in this study were no exception. After revealing the pros and cons of attending school off-reserve and on-reserve, they all concluded that the development of a community-based model of education is a fundamental responsibility and requirement for which they as parents need to be accountable.

Not only has this work elaborated upon the context of parental school choice for First Nations parents who are living on two reserves in Alberta, it also has the potential to deepen and broaden public understanding about school choices being made in First Nations communities. This is significant because there is a huge gap in the available information on First Nations band-

---

[5] A *band* is "a body of Indians as defined in the Indian Act" (Indian and Northern Affairs Canada, 2005); it is also referred to as a First Nation.

operated or band-controlled schools and how and why First Nations parents make the choices they do, especially in the context of the racism and other issues that parents and First Nations people often identify in talking about their relationships with non-Aboriginal systems, institutions, and service agencies that are often located in nearby towns and larger urban centers. They do not easily understand or articulate the bases and nature of these relationships, and yet, at the level of schooling, they are being acted upon and played out daily in that persons of authority and power are interacting with a vulnerable and powerless population in a setting of coerced relations.

The First Nations parents who participated in this study made their school choice decisions based on what they thought would be best for their children, and they presented their views from the position of caring parents. As will be shown in their comments and stories, they ended up identifying and dealing with significant consequences for every school choice decision that they made. The participants revealed that the process of decision making for their school choices has led inevitably to a situation in which they had to give up something significant to receive something else that they valued for their children. They made decisions based on the long-term decisions that, at times, seemed to directly contradict their claims that they wanted only what was best for their children. The complexities that surround the positions of these parents would dishearten and discourage any parent who wanted to engage meaningfully with the education or schooling of his/her children. That these parents found the strength and endurance to stay engaged with their children and with the schools (note that these are two separate situations) is a statement of their courage and a demonstration of the power that they gained through enduring their own schooling experiences. This work discloses pertinent and significant information about the educational journeys of two generations of Aboriginal students in both off-reserve and on-reserve schooling situations. It also tells the stories of the personal impact of two generations' parental school choices and reveals the perspectives and learning of one generation as a result of the choices of the earlier generation of their parents. A major element in the overall significance of this work lies in the type of self-analysis in which the participants engaged as they shared openly and willingly with me their own experiences as students and their children's experiences that resulted from their parents' and their own decision making in relation to school choices.

Significance

I hope that this work will constitute a significant contribution to scholarly research and the community practice of First Nations education. With its focus on parents' rationale for choosing between on-reserve and off-reserve schools, it will contribute to the literature on Indigenous education in an area that has hitherto been largely ignored. Except for oblique references found in federal and First Nations reports, the significance of this factor in First Nations schooling has not been directly addressed from any perspective or from within any educational or other context.

Although researchers have confirmed that Native education is a complex and multifaceted issue and that many factors have been identified as contributing to the high dropout rate or the low achievement and completion rates of Aboriginal students, no studies have directly addressed the impact that school choice decisions have had on the school dropout or school 'failure' challenge.

Parental school choice can be a critical factor in the integrity and endurance of First Nations education. This study works toward a deeper understanding for all educators of the relationship between parental choice, student identity, and student achievement as they pertain to First Nations communities. The insights and knowledge gained from, through, and with the participants in this facilitated process of critical analysis can be and are easily transferable to policies and practices relating to both on-reserve and off-reserve educational programs. For on-reserve situations, these policies and practices can easily include or cross over into the areas of health, economics, self-government, and new programs and services.

The nonstructured interview process and informal dialogue worked well because I chose to interview persons with whom I already had some form of past relationship. Because we had a sense of mutual trust prior to the interviews, the participants entered into the process with openness and gained and helped to create deeper understanding of the educational issues that challenge them as parents and their own children as students. As the participants told me their stories, the inevitable process of self-observation, listening to themselves, and analyzing their own words led naturally to a more critical awareness of the issues surrounding their own decisions related to parental school choices. This research study provided an opportunity for me as the researcher to facilitate a process that allowed parents to share their own and their children's stories. Through this sharing, the parents became involved in the critical analysis, not only of their school choices as parents, but also of their own political and economic involvement in their communities and their own and their children's well-being and identity-formation processes, as well as how all of these were directly connected to the schools they attended and their experiences in these schools. The parents' realization that, in fact, their situation did not portray any real 'school choice' is a significant outcome of the research process.

Summary/Organization of the Chapters

This chapter has introduced the study, described its purpose and significance, outlined the design of the research, and defined its delimitations and limitation. It is also in this chapter where I located myself as the researcher.

The Chapter 2 literature review describes the history of First Nations in Canada and discusses the phases of Native education. It also includes a brief overview of the topic of school choice as it relates to the non-First Nations population.

Chapter 3 describes in detail the methodology that I used in conducting this research. Using an Indigenous research methodology was important to me, and here the reader will learn why.

Chapters 4 and 5 report the results of the analysis of the interview data. Chapter 4 presents the challenges of off-reserve schooling and Chapter 5, the challenges of on-reserve schooling. In each of these chapters, the participants' voices will be heard. My personal stories and relevant literature have been interwoven in these chapters as well.

Three main themes emerged as a result of the discussions in Chapters 4 and 5, and Chapter 6 focuses on these themes of relationship building, parental involvement, and Native teacher presence. Chapter 7 includes the final discussions, the summary, and the concluding statements.

Definitional Aspects of the Work

Delimitations and Limitations of the Study

My study examined how parents within two Northern Alberta First Nations communities choose the schools to which they will send their children when they have the option of on-reserve schools or off-reserve provincial schools that have been designated for their use. Therefore, this study was delimited by location to those two Cree communities in Northern Alberta. The study was limited by the numbers of interviewees who participated because I did not have the time or resources to interview all members of each community. The two reserves are very different in size, and I took this into consideration in deciding how many community members from each reserve I would interview.

A concern for me throughout the study was whether or not I was fully capturing my participants' perspectives. Sometimes this concern surfaced when they spoke Cree only, but most of the time I was concerned only about interpreting their thoughts. Although I consider myself a fluent Cree speaker and I have a good grasp of the English language, I was still concerned. Was I interpreting what they were telling me correctly? Denzin and Lincoln (2000) provided some comfort when they stated that "there is no single interpretive truth" (p. 23). Ellis (1998) concurred and added, "Sometimes new researchers feel uncomfortable about the idea that their interpretations can count as knowledge. The prospect of this responsibility raises concerns about relativism since each person perceives differently" (p. 8). She concluded, however, that each person "has a consciousness open to a reality shared in a community," but that "a person's interpretations will rarely be bizarre or arbitrary, but rather will probably reflect an historical moment" (p. 8). Kluczny (1998) had a similar concern when he was writing his research proposal. He concluded that as researchers we may never be sure whether we have captured the true meaning of an experience as described by another and that all we can hope for is that we are able to "capture that which is meaningful, real and true for the participants at the point of asking" (p. 8). Returning to some of the participants to clarify certain things that they said helped to alleviate some of my apprehensions.

Definition of Terms

First Nations: Used by persons or group of people whose ancestors inhabited this land prior to the arrival of Europeans; a political term in Canada used by Aboriginal people to identify themselves as distinct nations apart from Canada: organizations that are owned and operated by First Nations people or governments. Sometimes used interchangeably with *Aboriginal, Indigenous, Indian, Cree,* or *Native. First Nation* is preferred to the terms *Indian, tribe,* and *band,* which the federal, provincial, and territorial governments in Canada have formally adopted and frequently use. There are over 600 First Nations across Canada and 46 in Alberta (Alberta Learning, 2002).

Indian: Used to define Indigenous peoples under Canada's Indian Act. According to the Indian Act, an Indian is a person who is registered or entitled to be registered as an Indian (Alberta Learning, 2002). Three legal definitions apply to Indians in Canada: Status Indian, non-Status Indian, and Treaty Indian (Alberta Learning, 2002).

Indianness: As used in this paper, refers to the cultural, spiritual, and traditional holdings that a Native person uses for his/her personal identification. It is a state of being.

Treaties: Legal documents between government and a First Nation that confer rights and obligations on both parties. No two Treaties are identical, but the Western Treaties provide certain treaty rights including, but not restricted to, entitlement to reserve lands and hunting, fishing, and trapping. To First Nations peoples, the Treaties are more than simply legal commitments; they are sacred documents made by the parties and sealed by a pipe ceremony. Prior to Confederation, Treaties in Canada were made between First Nations and the British Crown. Subsequent Treaties, including the Western Treaties, were made with the Crown in right of Canada (Alberta Learning, 2002).
Indian band: A body of Indians as defined in the Indian Act. Also referred to as a First Nation (Indian and Northern Affairs, 2007).
Reserve: A tract of land, the legal title to which is vested in Her Majesty, that has been set apart for the use and benefit of a band, as defined in the Indian Act (Indian and Northern Affairs, 2007).
School choice: In the mainstream, school choice means the opportunity granted to all parents to make choices about where to send their child and the right to choose a school that best fits their children's educational needs. Mainstream parents normally have the option of choosing between various private and public schools. In First Nations communities, school choice is limited to the on-reserve community schools or the off-reserve public or private schools with which the First Nations communities have negotiated tuition agreements.

CHAPTER 2:
LITERATURE REVIEW

Despite the diversity, Native people have many commonalties, including their relationship with nature, the historical relationship with Canada, and the ways that education has affected them. (Jules, 1999, p. 41)

Native education is a very complex topic and one that usually requires much explanation in talking with people from outside the Aboriginal circle. Therefore, to alleviate any confusion, I have decided to start this chapter with a brief history of Native education and to describe how Native education has evolved as a result of this history. Although this history is long and rich in details and complexities, I have chosen to highlight only those basic elements that will assist the reader in situating the study within it and thus contribute to a deeper and better understanding of some or all of the issues that the parents as the research participants in this specific study on Native education have identified.

History of First Nations in Canada

First Nations people lived as sovereign Nations prior to European contact. They were self-sufficient in every way, living off the land, where they obtained everything that they needed from their environment, and living in harmony with the Creator and with nature. Most of the Indigenous peoples who were the ancestors of the people involved in this study lived fairly nomadic lifestyles, hunting, fishing, and gathering from the abundance of the land in ways that recognized and honored traditional territories and territorial rights of the group as well as the rights and claims of other tribes and peoples. Snow (1977) painted a picture of this time:

> There were literally millions of buffalo roaming the plains along the foothills and even into the Rocky Mountains themselves. There were game animals of all kinds—moose, elk, deer, wild sheep, and goats, readily available for hunting animals, but the hunt was never for the sake of killing them. . . . When we were in need of meat, when we were hungry, the medicine men of the tribe performed sacred ceremonies before the hunters went out. (p. 7)

From the time of the arrival of the first Europeans, life began to change for the First Nations peoples. Mutual respect and relations of recognized interdependence and independence slowly changed to relations of dependence on the part of the Indigenous peoples. The equal partnerships that they had initially shared with the Europeans changed slowly to relationships governed by European objectives of control and eventual colonization of First Nations peoples. These policies and practices resulted in states of ongoing oppression and powerlessness for the Indigenous peoples. The newly established Euro-Canadian governments utilized their governing systems, churches, education, laws, and economic powers to suppress First Nations' efforts to sustain themselves and to reduce their Indigenous homelands. The First Nations were herded onto infertile reservations, and European settlers were encouraged to immigrate and take ownership of recently vacated rich farmlands and to reap the benefits that accrued from the harvesting and mining of natural resources, many of which had never been seen in Europe.

Legislation

When the Europeans arrived, they were already a well-structured, highly stratified society with an acquisitive economy (Miller, 1989). It was not long after entering the Americas that they began applying these structures in an attempt to establish their ownership of the land. They saw much potential in these lands, and they had no qualms, or at least made no secret, about wanting a part of the country's resources. However, the dilemma in which the Europeans and the Indigenous peoples now found themselves was one of incompatible worldviews and values. The Europeans had to deal with the fact that there were already First Nations people living on these lands when they arrived, and their own European laws required that they recognize the rights of the people who lived there to original land ownership. The Indigenous peoples, on the other hand, had no conception of private ownership of land and resources. This was a foreign notion that could not be ascribed to the reality of their relationships with the lands on which they had traditionally lived. In fact, the First Nations people interpreted the concept of owning land as "similar to one owning air; nobody owns the air that we breathe" (Makokis, 2001, p. 28). The First Nations believed that "Mother Earth would provide for them in a reciprocal relationship" (p. 29), and they had no right to even talk about selling or owning Mother Earth. The European paradigm, however, was one in which the land could be bought and sold. This basic difference in how the land and natural resources were viewed and held in relationships resulted in a great deal of resistance from the Indigenous peoples to the European proposals to purchase, trade, or 'treaty' for the land.

Royal Proclamation

This resistance from the First Nations did not stop the Europeans from moving onto the land, and in 1763 the British monarch issued the Royal Proclamation to stabilize relationships with First Nations through regulations that guided European conduct and practices around trade, settlement, and the purchase of land on the Western frontier, as Canada was then known. "The proclamation involved the establishment of the three new governments in the newly acquired territories of Quebec, East Florida, and West Florida, and provided guidelines for dealing with aboriginal peoples" (Wotherspoon & Satzewich, 2000, p. 20). The proclamation was to be used to protect Indian lands, and it instructed settlers who were living on Indian lands to remove themselves. It also clearly stated that lands could be purchased only through an authorized Crown agent. Wotherspoon and Satzewich explained:

> In relation to land and land rights within the territorial confines of the three new governments, the proclamation stated that because "it was just and reasonable, and essential to our Interests, and the security of our colonies," land that had not been formally ceded by the Indians "are reserved to them or any of them, as their Hunting Grounds." In lands outside of the territories of the new governments, the proclamations attempted to block further settlement. (p. 20)

Many other pieces of legislation followed, many of which were presumably "for the benefit" of First Nations people, but Makokis (2001) and others would agree that most of this legislation benefited everyone but the First Nations. Makokis explained:

> All of these European and Canadian legislative tools were intended to initially annihilate and eventually to assimilate the rest of First Nations people so there would be no "Indian problem" and the lands and resources could be dispersed among the Euro-Canadians. (p. 15)

Indian Act

Of all the legislative tools that the government uses, it was the Indian Act that has had the most detrimental effect on First Nations peoples. "The Indian Act was unilaterally designed to abolish First Nations status as independent, self-governing peoples, legislating the rules for band membership, abolishing traditional political systems, imposing federally controlled election systems, banning spiritual activities, and creating residential schools" (Steinhauer, 2004, p. 16).

The Indian Act is the principal instrument by which the federal government and, indirectly, the provincial governments have exercised control over the lives of First Nations peoples (Frideres, 1997). The Indian Chiefs of Alberta (1970) in *Citizen Plus* stated:

> The Indian Act provides for the basis for the Indian Affairs Branch. It confers on the Minister's very sweeping powers. It often frustrates Indians in their individual efforts to earn a living and the entire tribe in its attempts toward self-government and better stewardship of the assets of the tribe. (p. 12)

Examples of the Minister's powers include the following:

> The Minister may . . . authorize use of lands for schools or burial grounds, . . . authorize surveys and subdivisions, . . . determine and direct the construction of roads, . . . issue certificates of possession, . . . direct an Indian person or the tribe to compensate another Indian, . . . call a referendum, . . . appoint executors of wills, . . . declare the will of an Indian to be void, . . . issue temporary permits for the taking of sand, gravel, clay and other non-metallic substances upon or under lands in a reserve. . . . All of these things, and many more, the Minister may do without consulting anyone. (p. 13)

Basically, the Indian Act was administered in "the interest of benign rule, but its implementation created isolation, control, and enforced poverty" (Makokis, 2001, p. 21). Wotherspoon and Satzewich (2001) explained that

> there were three central elements to the Indian Act of 1876: 1) it defined who was an Indian; 2) it provided protection over lands; 3) and it provided for the concentration of authority over Indian people in the hands of the federal government. (p. 30)

According to Frideres (1997), it has become the most vicious mechanism of social control that exists in Canada today. On one hand, it accorded Indians special status, legally and constitutionally; and on the other hand, it has denied them equality in any realm of Canadian life (Berger, 1991). The federal government did not take its responsibility for Native people lightly and almost immediately started implementing strategies that would fix what they perceived to be the "Indian problem," to use the words of Duncan Campbell Scott, one of the highest ranking officials responsible for matters relating to Indians in the early to mid 1900s. Scott's efforts centered on educating the "Indian" out of the Indians. Chrisjohn and Young (1997) reported that Duncan Campbell Scott[6] said:

> "I want to get rid of the Indian problem. I do not think as a matter of fact, that this country ought to continuously protect a class of people who are unable to stand alone. This is my whole point. Our objective is to continue until there is not a single Indian in Canada that has not been absorbed into the body politic." (p. 42)

Phases of First Nations Education in Canada

Educating Native children became a priority for the federal government after the creation of the Indian Act, and especially after the signing of the treaties (Buckley, 1992). Within the treaties—namely, Treaties 1-7—First Nations tribes asked for the inclusion of an education clause, because they knew that if they were to survive in this New World, they too would have to learn to read and write. This clause was probably agreed upon, not so much because the government wanted to ensure that Native children received an education, but rather because it used schooling as a "device for the political containment of native peoples as a means to prepare them for possible labour force participation" (Wotherspoon & Satzewich, 2000, p. 116) and to get rid of the "Indian problem" once and for all.

Indian education can be said to have passed through five different phases: (a) traditional education, (b) education by missionaries, (c) residential schools, (d) integrated education, (e) Indian control of Indian education (Goddard, 1993; Hampton, 1995; Hebert & McCaskill, 1987). These phases will be covered in more detail below.

Traditional Education

> For thousands of years Aboriginal peoples had a very effective education. We knew how to prepare our children to handle the challenges they would face when living on the land. The harshness of our environment imposed a discipline that produced resilient, proud, and self-reliant people. Then things changed. (Watt-Cloutier, 2000, p. 114)

Long before European contact, First Nations people had highly developed systems of education. In their education system the community and the natural environment were the classroom, and they perceived the land as the mother of the people (Binda & Calliou, 2001; Kirkness & Bowman, 1992; Makokis, 2001; Snow, 1977). Education was interwoven into the life of the tribe, and all adults were responsible for "ensuring that each child learned how to live a good life" (Kirkness & Bowman, 1992, p. 5). I have included references from

---

[6] Duncan Campbell Scott (1862-1947) is best known as one of Canada's prominent early literary figures; however, in the eyes of many First Nations people, he has had another, less honorable impact on Canadian history. From 1913 until 1932 Scott was responsible for the implementation of the Canadian assimilation programs imposed on First Nations peoples, but his influence on Native history started in approximately 1879, when he was hired as a copy clerk in the Department of Indian Affairs. Over the next 50 years he received various promotions and became well-known as the Indian expert. In 1913 his perceived knowledge led to his position of deputy superintendent—a position in which he stayed until 1932. Scott played a pivotal role in seeking resolutions satisfactory to the Department of Indian Affairs, and his work has had and continues to have a major impact on all aspects of the lives of First Nations people, including Native education (Titley, 1980).

Indigenous/Aboriginal educators, but I also grew up and learned these historical facts as teachings from my own family and community.

Surviving off the land was difficult, and Aboriginal children had a great deal to learn before they could survive on their own: "Learning was for living—for survival. Boys and girls were taught at an early age to observe and to utilize, to cope with and respect their environment" (Kirkness & Bowman, 1992, p. 6). Through observation and active participation, children "learned the nature of sources of their food, community, and life relationships. They learned that everything in life was a matter of kinship with all nature" (Cajete, 2000b, p. 101).

Elders, parents, and extended family passed on not only survival skills to their children, but also their history, language, music, artistic ability, and religious values: "Parents, grandparents, and elders told and retold stories and legends to the children by the campfires, in teepees, on the hillsides, in the forests, and at special gatherings during the day and at night" (Snow, 1977, p. 6). Snow added:

> It was an ongoing education process about religion, life, hunting, and so on. Other topics were bravery, courage, kindness, sharing, survival, and foot tracks of animals, so it was a very extensive study of many things. With an education based on religion, the child was established in . . . tribal society. He or she was one of the Great Spirit's people. (p. 6)

The young were trained to live in balance with the forces of nature, and children learned at a very young age that wisdom is "acquired through a lifetime of study, experience, and prayer" (Snow, 1977, p. 7). "Very early in the lives of children, the role the child would play as an adult was determined. Training continued until the person was regarded as ready to perform his or her function" (Kirkness & Bowman, 1992, p. 7). Through story, Makokis's (2001) participants provided examples of how children learned in these traditional times. She shared Bernie's story:

> The children learned under the Elders, so they became quick learners, and there were always things that happened. The way that my grandfather told me was that, at a certain age, children were informed of their responsibilities. They would relate the events to a saskatoon branch. My grandfather said, "This is a woman saskatoon branch and where the root grew is the baby. As they would get older they would become flowers and the flowers is the time of change for women and they bear fruit which means that the woman can now bear a child." They always had ceremonies for that. They knew exactly when this process would happen and the old ladies would take the younger women and tell them about the facts of being a woman and the responsibilities of being a woman. On the other hand, the younger men had to seek a vision by the time they were 13 or 14 years of age. That vision was more or less to look at themselves as human beings and what their responsibility was. So at a very early age, the young women and young men knew exactly what their roles and responsibilities would be in the future. The education system was there, and they had the leadership and Elders to train and guide them through the process. (pp. 125-126)

Bernie related a story of a traditional education system that provided the youth with the specific skills, attitudes, and knowledge that they needed to function in everyday life within the context of a particular spiritual worldview.

Teachings within such systems would take many years for students to fully comprehend and appreciate. Children would not necessarily be aware that teaching moments were occurring because much of the teaching and learning took place during everyday activities. Practical knowledge developed over the years. In similar ways, but supported by structured, ceremonial practices and events, learners acquired knowledge of spiritual and metaphysical matters. Whereas these forms are often described as informal and unstructured pedagogies and systems of education, in fact, children and youth were recognized formally as learners; and as learners, their activities were monitored, and their learning experiences and teachings were based on ancient systems of thought that had been validated and legitimized through thousands of years of research, analysis, and practice. Cajete's (2000b) words sound simple: "The key to learning was continual experience of the natural world through work, play, ritual, food gathering, hunting and fishing" (p.101), but the layers of meaning that are carried through the actualization of this principle of traditional education are rarely unfolded or elaborated upon. By interacting with nature in accordance with this principle, each child developed his or her mind, body, and spirit according to an ancient and carefully structured system of individual and social education.

Cajete (2000b) pointed out that, traditionally, Native peoples lived "a kind of communal environmental ethics that stemmed from the broadest sense of kinship with all life" (p. 95). He described, for his people, the ecology of their community and expanded upon the following key elements that "structured and formed the experience of each Indigenous community member from birth to death" (p. 95):

- *Environment.* Nature was the frame of reality that formed the learning experiences.
- *Guidance.* Adult members of a child's extended family, clan, and tribe actively undertook parenting.
- *Kinship.* Children learned early the significance of family, responsibility, respect, and the foundations of relationship, and kinship.
- *Diversity.* In the close-knit, interdependent community, children . . . interacted with all types of people on a daily basis in the course of living in community.
- *Special status.* In Indigenous communities, all children were considered to be special, sacred gifts from the Creator, and thus, were respected and prized.
- *Ethical models.* Morals and ethics were modeled by the family and community.
- *Clear roles.* Everyone knew his/her relationship to other people, nature, and the things of their society.
- *Customs and practices.* Customs associated with each community role . . . defined specific relations and reinforced key values and activities.
- *Recognition.* Naming, rites of passage, gifting, feasting, and other social events honored achievements that benefits and enhanced individuals.
- *Unique ways of learning.* The unique qualities of each child as a learner were naturally accepted and honored.
- *Community work.* Community interdependence characterized activity related to all major events and tasks.
- *Spirit.* A sense of the sacred permeated all aspects of Indigenous community. (pp. 95-98)

I find that these principles can easily fit within the traditional values and practices of my own community and people. However, based upon my observations and experiences as a Cree woman, I note that many of these Indigenous education principles have been disrupted. I attribute this to the historical fact that Native communities, including mine, were forced to adopt Western systems of community governance and social structures as part of their displacement from their tribal territories. Our ways of knowing, ways of being, and ways of doing have been under assault since the formal establishment of Canada as a nation: "Aboriginal people have been bombarded with the message that what they know from their culture is of no value" (Sefa Dei et al., 2000, p. 25). Because intergenerational transmission of knowledge has been disrupted and Native children are no longer privy to the traditional ways of doing, knowing, and being, they are now struggling to achieve even those recognized minimum standards of success in current school systems. A participant in Steinhauer's (2007) study commented on these struggles:

> I think that's a big thing about why our students struggle or why our education system is not working. It is because in our traditional ways as parents, we were always involved with our kids' teaching and doing things. . . . [Today] kids are out of the home and they are learning separately from their parents and their parents are out working so there's already a cut off there. . . . It's not going to work. It's not going to work no matter how much culture and tradition we bring into the school. It's those whole processes of how to make that link again, that connection in our busy mainstream life today. (p. 89)

Education by Missionaries

> Traditions seem right and natural to those who follow them, and seeing that we did not have schools, people from the south concluded that we needed them. (Watt-Cloutier, 2000, p. 114)

Building day schools on the reserves was the first step taken to honor the educational component of the formal treaty agreements signed between the First Nations or Aboriginal tribes of Turtle Island and Canada on behalf of Britain. The churches were given the privilege of running these schools, with the government providing financial support and formal supervision and administration (Buckley, 1992). This form of education suited the Native families very well because, in addition to the children's receiving formal education at school, they could continue to receive a traditional education at home and in their community.

It was not long before the missionaries and the government decided that this form of schooling was not working. Native children were not adopting the lifestyles and teachings of their teachers, and Native traditions were not diminishing. The churches felt that parental influence was disrupting the learning and training of the children. Consequently, they decided that it would be best to remove Native children from all family and community influence. Buckley (1992) suggested that the government had an ideological commitment to "suppress the native culture as rapidly as possible and fashion a new generation of Indian children raised in isolation from their parents, in the image of whitemen" (p. 47). This movement was the beginning of residential schools in Canada.

Residential Schools

> Rather than make us stronger, they tended to undermine our confidence and identity. (Watt-Cloutier, 2000, p. 115)

When the government turned to address the constitutional responsibility for Indians and their lands assigned by the Constitution Act of 1867, it adopted a policy of assimilation: "It was a policy designed to move communities, and eventually all Aboriginal peoples, from their helpless 'savage' state to one of self-reliant 'civilization' and thus to make Canada but one community— a non-Aboriginal, Christian one" (RCAP, 1996, p. 2). To accomplish this vision of assimilation, the government adopted a system that was similar to the industrial school system that already existed in the United States. Because the industrial schools in the United States had already had the experience of bringing Native children into residential school settings, they were instrumental in convincing the Canadian government that Native children were better candidates for assimilation if they were taken away from the negative influences of family and community.

With the help of missionaries, the government began its recruitment of residential school students. Although it was successful in convincing some Native parents that this experience would be beneficial to their children, it faced much opposition. With major reluctance, however, many parents allowed their children to attend these schools.

From my experiences and discussions over my lifetime in a Cree community, the first people to send their children to these schools did not know that the aim of the schools was not just to teach the Native children to read and write, but also "to prepare the children for a new way of life, make them give up accustomed beliefs, take white people as their models, and aspire to live as much like them as possible" (Buckley 1992, p. 48).

As time went by, the parents began seeing the negative effects of these schools, and, more and more, they began to resist this type of education. By this time, however—the 1920s— the government had amended the Indian Act, making it mandatory for Native parents to send their children to residential schools. From ages 3 to 16 the children were removed from their homes and placed in the schools, where they stayed from September until June of each year (Lafrance, 2001). During this annual 10-month period, they were isolated from their siblings, their parents, and the rest of Canada. They were not permitted to speak their Native languages, and in some places their supervisors and teachers spoke only English or French to them. The children were punished if they reverted to their own languages. The government's stated objective was clearly total assimilation of the Aboriginal peoples into mainstream Canada, and the residential schools represented the most promising means of achieving this end.

Breaking up First Nations families was encouraged from an early date by government legislators and enforced by representatives of the church and federal government Indian agents. The government's stated purpose of this policy was assimilation of the Aboriginal people into Canadian society. Not only were children educated separately from the dominant culture of Canada, but they were also educated away from their own cultures and led to believe that everything about their cultures was paganistic. Persson (1986) gave an example of how powerful the message was to the children:

> Many students from the 1930s remember the pictorial catechism used at Blue Quills: "They had two roads going up, the one going up to heaven had all the white people and the one going up to hell had all the Indian people." For one student, the catechism left the message that "if you stay Indian you'll end up in hell." Students were encouraged to try to change their parents' religious attitudes, to have for example, Catholic prayers in their homes on the reserve although they were not at home themselves. (p. 154)

The students were constantly reminded that their traditional lifestyles were substandard and that they should work hard to mimic everything they were being taught so that when they went home, they could demonstrate the right way to their families. The students came to see their homes as dirty and substandard and everything about their lives prior to residential school as wrong. They quickly learned that ceremonies and rituals that harmonized the spiritual and social life of their communities were "paganistic" and of the devil. The immaculate and orderly state of the residential schools sent a clear message to the students that this way of life was far superior to the "primitive" ways of their traditional lifestyles.

Haig-Brown (1995) quoted one of her participants on the powerful impact of residential schools:

> "By the time I went through the residential school system, I had a very negative attitude towards my parents and towards my friends. . . . I started seeing some of my brothers and sisters as ugly looking because they were Indian. . . . If my friends ever tried to talk about Indians, I'd just change the subject." (p. 281)

A great deal of literature exists on this topic (e.g., Assembly of First Nations, 1994; Bull, 1991; Chrisjohn & Young, 1997; Haig-Brown, 1995; Ing, 1991), and each piece of writing reveals the devastating effect of this genocidal process on the Aboriginal peoples of Canada and the United States. Languages, traditions, self-respect, community cohesiveness, parental skills, survival skills, and much more have been lost as a result of their experiences in the residential school system. Those losses in the areas of self-esteem, parenting skills, and language have had and continue to have a huge impact on Native communities (Chrisjohn & Young, 1997; Hanohano, 2001; Kirkness, 1998; Lafrance, 2001; Martin, 2002; Steinhauer, 2002; Weber-Pillwax, 2003). In Kirkness's words:

> Every Aboriginal person is affected even today by residential schools despite the fact that they no longer exist. The breakdown of our societies is attributed to the effect of the separation of Aboriginal children from their parents. Many generations of children were denied the association with their nuclear family, with their extended family's culture, their values, their language, their customs, and their spirituality. (p. 101)

Most residential schools ceased to operate by the mid 1970s, and only seven remained open through the 1980s. The last federally operated residential school in Canada closed in Saskatchewan in 1996.

Integrated Education

After recognizing that residential schools were not accomplishing what they were designed to achieve, a new policy was implemented—integrated education—that had as its stated purpose the complete integration of Indians into mainstream Canadian society. Titley (1980) explained:

> What the policy of integration meant in practice was that wherever possible Indian children would be enrolled in the predominantly white public schools operated by the provincial governments. Provincial education authorities concurred with this new departure and over the following two decades the gradual transfer of large numbers of native children from all-Indian schools to integrated ones took place. By March, 1968, the Minister of Indian Affairs was able to announce that over 50 per cent of Indian

children of school age were attending schools operated by the provinces.
The first major assessment of integrated education was carried out between 1964 and 1967 by a research group under Dr. H. Hawthorn of the University of British Columbia.... The report documented the alarmingly high drop-out rate of Indian students in school and showed that this rate intensified when Indians transferred to public schools. (p. 1)

Although the Hawthorn report showed that integration was not working, an intensification of the process was suggested as a solution. Titley (1980) described the policy of integration as assimilation in disguise: "Integrated education meant cultural modification on the part of the weaker and numerically inferior group—the Indians. They were to be assimilated" (p. 2). Assimilation became an obsession for the government, and in 1969 Prime Minister Trudeau presented the *White Paper on Indian Affairs* to Parliament. This paper suggested that the Indian Act be repealed and that First Nations be incorporated into the mainstream. The proposed legislation met major opposition from First Nations groups, and it was quickly withdrawn when the Indian Association issued a counterproposal that became know as the *Red Paper*, a document that asserted First Nations sovereignty.

Indian Control of Indian Education

Shortly after the withdrawal of the 1969 federal *White Paper*, the NIB (1972) issued the *Red Paper*, a position paper entitled *Indian Control of Indian Education*. This paper was premised on two educational principles widely "recognized in Canadian society: Parental responsibility and local control of education" (Barman, Hebert, & McCaskill, 1987, p. 2). The federal government eventually accepted the document, and since 1972 numerous First Nations have assumed control of their schools within the limitations that the Department of Indian Affairs defined and regulates. It is not surprising that with Indian Affairs still directing regulations and policies on education, the statistics with regard to Indian control of Indian education have not changed significantly. The federal government has agreed that Native people must take control of their own education and that Native people must provide their own answers, but this recognition has not been enough to inspire significant changes in the statistics on the schooling success of First Nations students. Knowing the answers and implementing changes are two different things, and, unfortunately, even with the local control that has been afforded to Native communities, the federal government continues to exercise most of the control (Abele, Dittburner, & Graham, 2000).

First Nations communities were granted local control of education as a result of the NIB's (1972) document, but as this policy was being operationalized, it became evident that the term *control* did not carry the same meaning for each of the parties involved. Abele et al. (2000) explained that this term could be problematic:

> While the Summary Report of the Task force on the Educational Needs of the Native Peoples of Ontario defines control, in terms of input, Aboriginal documents define it as a total or partial transfer of jurisdiction over education to the local community level. (pp. 9-10)

Therefore, the question remains, Do First Nations have control of Indian education? Brady (1995) argued that we do not have full autonomy from restrictive federal control:

Whereas the federal government may have agreed with the principle of Native control of Native education, it has done little to transfer legislative control over education to First Nations Government. . . . The result is that the term 'band controlled' somewhat misrepresents reality. As long as legislative and legal authority continues to reside in non-Native legislative bodies, Native people's ability to control their children's education will be, to all intents and purposes, severely restricted. (pp. 357-358)

The development of policies in Alberta, such as the recent First Nations, Métis, and Inuit Education Policy Framework (Alberta Learning, 2002) and, more recently, the Alberta's Commission on Learning (2006) seem to offer potential for more focus on Aboriginal-led education initiatives. The provincial government provided significant funds to expand the implementation of the First Nations, Métis, and Inuit Policy Framework, but the processes and methods used in the implementation strategies demonstrated that Aboriginal peoples still have not been granted complete autonomy even to participate fully in such initiatives as the government-led policy objective of infusing Aboriginal knowledge and perspectives into mainstream school programs and curricula. Although some Native people were involved in the public discussions and participated in the community consultations on the policy framework and the ensuing curriculum projects, according to Battiste (2002) and individual community members, it remains questionable whether their voices were heard and whether their ideas were actually incorporated into the policy or its implementation strategies. In their review of the policy framework, Wilson and Wilson (2002) were very skeptical of the policy: "On the surface, the concept sounds good. . . . The point is that the power differential remains as it has since formal education began" (p. 67). They added:

Current provincial curricula were developed out of mainstream Canadian society and its own agenda for transmitting its own culture: colonizing its younger generation, as it were, to its own attitudes, values, and customs. . . . By simply infusing something into an already powerful and harmful system, we may be contributing only that—an infusion—and may in fact be perpetuating the problem.

The need is for the curriculum to emerge from the traditional Aboriginal culture, not the other way around. Then the Aboriginal culture would provide the framework to legitimize the curriculum. (p. 67)

First Nations Schooling Today

Though it has now been 35 years since the federal government granted First Nations across Canada the option of having locally controlled schools on their reserves, there has been very little change in the outcomes of schooling. Native education has still not reached parity with non-Native education in Canada (Minister of Public Works and Government of Services Canada, 2000):

The Department reports an improvement in high school completion rates for Indian students over five years, from 31 percent to 37 percent. This compares with a 65 percent high school completion rate for the Canadian population as a whole in 1996. At this rate of progress, it will take approximately 23 years for the Indian population on reserves to reach education parity with the overall Canadian rate for high school completion, if that rate remains constant. We believe that more and faster progress is urgently needed. (p. 4)

Statistics Canada (2001a) reported similar findings from its Aboriginal people's survey:

> Education attainment among the Aboriginal population in Canada has increased over the past few years (Siggner, 2003; Statistics Canada, 2003). In 1996, just over half (52%) of the Aboriginal population aged 20 to 24 living in non-reserve areas had not completed secondary school. By 2001, this proportion had dropped to 48%. Nevertheless, there was still a huge gap in comparison with the Canadian population as a whole. By 2001, only 26% of the general population aged 20 to 24 had not completed secondary school. (p. 2)

These statistics hold true regardless of whether the Native children attended a public (provincial) school or an on-reserve school. Kirkness (1999) wanted Native people to turn these statistics around, stating that our objective has to be

> learning to appreciate and use all our resources to realize quality education, not only for the children, but for all Our People regardless of their level of study. Education into culture, not culture into education, must be our practice and we must believe that the answers are within us. (p. 25)

Referring to the work of Mackay and Myles (1989), Breen (2003) identified at least 18 different factors that might contribute to students' dropping out of school, 8 of which he focused on in his study: low English-language skills in reading, writing, listening, and speaking; low academic achievement; poor student-staff relations; inadequate parental support; poor home and school communication; impact of peer relationships; inadequate future plans; and irrelevant curriculum (p. 35).

The non-Native educators in Breen's (2003) study reported that they often struggled to find ways to reach the children they taught and were often "frustrated with the fact that they were not in a position to provide an education that is tailored to meet the learning needs, styles, and comfort of the community and its students" (p. 84). Many concluded that much of the failure that children experience is a result of low parental and community involvement and a lack of parenting skills. Breen mentioned, however, that although many of his participants thought they had the answers, few "presented any sense of understanding of historical and contemporary Native issues that might affect families" (p. 136).

As revealed in studies such as Breen's (2003) and Tessier's (2003), many non-Native educators assume that Native children are failing because First Nations parents and communities do not care about their school achievements, but there is very little, if any, evidence to support such a position. To the contrary, studies have revealed that Aboriginal parents *do* care about their children's education and that they *do* want them to graduate from high school (Breen 2003; Friedel, 1999; Kavanagh, 2002; Makokis, 2000; Tessier, 2003). This brings to the forefront even more forcefully the need for educators in general to identify accurately and understand more deeply the factors and complexities that drive the low academic achievement patterns of Aboriginal students.

Each new decade brings forth new theories and new policies to address the issue of Aboriginal students' low academic achievement. Some scholars theorize that the effects of colonization and the residential school experiences are major contributing factors, whereas others continue to embrace theories that point to learning-style differences. Still other scholars point to inadequate parental involvement; low English-language skills in reading, writing, listening, and speaking; dysfunctional homes; and irrelevant school curriculum. It seems pointless for First Nations to engage in debates on the reason(s) for their children's low academic achievement; the facts of the current reality remain clear regardless of who or what is to be blamed: Native children continue to struggle in the area of academics in schools. Arguments amongst scholars and educators have been going on for decades and have not resolved the problem. According to the history of formal Aboriginal education in Canada, including ongoing statistics, Aboriginal people have little evidence on which to build their hopes for solutions from this particular segment of mainstream society.

Parental School Choice in First Nations Communities

As a Native educator myself, I have always been confident that, as is true for most non-Native parents, most Native parents are concerned about the welfare of their children and want them to be successful, independent individuals. All of the parents whom I know want their children to receive at least enough education to enable them to function in today's competitive world, and, in fact, studies have shown that Native parents generally want at least a Grade 12 education for their children (Breen, 2003; Friedel, 1999; Kavanagh, 2002; Makokis, 2000; Tessier, 2003).

In 1867, through section 91(24) of the British North American Act (now the Constitution Act, 1867), the federal government assumed jurisdiction over Indian lands reserved for Indians. Shortly after, with the establishment of the Indian Act, the Canadian government also assumed total jurisdiction over First Nations education. It was the federal government that decided where First Nations children would attend school. Parental school choice for First Nations families was not a reality until sometime in the late 1960s when the federal government began dismantling the residential school system and, through its integrated education policy, encouraging Native parents to send their children to local public schools under the control of the provincial or territorial governments.

Today, with schools in almost all First Nations communities across Canada, parents have some choice as to where they will send their children, but the choices are limited. The federal government has committed to pay the tuition for only those students who attend schools where transfer agreements have been established with their administrative systems (Director of Education, personal communication, June 18, 2006; Makokis, 2000). Therefore, in most First Nations communities, parents must make a choice between the First Nations community schools and the surrounding off-reserve provincial schools that have tuition agreements in place between their own school system and the provincial and federal governments. In her study Morgan (2002) reported that "of the 120,000 eligible on-reserve First Nations students, 65% attend the 487 band-operated schools, while about 35% attend provincial schools" (p. 15). These numbers vary, often widely, depending on the reserve's proximity to rural towns with provincial schools. Where there is closer proximity, up to 75% of First Nations children might attend provincial schools (Morgan, 2002; Northern Affairs Canada employee, personal communication, June 13, 2006).

Assuming then that the factor of proximity is not one of heavy weighting in a particular situation, how do First Nations parents decide where to send their children to school? Some researchers (e.g., Breen, 2003; Kavanagh, 2002; Makokis, 2000) have alluded to this topic, but the research and literature that speak directly to the topic of First Nations parental school choice are sparse. Because this topic carries major significance in the lives of my own people as well as those of other tribal peoples in Canada, I focused my literature searches on gaining a better understanding of the factors that influence parental school choice in the wider population. A description of these factors follows and I hope will provide the reader with an appropriate context for the stronger emphasis of this work on parental school choice for First Nations parents who are living on reserves. The intent of this discussion is to make educators and policy makers aware of some of the complex processes and factors that influence First Nations education in general and First Nations parental school choices in particular.

The perspectives of First Nations parents on the educational experiences of their children within the context of Canadian "schooling" have been widely disseminated. However, to my knowledge, First Nations parents have never openly revealed how personal experiences and perspectives ultimately lead to parental school choices. This work may well be the first attempt to give space to those voices on this topic.

Parental School Choice Within non–First Nations Communities

Research has revealed that the increasing economic uncertainty influences most school choice decisions (Cowley, 2004; Ungerleider, 2004). "Today's parents want their children to grow up well educated and able to find meaningful work. They know that their own wellbeing, and that of their children, is connected to the quality of the schooling their children receive" (Ungerleider, 2004, p. 20). Therefore they want their children to attend good schools—schools that will meet their expectations. *Good* schools in this case seems to refer to those that will move their children successfully into good employment positions.

What constitutes a good school? Cowley (2004) affirmed that a good school always strives for high academic achievement, and he identified four criteria that might help parents determine whether the school is, in fact, a good school: It (a) has a very public mission, (b) knows how to succeed and tells everyone what it knows, (c) maintains rich communication with its families, and (d) measures its performance and succeeds in its mission (pp. 10-11).

Hoxby (2001) charged that Cowley's (2004) criteria might be a little too idealist and reported that many parents do not have the option of shopping around, let alone of reviewing mission statements or investigating whether or not the schools are actually meeting or succeeding in their mission. Realistically, many "parents are not all equally able to exercise choice" (p. 75), and therefore they become less concerned about the criteria listed above. "High-income parents routinely exercise more choice than low-income parents because high-income parents have more school districts and private schools within their choice set" (p. 75). Canada is a diverse country in all aspects, and people from different economic and social backgrounds may use different criteria when they select schools for their children.

COMPAS Research conducted a poll in 2001 for the *National Post* (Hoxby, 2001) that revealed several different parental values and ideas on the purpose of education. The results showed that up to 32% of parents identified training youth for the work world as most important or valuable to them, 23% chose creating good citizens as most important, and 17% selected creating inquiring minds as most important. A further 7% considered creating happy people as important, 4% felt that teaching religious values is very important, 3% thought that producing good parents is important, and the remainder had various other thoughts about the purpose of education (p. 57).

Taylor and Woollard (2003) focused their study on how middle-class parents and their children choose a high school, and it became very clear that school choice was more than just a matter of academics. Although these parents thought that academics are important, other factors contributed to their decisions. Some parents were looking for schools that focused on religion, culture, and language; whereas others were looking for special-interest programs that focused on fine arts, sports, the military, or technology. Still others desired schools that would ensure entry to university, and some searched for schools tailored to vocational training. Whatever the factors, most of the parents in Taylor and Woollard's study hoped that, in addition to academics, the schools that they chose would promote a sense of belonging and be places where their children would be safe and happy. They shared the following parental considerations:

> John and Sandra . . . comment on the pressure imposed by channeling all eligible students into elite academic programs. . . . Arlene . . . was torn between her concern that school continues to be fun for her son and her feeling that he needed to be pushed to develop a strong work ethic and academic discipline in preparation for further education. . . . Dave comments that the reason they chose the school they did was because administrators and staff appeared to care about the well-being of students and promoted the value that 'people come first.' The issue of his son's comfort was paramount. (pp. 626-627)

Responding to dissatisfaction with public schools, parental school "choice in education has become a common reform theme in recent years in several industrialized countries" (Taylor & Woollard, 2003, p. 617; Froese-Germain, 1998; Stein, 2002), and although this may be viewed as a good thing, the effects of choice are difficult to measure. Discussing the work of Ball (2003), Taylor and Woollard argued that "the education market works as a class reproduction strategy for the middle classes" and that "school choice can lead to increased segregation" (p. 317).

Tomlinson (1997) agreed that school-choice policies increase segregation: "A major result of these choice policies globally has been to increase social class and segregation in schools" (p. 9). Minority students, she pointed out, will ultimately be the losers because

> it was apparent and acknowledged that the 'choice' legislation would increase ethnic and white school segregation. Minority students now bear additional market burdens. They are likely to be regarded as undesirable, attending 'failing' schools and schools with severely reduced budgets. Afro-Caribbean students are faring particularly badly in the market, and minority parents who initially perceived the educational reforms to be positive are becoming disillusioned. (p. 9)

Taylor and Woollard (2003) concluded that although school choice appears to be a positive move, even middle-class parents sometimes find it overwhelming to have to make such a decision for their children. Two of the parents in their study commented on this very issue:

> Mary: I wish it was back the way it was when I was a kid. I mean, there was an elementary, a junior, and a senior high school in your neighborhood and you went to school near where you lived, everybody knew you, the neighbors all knew you. I think we've lost something with the moves to choice and out of our communities.
> Arlene: I think we've lost the sense of communities building and that anchor that schools were. . . . In the area of town where I live, they're never going to build any new schools. . . . And the schools we have are falling to pieces and they don't have a lot of the amenities that the newer schools have. So . . . is that fair to our students in those

neighborhoods? It's becoming elitist.
Mary: It is becoming very elitist. And it's becoming very much a form of privatization because you can only go to certain schools if you meet the criteria, can pay the extra fees, can get there somehow. That's not a public school in terms of open to all.

Education is an important factor in determining quality of life, and more and more Canadians identify education as the key to economic opportunity and advancement (Baker, 2003). New technologies and educational techniques are helping to bridge the gap between rural, remote, and northern communities. However, the largest gap that exists between rural and urban centers is in the area of school choice. It seems natural and logical that living in a rural community means fewer choices when it comes to choosing a school, but Baker suggested that this lack of options for school choice does not appear to be a large concern for those who choose rural living. In fact, he maintained that parents appear to be generally satisfied with the schools that serve their rural communities. However, in my review of the literature I found it difficult to find other research that would confirm Baker's statements. Documentation on school choice in First Nations communities is even more limited, and the following research questions remained unaddressed in the review of literature on parental school choice: How do parents who live on a First Nations reserve decide where their children will be schooled when they have the option of choosing between an on-reserve and an off-reserve school? What criteria do they use to make this very important choice?

Overview of the Literature

This brief examination of the literature on parental school choice shows a huge gap in addressing this topic as it relates to First Nations/Aboriginal parents and communities. Although a great deal of documentation can be found in the area of Native underachievement, discussions about parental school choice are almost nonexistent. Because Makokis (2000), Tessier (2003), and Breen (2003) are among the few scholars who have alluded to this topic, it is their works that I have cited in this study. In attempting to better understand parental school choice in relation to First Nations education, I searched both past and present literature and used the writings of both Native and non-Native writers. The literature that exists on the topic of school choice decision making is vast, but because none of it directly refers to school-choice decision making for First Nations parents and, in particular, those who live in reserve communities, I have cited and commented on only a small portion of the literature. The literature revealed that the trend toward school-choice decision making is a reaction to the rapidly changing economy. As indicated earlier, the literature on school choice demonstrates that many non-Native parents are looking for schools that will best prepare their children to compete in the market economy; this may not be the basis for parental school choices for First Nations parents who are living on reserves. Because the available literature does not address this aspect of parental school choice, in this work I have relied heavily upon the integration of multiple sources to speak to the topic—literature references and citations, the participants' words and narratives, and my own words and narratives—and, as a result, I developed the presentation style itself to encapsulate that crucial integration of knowledge sources.

CHAPTER 3:
INDIGENOUS RESEARCH METHODOLOGY

An Indigenous research methodology fits within a research paradigm that draws upon the inherent wisdom, morals, and beliefs of Indigenous peoples. It encompasses the natural laws of love, respect, courage, honesty, humility, wisdom, and truth that my people believe have been given to Indigenous people by the Creator to ensure a vision of unity whenever they "came together to share and celebrate their ways of knowing" (Makokis, 2001, p. 50). As a research concept, an Indigenous research methodology allows Native people to move beyond the limitations posed by modern Western theories to conduct research and move into new spaces that embrace Indigenous knowledge. "The recognition and intellectual activation of Indigenous knowledge today is an act of empowerment by Indigenous people" (Battiste, 2002, p. 4). As a result of this movement, there is a renewed appreciation within the sphere of Western academia for the wealth and richness of Native languages, worldviews, teaching, and experiences.

Battiste (2002) spoke about the significance of Indigenous knowledge to contemporary Western forms of education and pedagogical systems:

> Indigenous knowledge benchmarks the limitations of Eurocentric theory—its methodology, evidence, and conclusions—reconceptualizes the resilience and self-reliance of Indigenous peoples, and underscores the importance of their own philosophies, heritages, and educational processes. Indigenous knowledge fills the ethical and knowledge gaps in Eurocentric education, research, and scholarship. By animating the voices and experiences of the cognitive "other" and integrating them into the educational process, it creates a new, balanced centre and a fresh vantage point from which to analyze Eurocentric education and its pedagogies. (p. 5)

The integration of Indigenous knowledge systems into the educational processes of schooling for First Nations or any other Aboriginal students must be preceded by formal recognition and acceptance of the substance and meanings of Indigenous knowledge. The concept of Indigenous knowledge is not usually heard in discussions outside the settings of academia, and as an educator I believe that this limitation offers a plausible and convincing explanation for the lack of development of new and more effective forms of education programs and curricula for Aboriginal students and communities.

Although this work does not directly address the concept of Indigenous knowledge, the Indigenous research methodology that I used to guide the research process is based upon a specific Indigenous knowledge system—that of the Plains Cree. Key points in this knowledge system refer to our relationship to space and time, to living and nonliving things, to the physical and the spiritual aspects of life. These aspects connect knowledge with understanding and involve the formal recognition and place of dreams and visions in everyday individual and social life. Relying upon a research methodology that permits and supports my efforts to draw on and include the experiences, thoughts, feelings, and spirituality of our people in this work is one way that I am able to honor the knowledge that is available to me from my own way of being and knowing. Grounding my research in this Indigenous research methodology, and therefore within this particular knowledge system, assisted me in ensuring that my research would maintain the integrity of the participants and the communities with which I engaged.

The research process that I set up and within which I conducted this research, using an Indigenous methodology or framework, reflects a spiritual base. Ermine (1995) explained Indigenous ways of seeking knowledge:

> Aboriginal epistemology is grounded in the self, the spirit, the unknown. Understanding of the universe must be grounded in the spirit. Knowledge must be sought through the stream of the inner space in unison with all instruments of knowing and conditions that make individuals receptive to knowing. Ultimately it was in the self that Aboriginal people discovered great resources for coming to grips with life's mysteries. It was in the self that the richest source of information could be founded by delving into the metaphysical and the nature and origin of knowledge. Aboriginal epistemology speaks of pondering great mysteries that lie no further than the self. (p. 108)

To build on Ermine's words, the individual who engages in the seeking or, in the current context and terms, carries out the research does so as spirit first. An Indigenous research framework, then, will reflect this perspective, and in this study I as the researcher was aware of the need to carry out all research activities and processes in the context of that spiritual aspect.

Indigenous research is a growing form of inquiry, both nationally and internationally, and is of "great importance to Indigenous people because it allows for the development of Indigenous theory and methods of practice" (Wilson, 2003, p. 25). Science "has not been able to deal with the things that make up, for example, Aboriginal wisdom" (Friedel, 1999, p. 147). It has failed to recognize that Indigenous peoples have a "complete knowledge system with its own concepts of epistemology, and its own scientific and logical validity" (Battiste, 2002, p. 8). As Friedel stated:

> Science has failed in its endeavor to measure Indigenous knowledge; it has not been able to capture our emotions; it has not been able to understand the essence of our spirits; and it has no way of doing justice to our experiences. Although qualitative methods have experienced greater success in trying to explain certain phenomena, it may be that an Indigenous methodology is the only true way of doing research involving aboriginal people. (p. 147)

A researcher who claims to be using an Indigenous methodology in his/her work understands the presupposition that is inherent in that claim: The researcher's personal life is guided by the natural laws of love, honesty, kindness, and determination. The researcher also recognizes that expectations from the community must be considered and upheld. Weber-Pillwax (1999) outlined several principles as foundational to an Indigenous research methodology, and these, I think, could be related to crucial aspects of community expectations of Indigenous and non-Indigenous researchers. The principles, in summary, included the interconnectedness of all living things, the impact of motives and intentions on person and community, research as lived Indigenous experience, the groundedness of theories in Indigenous epistemology, the transformative nature of research, the sacredness and responsibility of personal and community integrity, and the recognition of languages and cultures as living processes (pp. 31-32).

Indigenous research methodologies are very holistic in nature, and many Aboriginal scholars (e.g., Bruno, 2003; Chisan, 2001; Hanohano, 2001; Martin, 2002; Weber-Pillwax, 1999; Wilson, 2001) have expressed the need to rely upon such principles when they conduct research within Native communities. Although Martin (2002) argued that "frameworks such as historiography, ethnography, phenomenology, and particularly hermeneutics have some congruence and cultural safety" (p. 11) for the Indigenous researcher, Wilson suggested that these Western methodologies do not completely fit within our Indigenous way of thinking.

> One major difference between those dominant paradigms is that they build on the fundamental belief that knowledge is an individual entity: The researcher is an individual in search of knowledge, knowledge is something that is gained, and therefore knowledge may be owned by an individual. An Indigenous paradigm comes from the foundational belief that knowledge is relational. Knowledge is shared with all creation. It is not just interpersonal relationships, not just with the research subjects with whom I may be working, but a relationship with all of creation. It is with the cosmos, it is with the animals, with the plants, with the earth that we share this knowledge. It goes beyond the idea of individual knowledge to the concept of relational knowledge. (pp. 176-177)

I agree that an Indigenous paradigm comes from the foundational belief that knowledge is relational, and I also think that an Indigenous researcher must have a deep understanding of the meaning of such relationality. As I understand knowledge in my own Cree world, knowledge can be acquired through personal effort, or it can come to us as a gift from the Creator. Being blessed with the gift is an honor, and if I have been blessed with that honor, I understand the responsibility that goes with it. My responsibility is to pass on or share that gift with all other parts of my world, including people and other living elements of my environment.

Battiste (2002) stated, "Knowledge is not secular. It is a process derived from creation, and as such it has a sacred purpose. It is inherent in and connected to all of nature, to its creatures, and to human existence" (p. 14). Maintaining the integrity and/or coherence of Indigenous research depends on the overt recognition, in words and actions, of the connection between Indigenous knowledge and Indigenous research.

Using Indigenous methodologies does not mean that Indigenous researchers dismiss other theories and/or methodologies (Steinhauer, 2002). Rather, it means that we as Indigenous researchers are engaged in the processes of developing theoretical understandings and practices that arise out of our own Indigenous knowledges. Smith (1999) emphasized the importance of this engagement in understanding the past, often negative experiences that our own peoples have had with research.

Accepting the Responsibility of Conducting Research

As I was preparing to begin my research, I was very cognizant of this privilege of doing advanced research. The most serious consideration for me as a researcher was the assurance that I would be able to uphold the personal responsibility that goes along with doing research with and amongst my own people, using an Indigenous research methodology. Throughout my study I was always conscious of making sure that I was doing the "right" thing and that what I did and said would not harm anyone in the process. It did not take long for me to realize that I could not do this alone. I prayed often, asking for guidance and direction and giving thanks for having been given the opportunity to study at this level. As a researcher, I have a tremendous responsibility. Weber-Pillwax (2003) pointed out the significance of personal responsibility for Indigenous researchers who are doing "formal research" with Indigenous communities. She suggested that, as a researcher, "I am accepting responsibility and accountability for the impact of the project on the lives of the community members with whom I will be working" (p. 2).

The challenge of pulling out the words of my limited English vocabulary to articulate a part of the reality in which I am immersed is extremely demanding both intellectually and emotionally. I asked myself whether I had earned the right to even talk about Indigenous research methodologies. I was raised with the understanding that although I was physically capable of doing something, this did not necessarily grant me the right to do it. For example, knowing the procedures for conducting a sweat does not grant me the right to host one. Second, coming into this study as a Native person with traditional beliefs, I was not sure whether my claim to using an Indigenous research methodology would send out the message that I am an expert in the area, which I am not. As I shared earlier, all of my teachers have always emphasized humility, and they taught me never to act as though I knew everything. These personal reservations may be interpreted as weaknesses, but they were significant considerations in my effort to articulate how the concept of an Indigenous research methodology applies to my own work. Lightning (1992) shared a story about experiencing a similar apprehension:

> I said to him in Cree, "Grandfather, I don't know how to do these things. I am trying to prepare the protocol but I realize that basically I don't know anything. As a matter of fact, I have no idea what I'm doing. Please, I implore you, have compassion for what I am doing."
>
> Elder Art Raining Bird, for all of his stature and knowledge, was a living example of humility. He looked at me and answered with a deep kindness, and understanding, saying, "It's nothing my grandson. We don't know anything." (p. 216)

Although we may know a great deal about the topic we are researching or studying, we never become experts because there is always so much more to learn. Elder Raining Bird explained to Lightning that learning is a lifelong process and that knowledge can be attained only in stages:

> The Elder then took a stick about 16 inches long from the ground a few feet away from where they were sitting on the grass. He scratched a notch at about the middle of the stick, and then indicating one end of the stick and that notched mark said, "This is when you are born and this notch is 50 years old. In this area between being born up to 50 years of age, you do not know anything." He then pointed from the notch at the middle of the stick to the other end and stated that from 50 years of age to 100 years of age you can say that you begin to have a hunch, and intuitive feeling, for knowledge. From 100 years of age and on, you have entered an area, a stage in your life, where you know something. (p. 217)

This story has had a strong impact on me, and Elder Raining Bird's words have humbled me into having a much deeper respect for the culture into which I was born. Regardless of my own apprehensions about personal worthiness, using an Indigenous research methodology to conduct my research is a privilege and an honor with which I have been blessed just by being a Cree woman. It is important, however, to note here also that Indigenous scholars did not and still do not always have this opportunity to carry out formal research using a research methodology that honors and is based upon their own ways of knowing. Therefore, I embrace this particular form of Indigenous research methodology and will use it with a good heart, respectful of my own Cree traditions and values.

When Hanohano (2001) was doing his research, he designed a set of guidelines for himself, and I found that his description is very similar to the process that I followed in my own interactions within my community. He advised:

> When doing research in Aboriginal communities, always begin with prayer; give and share gifts; build and establish relationships of trust. Be humble and approach in a humble way; to gain knowledge, you need to acknowledge that you lack some; follow the Spirit and listen to what the person has to say; before closing, express gratitude and commitment to preserving the voices and intent of those involved in sharing their knowledge. (p. 65)

Hanohano's guidelines convey humility, and humility is a key ingredient in Indigenous research. Our people know that humility can be the most difficult virtue to learn and maintain, so they begin early to teach the children how to behave appropriately and respectfully. These ways are the ways of humility. Marshall (2001) commented on this virtue:

> A humble person rarely stumbles, the old ones say, because such a person walks with his face toward the Earth and can see the path ahead. On the other hand, the arrogant man who walks with his head high to bask in the glory of the moment will stumble often because he is more concerned with the moment than what lies ahead. (p. 19)

Indigenous Knowledge in Indigenous Research

Indigenous knowledge is said to be personal, oral, experiential, holistic, narrative and metaphorical in nature (Castellano, 2000) and is retained and expressed, expanded and contracted according to social, political, historical, and spatial dimensions of individuals and the group. "The knowledge valued in Aboriginal societies derives from multiple sources including *traditional teachings, empirical observations, and revelations*" (p. 23), all of which are equally important. Brief summaries of Castellano's descriptions of these sources follow.

Traditional knowledge (Castellano, 2000) is something that has been handed down from earlier generations, often through creation stories, the treaties, and all the events that occurred throughout history. Elders play a major role in passing on traditional knowledge and teachings. In Cree societies we have two types of stories, *atchimona* (mere stories, accounts, reports) and *atayohkana* (sacred stories).

Empirical knowledge is gained through watching and listening. Before the arrival of Europeans, much of an Indigenous child's empirical knowledge was attained through this type of instruction. Castellano (2000) quoted Waldram, who described how knowledge is created through this mode: "This information processing forms a constant loop in which new information is interpreted in the context of existing information, and revisions to the state of knowledge concerning a particular phenomenon are made when necessary" (p. 23). In Cree communities everyone was a teacher. But there were specialists as well. There were also particular roles and functions to guide the establishment of learning environments, methodologies, and content.

Revelations or revealed knowledge is acquired "through dreams, visions, and intuitions that are understood to be spiritual in origin" (Castellano, 2000, p. 24). Traditionally, much of what we did was influenced by our dreams, our visions, and our intuition. Brody (1983; as cited in Castellano, 2000) described the power of dreaming and explained that some Beaver people of northeastern British Columbia still use dreams:

> Some old-timers, men who became famous for their powers and skills, had been great dreamers. Hunters and dreamers. They did not hunt as most people do. They did not seek uncertainly for the trails of the animals whose movements we can only guess at. No, they located their prey in dreams, found their trails, and made dream-kills. Then, the next day, or a few days later, whenever it seemed auspicious to do so, they could go out, find the trail, re-encounter the animals, and collect the kill. (p. 24)

Cree and Dene people, who live close to the land and to animals as trappers, hunters, or fishermen, also rely on revealed knowledge. Lives of solitude or lifestyles that encourage revelations or altered states of awareness accept revealed knowledges as a part of everyday reality and a normal, ordinary source of knowledge or information and understanding.

Stan Wilson (1995) shared a story that is also a good example of revealed knowledge. He spoke of an experience that he had while he was in Georgia several years ago:

> As I walked I had an overwhelming feeling of being welcomed in a powerful way. Yet at the same time there was a sadness, almost a melancholy feeling. It was a wistful feeling and yet I knew that I was welcomed. . . . Later that night an image came to me. I don't know if it was a dream while I was sleeping or if it was a vision that came to me as I was waking up. Whatever it was, it woke me with a start. The image was clear and remains clear to this day. (p. 62)

When Stan told his friend, Lionel Kinunwa, about this sad, yet welcomed feeling and about his vision, Kinunwa's response was, "You've had a ten thousand-year-old experience. Your ancestors were happy to see one of their own kind" (p. 65). The dream or vision had a teaching attached.

Cardinal (2001) also spoke of this revealed knowledge in his story about Elders whom he had observed at an Elders' think tank:

> They would say, "Let's sleep on it," and the meeting would end. They would have their own personal ceremonies, maybe go into the sweat lodge, or they would go into a pipe ceremony. Early the next morning, by 6 o'clock, they would already be meeting while government officials were trying to wake up.
>
> The Elders would talk about their dreams. They would say something like, "I saw this bear walking around the mountain and I was standing there and he took me by surprise," and so forth. The other Elders would listen closely, trying to understand what this could mean. Then they compared information from their dream or vision work. The process of Circle work and Dream work are methods: Indigenous methods that speak clearly to an Indigenous perspective, and Indigenous worldview. (p. 181)

I too had a very significant dream while I was writing this dissertation. At the time a battle was occurring between my head and my heart. I was having major doubts, and a nagging uncertainty plagued me about writing this dissertation. Throughout the data-collection process I often asked myself the following questions, which placed a separation between myself and the research methodology I had selected: Am I worthy? Do I know enough about an Indigenous research methodology to use it? I never want to be considered an expert in this area, and if I use it, will I be placing myself in a category in which I do not belong? And if I am, is that deception? These and many more questions plagued me. Then one day Shawn Wilson (2003) sent me a copy of his dissertation. I have always been in awe of Wilson's work in the area of Indigenous research, and after I read his dissertation from front to back, my anxiety and fear escalated: Shawn knows so much, and I know so little. The night that I finished reading his dissertation, I had a dream, and it was this dream that changed my thinking. Although it took months to sift through the whole dream, a partial answer finally came to me. I was being granted the permission to use this framework. This is why I had this dream! I realized immediately after I awoke that this dream would be an important vehicle for my understanding. I did not know how, but I knew it would be, so I recorded it immediately. I share this dream exactly as I recorded it in my diary:

> It is 4:30 a.m. and I just had the weirdest dream. I am sure it would have continued had the fire alarm not gone off, but I think this is where it was meant to end anyway. I don't really understand what it means, but I am confident that the answer will come to me in time....
>
> In the dream several people were standing along side a body of water, it was a river. The people were cheering, getting themselves ready to jump onto a huge piece of ice that was coming downstream. (It must have been a river for the huge piece of ice, possibly an iceberg was moving swiftly in our direction.) I had no idea why all this was happening, and why everyone there wanted to get on board that large piece of ice. Why, why did they want to get on? I was questioning myself in my dream. From where I was standing downstream, I could see people taking a run at in, only to land in the chilling waters. I saw the iceberg moving closer to where I was standing, and suddenly I had the urge to do the same. Without thinking, I ran as fast as I could. I jumped off the embankment and landed right on the ice. Oh my gosh, I was on!! But why was I on? What an exhilarating feeling! I was on the ice, floating downstream! As I was floating downstream, others tried to jump on, but no one made it, except Shawn Wilson. Although dozens of people tried to jump on, why were there only two of us that made it? Was it because I had just finished reading his dissertation that he was on there too? Did this dream have anything to do with his work? Was this dream about Indigenous research? What did the iceberg represent? After reading his dissertation, I had a clearer understanding about the importance of using an Indigenous framework, but I don't know why I made it onto the piece of ice, while others did not.

Another concept that might be categorized as a form of revealed knowledge is *cellular memory*. The basis of this concept is that knowledge is carried in our cells and through various means may be revealed or brought to our consciousness. I was introduced to this concept of cellular memory in 2001, and since then it has fascinated me. When I first heard about this way of knowing, I was skeptical, yet as I listened to various students talk about this theory, it began to make sense. The students who shared this knowledge had been exposed to the concept by a traditional teacher, the late Lionel Kinunwa. He had taught that memories are stored in our cells. One of his students elaborated on what this meant to her: "You know how sometimes you just know something without being told, or how sometimes you get the feeling that you know someone? This is cellular memory" (P. Steinhauer, personal communication, November 15, 2002). To elaborate further, I quote Stan Wilson (1995) on this topic:

Lionel said, "We have memories. Our ancestral memories are in our blood, they're in our muscles, they're in our bones, they're in our hair." He said that many of us do not pay attention to these memories because we are too busy paying attention to what's going on in the modern world. We don't pay attention to our historic memory. This is why when we hear the drum, our spirit is moved. The vibrations of the drum stir old memories—our ancestral memories. These memories come out of the molecular structure of our being. This is also why when you hear someone speaking your language, your molecular structure picks up those vibrations, because each language has its own peculiar patterns, and you feel good that somebody is speaking your language.

Does this cellular memory explain intuition? From where does that nagging sense of knowing, yet with no concrete proof, come? Cardinal (2001) asserted, "One thing we all have in common, however, is our intuition" (p. 182). He, too, spoke about Lionel Kinunwa:

Lionel Kinunwa spoke of this as molecular or cellular memory. I have met many young Native people who have come to me and said, "I've always felt different, but not in the sense that I was an Indian and I looked different from the rest, but there is something different down inside." I think as human beings we have a deep connection to our Indigenous roots. Young people in the cities or even on the reserves who do not have connections to their culture and traditions look for these connections. (p. 182)

For many of us, revealed knowledge is a way of knowing. This type of knowing, often guides what we do and say, as well as what we do not do and say. When I applied at the university to do my PhD, it was my intention to study the divisive conflicts between the various religious groups in my community. I wanted to know why religion mattered so much to a people who were already so spiritually grounded. It was my theory that there was a correlation between cultural loss, high school dropout rates, low self-esteem, and the religions that had been forced upon us. But within weeks of starting the program I knew that this was not the work that I was going to do. There was something else for me to study, but I did not know what it was. Then one day I suddenly knew that my research would be about parental school choice in First Nations communities. I had not gone through the intellectual exercise of trying to determine what I would be studying, but something within me told me that this would be my research topic. Was my late father guiding my decision making? Perhaps the revelation that I spoke of in the first chapter (learning about my father's passion about Indian education) was already trying to reveal itself at the time that I changed my topic.

Do the active connections to our past, this capacity and practice of tapping into or accessing consciously revealed knowledge through our dreams and visions, speak directly to a worldview that is different from those of the educators and teachers in standard, non-Indigenous schools? If this is so, as my personal experiences have indicated, then parental school choice becomes a crucial topic, linked inevitably to the survival of this Indigenous worldview.

Indigenous Worldview

According to Henderson (2000):

An Indigenous worldview assumes that all [life] forms are interconnected, and that the survival of each life form is dependent on the survival of all others. Aboriginal worldviews also note that the force to the life forms is derived from an unseen but knowable spiritual realm. (p. 261)

All life is sacred, and all life forms are connected. Humans are neither above nor below others in the circle of life. Everything that exists in the circle is one unity, one heart:

> The Aboriginal worldview teaches Aboriginal people, to feel humble about their existence. They are but one strand in the web of life. In the circle of which all life forms are a part of, humans are dependent upon all the other forces for their survival. Aboriginal worldviews also teach that humans exist to share life according to their abilities. They exist to care for and renew the web of life, and therefore they must respect and value all forces of life. Often this worldview is called the process of humility. (p. 259)

Our worldviews are reflected in our language, knowledge, unity, and social order. Although Indigenous worldviews are distinct and connected to particular locations and groups of people, the one thing that binds us together as Indigenous people is the shared understanding of interconnectedness, the understanding that all things are dependent on each other. Graveline (1998) explained: "We are like one big family with all our relations. Nothing we do, we do by ourselves; together we form a circle. That which the trees exhale, I inhale. That which I exhale, the tree inhales" (p. 56). An Indigenous worldview is different from the Western worldview in that "western thought conceptualizes history in a linear temporal sequence, whereas most Native American thinking conceptualizes history in a spatial fashion" (Duran & Duran, 2000, pp. 90-91).

Temporal thinking means that we think of time as having a beginning and an end, whereas with spatial thinking we view events as a function of space where the event actually took place. Duran and Duran (2000) added:

> The Native American worldview is a systematic approach to being in the world that can best be categorized as process thinking as opposed to content thinking found in the Western worldview. Process thinking is best described as a more action and 'eventing' approach to life versus a world of subject/object relationships. . . . Thus the Native worldview is one in which the individual is part of all creation, living life as one system and not in separate units that are objectively relating with each other. The idea of the world or creation existing for the purpose of human domination and exploitation—the core of most Western ideology—is absent in Native American thinking. (p. 91)

Duran and Duran discussed worldview in relation to Indigenous ways of conceptualizing or thinking. At the same time, however, Indigenous methodologies have been inextricably connected with the spirit as the key element of the being of a person or a people. Within this perspective then, an Indigenous worldview cannot solely be described as an Indigenous way of thinking; it must also be recognized for its connection to Indigenous ways of being.

The integration of the individual as an emotional, physical, intellectual, and spiritual being is the expression of a worldview. An integrated individual in the Cree world will think and live from within an integrated Cree worldview. The stronger that an individual is rooted in his/her own Cree ways of being and ways of thinking, in traditions and worldview, the more difficult will be his/her experiences of learning within the context of another foreign worldview, as in the situation that Canadian schooling presents.

Therefore, how does one provide a detailed description of an Indigenous worldview when so much of this view is derived from our ways of being? Worldviews are not something that individuals or groups discuss and deliberately set about to learn; they become part of a person or a people right from birth (Steinhauer, 2002). Worldviews are shaped by the interaction between individual/community and the physical, social, emotional, and mental aspects of the person's environment. Graveline (1998) explained:

> A spiritual connection helps not only to integrate our self as a unified entity, but also to integrate the individual into the world as a whole. Spirituality is experienced as an ongoing process, allowing the individual to move towards experiencing connection—to family, community, society and Mother Earth. (p. 55)

Descriptive and convincing explanations of Indigenous worldviews as distinct and useful in the world of academics or to scholarship in general is not now accepted as meaningful, nor is it likely to ever be accepted until it has been presented in application and practice in ways that have an impact on mainstream Canadian non-Aboriginal lives. What I have presented is only enough to point out that a Cree worldview exists as an Indigenous worldview, and it is from this perspective that I speak, write, and have conducted this research. There is no other perspective from which I may speak with integrity.

Readers of my work will not necessarily all read from an Indigenous worldview or perspective and it will not be obvious to them or me what points of the differing worldview will need to be clarified or pulled out as significant junctures where meanings do not "fit" with each other and cannot cross the worldview divide. These points of difference in meanings can only be identified and articulated, and perhaps resolved, only in mutually respectful dialogue. Duran and Duran (2000) addressed this: "The legitimization of Native American thought in the Western world has not yet occurred, and it may not occur for some time" (p. 99).

It is not the intent or purpose of this work to respond to or argue for the legitimization of Native American thought. I mentioned it here only to make clear the theoretical context of the participants' interviews and my own writing. Indigenous scholars have to adhere to universities' guidelines if they are to receive the credentials to which they aspire. Legitimization of their knowledge systems can be a huge factor in the degree of difficulty that they will face in achieving their goals. This is true at all levels of schooling (Curwen Doige, 2003; Duran & Duran, 2000). Although the struggle for legitimization and acceptance has largely been occurring in academies of higher learning, Indigenous scholars continue to struggle to articulate their own knowledge systems and to have them recognized formally. Battiste and Henderson (2000) commented on this situation:

> To attempt to evaluate Indigenous worldview in absolute and universal terms is irrational. Using Eurocentric analysis, one cannot make rational choices among conflicting worldviews, especially those held by others. No worldview describes ecology more accurately than others do. All worldviews describe some parts of the ecology completely, though in their own way. (p. 38)

Henderson's (2000) words provide a good summary here: "Learning another worldview is a lifetime project that requires time and patience" (p. 261).

Data-Collection Process

Using an Indigenous research methodology as the framework for my study presented me with another challenge—deciding on which methods I would employ for collecting data. Weber-Pillwax (2003) warned that this process of selecting the right method is very complex: "For Indigenous researchers, the complexity takes specific forms, usually forms that are embedded with the values and beliefs about human interaction. These values and beliefs are inherent to the culture implicated in the research" (p. 1).

Wilson (2001) too stressed the importance of choosing the right methods to employ, because not using the right methods could result in great insult to both the researcher and participants. He suggested asking oneself the following questions in evaluating which methods will be appropriate: What is my role as a researcher, and what are my obligations? Does this method allow me to fulfill my obligations in my role? Does this method help to build a relationship between myself as a researcher and my research topic? And does it build respectful relationships with the other participants in the research? (p. 178).

I knew that some methods would fit better into my research methodology framework than others. Talking circles, storytelling, personal narratives, and participatory action research are all appropriate methods to use with Cree people because each fits into the forms and protocols of respectful interpersonal interaction. In research, each also helps to build strong relationships between the researcher and participants. I also knew that regardless of which method I chose, I would have opportunities to develop relationships and spiritual connections.

"A whole base of research tools and methods for Indigenous people has yet to be realized and incorporated into the hunt for truth, the hunt for knowledge" (Cardinal, 2001, p. 180). Although I agree with this analysis, I was comfortable in relying upon the forms of interaction, dialogue, and sharing that grew from and were respected in Cree cultural traditions.

Choosing a Method

In conducting this research I employed two primary methods: individual one-on-one interviews and storytelling. These two methods complement each other and fit well within the oral nature of Cree people's social reality: "Cree and other Indigenous societies continue to function in a consciousness of primary orality, and this reality cannot be politely set aside" (Weber-Pillwax, 2001b, p. 155). Orality continues to be the foundation of Cree consciousness in the communities where I conducted my research, and the methods that I used to collect data needed to reflect and respect the fact that "orality systems govern communication, whether interpersonal or intrapersonal" (p. 152).

For most Aboriginal people, the word *interview* can conjure up a rather formalized and intimidating picture; but when the participants are made to feel at ease and when relationship building is deemed more important than getting through the interview questions, the process can be enjoyable and even inspiring. In these situations, participants will eagerly and easily express their views and opinions. "Trust is crucial to this method, and the researcher must have a deep sense of responsibility to uphold that trust in every way" (Weber-Pillwax, 2001a, p. 170). To develop and maintain these trust relationships with the participants, the data-collection process must be guided by the principles of respect, responsibility, and reciprocity. Wilson (2003) asked several questions related to trust that spoke to my experiences and stayed in my mind throughout my own research process: "What is my role as a researcher in this relationship, and what are my responsibilities? What am I contributing or giving back to this relationship? Is the sharing, growth and learning that is taking place reciprocal?" (p. 150).

In my case, establishing trust was not difficult because I conducted the study in my own community, in which my family and others on the reserves had developed trust relationships for generations. Of higher significance to me then was the challenge to ensure that I did not break the trust that was being shown to me because of a long-held trust of my parents or my grandparents. In other words, people trusted me because they trusted my grandfather or my father, and my responsibility was to uphold that trust through what could have been essentially the imposition of a foreign and interfering process.

Interviews

In planning the process of data collection, I decided that the ideal way to obtain the information that I needed for my research was to interview. I had specific questions that I needed to ask, and although I knew that a more structured interview might provide more direct responses, I also knew that conducting an interview in this format would not fit with the methodology that I had chosen for the study. Consequently, I decided to use an unstructured interview with a more free-flowing structure that is more supportive of Cree styles of communication, particularly Cree ways of providing information through indirect means, including personal narratives and stories.

Although I used a more unstructured approach in the actual interviews, I relied upon an interview guide to ensure that I collected the same general areas of information from each participant. In total, I conducted 19 interviews, each of which was very unique because every participant had his/her own stories to tell and in his/her own setting. This type of interviewing provided a culturally appropriate way for the Cree participants to share whatever it was they wanted to share about the school-choice decisions they had made and in whatever form of dialogue and physical setting they wished to use.

Prior to carrying out the audio-recorded interviews, I visited and had tea with each participant. These initial visits gave the participants a chance to relax and to feel at ease with me and the project, as well as more comfortable about being audio-recorded. Moving from an informal to a more formal context was therefore easier and felt less superficial to both of us. I considered this part of my research process the most important phase of the data collection because this was where the basis of the work and relationship building actually occurred. Weber-Pillwax (2001a) spent a great deal of time doing this when she was conducting her research. She shared a story:

> I took a trip with a friend from the community who gave me a history of the land area during three hours of driving. I saw where people had lived, and learned who they were and how they fitted into the lives of the people who still lived there. The history of the land became alive with people and their stories. It was critical stuff, not necessarily because I use it in my research, but because it helps me to establish and maintain the relationships I have with people who live there. It also helps me to contextualize and understand the information and the stories that I am given as I get to know more people and make deeper connections in the community. (p. 171)

In the same way, the participants in my study were much more than participants. By sharing their stories, they shared their lives, and their lives became more deeply connected with mine. It was not relationship building so that I could do the research; rather, it was the research allowing me to deepen, understand, and make real my relationships with people who already had had generations of intimate connection with me through my family.

The interview guide was useful because it kept the parameters of the data clear to me as well as to the participants. However, I did not permit the guide to take away from the data-collection process as a prescribed and rigid set of questions might have done. I felt that an intuitive, authentic engagement with the participants would more likely occur if we moved with the natural flow that evolved with each dialogue, and it proved to be a better way of collecting data. All of the questions in my guide received answers and information, and the responses had an unanticipated richness and depth to the issues that I attributed to the open-ended approach to the interviews. As a result, powerful learning took place for both myself as researcher and the participants who contributed and entrusted me with the stories of their own pasts, their own and their children's presents, and, essentially, the futures of both.

Storytelling

Within the context of the interviews, it became clear, almost immediately, that oral tradition and storytelling are still central to Cree personal and community identity. Everyone in the community has at least one story to tell, and every participant in the study had several stories to share. They shared real-life stories about their children's schooling experiences and gave stark accounts of betrayal and disruption as well as positive descriptions of success, joys, and achievements in their personal lives. Stories are very powerful ways of providing and generating information, and the best thing about them is that every story that is told generates another. Thomas King (2003) in *The Truth About Stories: A Native Narrative* commented, "The truth about stories is that that's all we are" (p. 32). Quoting the Anishnabe writer Gerald Vizenor, he added, "You can't understand the world without telling a story. There isn't any centre to the world but a story" (p. 32). The participants wanted me to understand their world, and they used stories to help me do that.

In most, if not all, Aboriginal societies, stories were used for teaching; and in most Cree communities, they still are. Stories are important because they

> allow the listener to draw their own conclusions and to gain life lessons from a personal perspective. By getting away from either abstraction or over-riding rules that one should adhere to, stories allow us to see others life experiences through our own lens. (Wilson, 2003, p. 22)

Tafoya (1995) observed, "We all have a lot of stories to tell.... Scientists say we are made of atoms, but I think we are made of stories. When we die people remember the stories of our lives and the stories that we told" (pp. 7-11). He added:

> Stories go in circles; they don't go in straight lines. It helps if you listen in circles, because there are stories inside and between stories, and finding your way through them is as easy and as hard as finding your way home. Part of finding is getting lost, and when you're lost you start to open up and listen. (pp. 11-12)

According to King (2003), "We live by stories, we also live in them" (p. 153). The participants in this study lived the stories that they shared, and by sharing them with me, they were giving them to everyone. They invited us not only to see their experiences with our lens, but also to walk with them through their experiences and to thereby understand their decisions and their actions. Without even knowing it, these participants were effecting change because, through their stories, the educational stories of future generations can be changed. If we can change our own stories and the stories of those who hear the stories, the stories of those who come after us might also be changed.

Community Selection

One day a colleague asked me why I wanted to pursue a PhD, and my response to her was, "I want to do it for my community. There is so much more that I have to learn. Now that I have had a taste of graduate school, I want more. The more I learn, the more I will be able to give back to my community." As I reflected on what I had said to her, I realized how important my community is to me. My identity is not formed in opposition to my community; rather, my community is a part of me, as much as I am a part of it.

When I say "my community," I am referring to Saddle Lake Cree Nation first, and to Whitefish Lake First Nation, also known as the Goodfish Lake Reserve, second. (From here on, I will refer to Whitefish Lake First Nation as Goodfish Lake reserve.) Although Saddle Lake and Goodfish Lake are administered separately, they are considered one band under the Indian Act—Saddle Lake Band #462. Separately, they are Saddle Lake Cree Nation #125 and Whitefish Lake First Nation #128. The fact that both reserves constitute one band is not the reason that I decided to do my study in both communities. Rather, it was because I consider both of these reserves "my communities." Although I was raised in the Saddle Lake First Nation, I spent a great deal of my youth at my grandparents' homestead just outside the perimeter of the Goodfish Lake reserve. Many of my relatives continue to reside on this reserve as well.

Because of the close kinship between Saddle Lake and Goodfish Lake people, there are many similarities. However, one of the major differences is the degree of adopted Christian influence. A participant from Goodfish Lake described the difference in this way:

> Saddle Lake is more traditional. Although many consider themselves Catholics and Protestants, most members practice Native spirituality. Goodfish Lake is predominately a Christian community, where Native spirituality is considered taboo by most. In fact, I could probably count on one hand how many people practice Native spirituality in this community. Henry Bird Steinhauer and his family had a big influence on this reserve, and that influence remains.

Another reason that I selected these two communities was that I thought that I might collect different data from the two communities, only because I believed that religious affiliation and/or Native spirituality might be an influencing factor in school-choice decision making. In fact, the data from both communities were fairly consistent, and, as I will reveal, my theory had very little to do with the parents' decision-making processes.

The goal of both Saddle Lake and Goodfish Lake is to create self-sufficient Nations that provide their members with a sustainable, high qualify of life, as Chief Eddy Makokis from the Saddle Lake Cree Nation clearly stated:

> I believe that Saddle Lake Cree people have the ability to develop a self-sustaining economic base so that the First Nation may control its own economic destiny. Saddle

Lake [Cree] Nation has no alternative but to develop a self-sustaining economic sector based on the needs of the growing population, depleting natural resources, limited land base, federal funding cuts attributed to the federal devolution process, and other factors. (Meyers Norris Penny LLP, 2006, p. 1)

Saddle Lake Cree Nation[7]

Population and location. Saddle Lake Cree Nation reserve is located 1.5 hours northeast of Edmonton, Alberta, and 20 minutes west of St. Paul, Alberta. It has a membership of 8,475 (Indian and Northern Affairs Canada, 2006). According to Indian and Northern Affairs Canada's residency breakdown, 68% live on the Saddle Lake reserve, 1% live on other reserves, and 31% live elsewhere. Approximately 60% of Saddle Lake Cree Nation's population is under the age of 30. It is estimated that by 2030 the band's population will have tripled to between 20,000 and 25,000.

Although Saddle Lake Cree Nation has at least four convenience stores on the reserve, three of which are privately owned, most of the shopping is done in the nearby town of St. Paul. At least 60% of St. Paul's income comes from Saddle Lake reserve, but despite this, Native people are not treated well in the town. Although most St. Paul residents would deny that racism exists, Native people would say otherwise. They would say that "racism prevails and flourishes in the town" (Marleen). It was because of these racist attitudes that the Saddle Lake Cree Nations boycotted the town of St. Paul in March 2005 for the second time. "Millions of dollars are spent in the town of St. Paul, yet you will not see any of our own people working in the stores or other businesses, so why should we continue to give them our money?" a band member wondered. "Racism prevails," suggested another.

Political structure and tribal council membership. One Chief and eight councilors, all democratically elected, govern the band. Elections are held every three years. The Chief and Council of the Saddle Lake First Nation are the band's recognized responsible governance body in all matters including education.

Employment/unemployment rate. Like many other First Nations in Canada, the current unemployment rate on Saddle Lake First Nations is high, estimated at about 80%–85%. However, of this figure, Saddle Lake needs to identify the percentage of its unemployed members who are employable.

Schools. Informally calculated, the school-age population of approximately 1,000 youth between the ages of 6 and 19 years is served by Saddle Lake schools and neighboring town schools. Approximately 75% of those students attend school off-reserve, which is a substantially high off-reserve number. Saddle Lake schools include Onchaminahos Elementary School (Grades 1 through 5) and Kihew Asiniy Education Centre (Grades 6 through 12). Since the takeover of the administration of the Saddle Lake educational programming in 1980, governance and policy decisions have been entrusted to a board appointed by the Chief and Council.

Economic development overview. The Saddle Lake Tribal Administration is the overall administrative body that delivers the Nation's programs and services. It was created in 1968 to transfer control to Saddle Lake Cree Nation to administer the delivery of its own programs and services. The programs on-reserve include Child and Family Services, Social Services, Public

---

[7] I extracted much of the information on Saddle Lake from the Saddle Lake Cree Nation Economic Development Strategic Plan (2005 to 2030) that Meyers Norris Penny LLP prepared in 2006.

Works, Economic Development, Finance, Agriculture, Education, Human Resources Development (HRD), and Health.

Currently, the community economic development activities fall under the responsibility of the Economic Development Office. This department and Peyasew Management Ltd.[8] both focus on generating sustainable wealth for the Saddle Lake Cree Nation. Peyasew Management Ltd. currently oversees five companies that the Saddle Lake Cree Nation owns, and it reports directly to the Chief and Council. Among several other business ventures, Saddle Lake First Nation and Whitefish (Goodfish) Lake jointly own Keyano Pimee Exploration Company Ltd., a First Nations–private sector venture to drill and produce natural gas on their reserves. Saddle Lake First Nation also owns 43% of Pimee Well Servicing, a company that operates seven service rigs. It also owns 51% of two drilling rigs, and Western Lakota owns the remaining 49%.

Whitefish Lake (Goodfish Lake) First Nation[9]

Population and location. Goodfish Lake is a First Nations community located two hours northeast of Edmonton, Alberta. It has an estimated membership of approximately 2,000, but only about 1,200 of that total population reside on the reserve. Like other First Nations, the population of this community is very young, and approximately 65% of the total population is under the age of 30 years.

Although the reserve has many of the amenities of a small town, including a bank, most people prefer to do their business outside the community. The larger centers are about 45 miles from Goodfish Lake; therefore most people will travel the few extra miles north or west to do their business.

Political structure and tribal council membership. A Chief and Council of four members is the band's governing body in all matters on the reserve. Programs on-reserve include Child and Family Services, Social Services, Public Works, Economic Development, Finance, Agriculture, Education, HRD, and Health.

Schools. It is estimated that there are about 500 children of school age in the community of Goodfish Lake, of whom only about 20% attend the local Pakan School, whereas about 70% attend school in the neighboring towns. The remaining 10% do not attend school at all (Veronica).

Goodfish Lake's elementary school, Pakan, has been on the reserve for several decades, but local management of education took place only in the mid 1990s. Approximately 10 years ago, shortly after the takeover, a new school was built approximately four miles north of the old school, but it still looks new. It is a beautiful facility that can accommodate approximately 350 students. At the time of data collection only 120 students attended Grades 1 to 9. Although there is no high school program, students can access high school courses via Cyber School. Most of the students who attend Pakan School are in playschool through Grade 6, with the majority in the lower elementary grades.

Economic development overview. Goodfish Lake has a solid economic base. The band has owned and operated a dry-cleaning plant and sewing centre since 1978. In 2006 a $5.4 million dry-cleaning and laundry facility was opened. The dry-cleaning plant has a long-

---

[8] Peyasew Management Ltd. became operational in April 2005 to oversee and provide management expertise to Saddle Lake's businesses and investments. It is owned and operated by the Saddle Lake First Nation and is 100% aboriginally owned and controlled.

[9] I obtained information on Whitefish Lake (Goodfish Lake) First Nations from a variety of band members, but I was unable to obtain an economic development strategic plan from this community.

term contract with Syncrude Canada to sew and clean industrial clothing. With the increase in demand from the oilsands development in the Fort McMurray area, this new plant could not have been built at a better time. The dry-cleaning and laundry centre is just one of four divisions that operate under Goodfish Lake Development Corporation. The band also owns and operates a sewing and garment division and a retail outlet in Fort McMurray under the name of Protective Clothing Supplies Ltd. Recently, this company branched out and purchased a bakery in the town of St. Paul. The company currently has over 90 employees, at least 90% of whom are Aboriginal.

Other major businesses include a cattle farm, automotive shop, and several additional off-reserve oil and gas investments. Private entrepreneurs own the two convenience stores that are located within a few minutes of each other. Most members purchase their cigarettes, gas, and convenience items there, and both stores do well. One of the stores supplies the school with all the food required for its hot lunch program.

Participant Selection

I gave a letter of invitation to the people who agreed to participate in my research and described the study to them. The participants were all members of the Saddle Lake Cree Nation and Whitefish Lake (Goodfish) First Nation. They included 15 parents and 4 youth. One of the parents interviewed was an educational administrator (principal) at the time of the study, and three were school teachers. The others held various jobs on- or off-reserve, and some were unemployed at that time. I interviewed a total of 19 First Nations members from these two communities. Of the 15 parents, 8 were from the Saddle Lake Cree Nation and 7 from the Goodfish Lake First Nation. Three of the youth were from Saddle Lake, and one was from Goodfish Lake.

All of the parents were First Nation members, and all were living on-reserve at the time of the study. I interviewed two groups of parents: those who were currently sending or had sent their children to an off-reserve public (provincial school) and those who were currently sending or had sent their children to the on-reserve band-operated school. All but one of the youth were still living within their communities. One was just completing Grade 12, another was attending a nearby college, and the other two were employed full time, one on-reserve and one off-reserve.

Initially, I intended to choose my participants as representatives of family clans[10] and to work with a manageable number of possibly 6 to 10 people; however, this process proved to be too complex. I decided that choosing from a band membership list[11] of almost 10,000 members was an unreasonable approach to take. Instead, I selected three members from each community whom I thought would represent certain clans, and I then contacted those people. At that point snowballing sampling[12] seemed to take over. Not everyone on my original list was able to participate, but they were able and eager to recommend someone else. Following that first round of interviews, each one of those participants recommended someone else that I should interview. After completing 13 interviews with parents, two more parents asked if it was too late to take part in the study. I was humbled by their interest in my work, and I invited them to participate. I recruited the youth in much the same way.

---

[10] A clan is a group of people united by kinship and descent, which is defined by perceived descent from a common ancestor. Even if actual lineage patterns are unknown, clan members nonetheless recognize a common ancestor.

[11] A list of persons that a band or INAC maintains under Section 8 of the Indian Act.

[12] A technique for developing a research sample in which existing study subjects recruit future subjects from among their acquaintances. Thus the sample group appears to grow like a rolling snowball.

Essentially then, through this process the community chose my participants and determined how many persons I would interview. I was committed to using an Indigenous framework when I set out to collect the data and select the participants, and I believe that by allowing the community to determine whom I would interview, I was living up to my commitment. Traditionally, this was the way that we have conducted activities and regular business in our communities. Those people who are best suited to perform different tasks or answer specific questions are recognized in the community for such skills or knowledge, and, in my case, interview referrals would have been made according to that traditional system. I am grateful that my research participants were selected in this way. It was no accident that after I became overwhelmed trying to figure out the band list, people were sent my way; the people of the communities are the keepers of the information I was seeking, and I am confident that those people who were supposed to participate were recommended and did participate. The community knew who would represent them in this study.

As I indicated above, of the 15 parents who participated in this study, 4 were educators who were currently working within the school system. I recognize that this may be perceived as a conflict of interest; however, in this context that perception is likely wrong. The following is a logical explanation that is grounded within the cultural practices and values of these particular communities.

As I pointed out earlier, in these two First Nations communities the people recognized that certain individuals possess specific skills and knowledge that would be particularly relevant to my study. It is those individuals who were called upon to speak for the community. Because they were referred to me by the people, and because I was an Indigenous researcher in those communities, I had to respect and accept this way of selecting the interviewees. If I had not conducted the interviews, that would have not only insulted the individuals, but also jeopardized my relationships and broken the trust that was already a part of my own family's heritage. Such action would have denied me the respect and social recognition that lie within the system of social interaction that has governed these communities for centuries. Furthermore, if I had not interviewed them, my actions would have been interpreted simply as those of another academic who had no real connection or integrity in relation to the communities; because of my own place in the community, the positive nature of my personal connections would have been severely threatened. In the end, there was no conflict of any type. I recognized that these specific individuals were asked to participate in this study because of their perceived or recognized ability to articulate the issues, the problems, and the concerns that the communities share freely and publicly about their schooling systems. The communities were confident that these particular individuals would be able to speak on their behalf, and as a researcher, so was I.

In total, I audiotaped 20 interviews. The 20th interview was with Brian Wildcat, a member of the Ermineskin Cree Nation of Maskwachees (Hobbema, Alberta). Brian is currently the Director of Treaty 6 Education and is working with a team to develop a strategic plan for education development for the schools in the Treaty 6 area.[13]

I conducted the majority of the interviews in my home and three at the participants' workplaces. The interviews varied from 45 to 120 minutes; most lasted about 60 minutes. I fully informed all of the participants about the study and of their right to withdraw from the study at

---

[13] The Treaty 6 area includes the following reserves: Saddle Lake Cree Nation, Whitefish Lake (Goodfish Lake) First Nation, Alexis Band, Beaver Lake First Nations, Cold Lake First Nation, Enoch Cree Nation, Ermineskin First Nation, Louis Bull Tribe, Montana Band, Samson First Nation, Frog Lake First Nation, Heart Lake First Nation, Kehewin Cree Nation, O'Chiese First Nation, Paul First Nation, and Sunchild First Nation.

any time without penalty, and I asked them to sign consent forms to participate and confidentiality agreements.

Cultural Protocol

I considered cultural protocols in every action that I performed during this study. Different community members required different sets of protocol procedures that I carefully followed. I knew that if I did not properly adhere to these procedures, I would not get the cooperation that I was seeking. I also realized that protocol is much more than just handing over a package of tobacco or the presentation of material gifts. Hanohano (2001) elaborated:

> Protocol can be formal or informal, private or public, individual or communal, personal or general, but in all cases, respectful. Protocol is the process that acknowledges and recognized the *mana* (spiritual essence or power) or the being or entity at hand. To ignore those steps reflects badly upon the individuals upbringing and parentage, and diminishes the sacredness of the person's status and being. (p. 62)

Protocol can be represented in the form of words and gestures, but everything that is done must be done from the heart, with respect and humility guiding the process. There is no set prescription for how to carry any of this out, and as an Elder once told me, "If you want to know anything or if you want to do anything, just ensure you do it with a good heart. The answers will come, and you will be shown the way." To achieve this humility, I had to become the student and accept the participants as my teachers.

I also had to make a commitment to myself that the work I was doing would never be used for economic or political gain or just to produce a thesis and earn a credential. I was conducting the research for the communities of Saddle Lake and Goodfish Lake, and, ultimately, these two communities own the data. I say this because the data that I gathered and the knowledge that I gained did not originate from me, but from those people who became my participants. "I might do the work, write up the findings, and determine the themes or patterns from the information shared; that knowledge did not originate with me, and thus does not belong to me" (Hanohano, 2001, p. 70).

I have been reminded many times that humility is a key teaching within Native societies. When I was a young child, my grandmother used to say to me, "*Kaya mamihcimo*," meaning "Don't brag" or "Don't elevate yourself." I carry these words in my heart, and I carried them into my research with me. Hanohano (2001) shared his thoughts on the importance of remaining humble:

> To approach members of my family and community properly, I must do so not as a 'researcher,' but as a 'humble seeker.' Because I am a member of the community—an insider, I could not and did not approach my community nor am I allowed to conduct myself as if I were outside the social norms and expectations that govern the behavior of our community. In other words, I could not appear to be above or better than my own family or community. In all ways, I acted and behaved as if I never left. I hold a place in my community, and while I may return possessed of new knowledge and teachings, the collective wisdom of my Elders and community supersedes anything that I bring. There will be a time and place for sharing the things that I have learned, but for purposes of my

place in my community, I am there to learn as if it were 'at the feet of my Elders.' (pp. 64-65)

Over the past several years I have read many dissertations, articles, essays, and books authored by Indigenous people all over the world, and the one thing that has always struck me is that anonymity does not appear to be an issue. Many of these scholars (Hanohano, 2001; Lightning, 1992; Makokis, 2001; Meyer, 1998; Wilson, 2003) used their participants' real identities. I attributed this to respect, and reading Hanohano's thesis affirmed this for me:

> For me to remove their names from their stories and teachings is disrespectful and presumptuous, and gives the appearance that the words are now mine. This would destroy the trust and respect of our relationship, is misappropriation of the common kind, and totally out of keeping with proper protocol and etiquette. (p. 82)

But in my study I also had to ensure that I respected those participants who did not wish to be identified. I ensured that their anonymity was protected through the use of pseudonyms. This decision also evolved from within the research process. Although five people clearly stated at the beginning that they did not want to be named, the others gave me permission to use their true identities if I felt that it would be useful to the study. Because being named or not named did not really matter to these parent participants, I decided to keep the anonymity consistent. Therefore, I have assigned pseudonyms to all of the participants, with the exception of Florence, the principal of the Saddle Lake Onchaminahos School (also a parent participant), and Brian Wildcat, Director of Treaty 6 Education (not a parent participant). Disguising the identity of the principal would have been impossible because of the way that I chose to present the data.

Ethical Behavior

"Many of the decisions that researchers will face are moral ones, rather than epistemological ones, so ethical behaviour needs to occur throughout the research process" (Martin, 2002, p.10). Research, to me, is about gaining trust and maintaining integrity. To be truly ethical, I had to recognize and respond to the duality of the research context and act in a culturally appropriate manner. For the Indigenous researcher, acting in a culturally responsive and responsible manner comes from a constant state of respectful being. As I conducted my study, it helped me to keep in mind the many to whom I was accountable for my actions: myself, my communities, and the University of Alberta, the educational institution of which I am a part. The University of Alberta Research Ethics Board outlined one set of the principles to which I had to adhere, but I had also to adhere to the ethics of my own community.

Trustworthiness

Ensuring the trustworthiness of the data was a consideration throughout my study. From the onset of my research plans I begin to think about the strategies that I could employ to ensure the trustworthiness and credibility of my data and of the process itself. Although anticipating issues of trustworthiness and credibility in this manner go against the Cree worldview, I knew that I needed to start thinking about these things immediately. I needed to find those validation techniques that I thought would best fit the Indigenous framework within which I was working. These techniques could not be offensive or evasive; they had to be respectful, and the participants could not perceive me as second-guessing them or putting my words in their mouths. The people who came to my study were deemed to be credible sources by the community, and I was afraid that going back to the participants in a manner that they could view as disrespectful would be a major insult not only to the individuals, but also to those people who referred them to me and, ultimately, to the community.

The two validation techniques that I decided would be the most culturally appropriate were member checks and peer debriefing. I conducted member checks by engaging the research participants in analyzing their own contributed data and confirming the findings. This technique proved to be very valuable and appreciated by the participants. Their input at this level was not only rewarding to them personally, but was also extremely helpful to my own understanding of their data contribution. It confirmed the significance and importance of this study for both myself and the participants.

In the peer debriefing sessions, I invited academic and community peers, including my supervisor, fellow Indigenous graduate students, and community members to the debriefing sessions. Their roles as debriefers proved to be extremely helpful in collaboration and clarification and offered a fresh perspective for the analyses and critiques. Sometimes these sessions were very informal, with only two or three people present; and at other times, as in an educational planning session in one of the communities where I presented some of the findings, approximately 30 people helped me to make sense of the data.

Analysis of the Data

Analyzing the data did not take place in one sitting or even after all of the interviews were finished. Consideration and analysis of what the participants had shared during the interviews was ongoing for me as researcher. Not only was I always conscious of the themes that were emerging, but also my thoughts were always replaying their words and stories. They had shared many stories during the interviews, and although on the surface the stories appeared to be straightforward and safe to take at face value, most of the narratives and comments required deeper analysis. Sometimes I was unable to sleep as the meanings of these stories grew further and further into the larger ideas inside my being.

Although my research question was specifically about school choice, the participants needed to process how they came to their decisions, and this meant that their interviews were heavy with embedded personal histories and emotions evoked by memories. It was a process of learning and healing as well as one in which I was inviting them to share a dispassionate view. Through this process I collected a massive amount of data, and sifting through it was very difficult. The participants had entrusted me with their stories; they had shared their lives, and clarity resulted only through tremendous landscapes of personal experiences. The responsibility loomed: How was I going to present this data?

I decided to analyze the data in three ways. First, I began the process by grouping concepts that seemed to pertain to the same phenomena into themes/categories by analyzing the interview text line by line. This process facilitated the emergence of larger categories and subcategories that logically related to the data. Second, I listened to the tapes again to hear what the participants were saying about the specific themes that I had chosen. Whenever possible, I contacted the participants and invited them to engage in the data-analysis process. Third, I used pertinent school-choice literature as a tool of analysis.

Reporting the Findings

In reporting the findings, I tried to ensure that I wrote the dissertation in a language and style that the communities with which I was working would be able to access. Research findings must, of necessity, suit an academic audience, but they can also be written in a style that accommodates the research participants and communities of nonacademics. The findings of this study were about and therefore for the communities. "Within Indigenous research, reporting is culturally regulated through respect of protocol to others such as: asking permission, using preferred language, terms and expressions and understanding that acknowledgement of a question is not always consent" (Martin, 2002, p. 10).

When I go back to the community to share these findings, I will be respectful and ensure that the community members easily understand them and that I honor all of my relations. I have tried to live by the guiding principles of respect, reciprocity, and relationality from the beginning to the end of this work.

Presenting the Findings

The data from the study are presented in Chapters 4, 5, and 6. Although, conventionally, the presentation of the findings represents only the voices of the participants in a study, these chapters stray from that traditional format in that I have included my own narrative as part of those findings. I chose not to separate myself as the researcher from the participants, but to include my own schooling experiences as a Native child of an on-reserve family with their stories. I did not make this decision to express a preference for one system or school choice over another (on-reserve versus off-reserve schools), but rather to allow me to use my own experiences and my stories as an integral part of the manner and context in which I have interpreted and presented the data. In addition, embedding my own stories within the text is a culturally appropriate way to contextualize my analysis and interpretations of the research participants' stories. It is one way to demonstrate openly that, as a researcher, I have not hidden or reserved anything from them in this work, either through my experiences or through my words. This is validation for the communities and the participants. "Putting yourself forward as a researcher tells the community whether or not you are connected and committed to those you are researching" (Absolon & Willett, 2005, pp. 118-119). Finally, sharing my personal stories is a significant way for me to contribute to the learning of the participants and the communities in recognition of the gifts of information and stories that they gave me.

Literature also is not traditionally presented in the findings chapters, but in this work I decided that the most effective way to discuss the literature that I found useful was to locate it within the text in direct connection with the voices of the participants. In this way I have used the literature to show that the participants' experiences and thinking are not to be interpreted as isolated cases or as confined or limited to persons from the participating communities. The literature confirmed that the experiences and issues presented in this study are not individual in nature, but rather that they represent patterns of experiences for First Nations children in particular schooling situations.

CHAPTER 4:
THE OFF-RESERVE SCHOOLING EXPERIENCE: FINDINGS

Introduction

In an effort to better understand how First Nations parents made decisions about where their children would be schooled, I asked the parents who had been selected for interviews the following question: "How did you chose the school that you would send your children to when you had the option of the on-reserve school or the off-reserve provincial schools?" Although this question generated some direct responses, most parents responded by telling me what was wrong with the current education system, both on-reserve and off-reserve. They also told me what they wanted for their children: They wanted their children to have the best education possible. They wanted them to graduate from high school and eventually become self-supporting, and they wanted them to feel happy and secure as they went through this schooling process.

The parents wanted their children to be proud of who they were, and they hoped that throughout their schooling, their children would embrace their Native heritage. However, as Pamela suggested:

> Unfortunately this [embracing one's Indianness] does not always occur. I know if I send my child to a provincial school, we will be sacrificing something because there they will not be in a position to embrace their Indianness. . . . Being Indian is not valued in these systems. . . . But we don't have much choice. We have to make the choice based on what we think will be best for our children in the long run; and for me, getting them through school and graduating them is the most important thing.

Although many of the parents whom I interviewed were not happy with the public school system, they considered it their best option if they wanted their children to graduate from high school. They did not have much faith in the reserve school system and were convinced, in addition, that the public schools provided a better education for their children. Approximately 75% of the children from both Saddle Lake and Goodfish Lake attend school off-reserve. This number indicates that the majority of the people from these two communities have serious questions and doubts about their own schools; yet most of the interviewees also repeatedly expressed dissatisfaction with the public school systems as well. First Nations parental school choices seemed to favor the public school system because the numbers suggested that their children would have a better chance of graduating from high school if they attended these schools. They offered few other reasons in support of this particular choice.

The parent participants seemed to recognize that sending their children off-reserve came with a price and that they were "making a tradeoff" (Marleen). These parents hoped that their children's schooling experience would be more than intellectual or mental exercises—that it would "meet the needs of the whole child, which includes the mental, emotional, physical, and spiritual needs" (Pamela). As will become evident in this chapter, however, this schooling system has fallen far short of meeting the emotional and spiritual needs of Native students. Despite this deficit, as most of the parents pointed out also, more and more children are leaving their reserves every morning to attend the surrounding provincial schools.

"When we live on reserve, we have only two choices: We send our kids to the provincial schools that we have tuition agreements with, or we keep them on reserve. But what kind of choices are those?" Marleen asked. She asked this question because she did not believe that the reserve school was really a choice for her. She wanted her children to have the academic rigor that they deserved, and from her perception, the reserve schools lack in this area. "But there is guilt sometimes for not supporting our own schools," a parent who had worked in the community schools admitted. Other parents shared similar concerns as well, because many knew that an exorbitant number of educational dollars were being pumped into the neighboring provincial schools each year, and very little money was actually remaining in the First Nation communities to support their local schools. Marleen expressed the conflict she felt: "What choice do we have if we want our children to graduate?" Most of the parents asked this question and felt strongly that, in fact, they had no choice.

The parents felt that they had no school choice for their children, and every one of them had endless stories to share about their own negative experiences in the public schools with which they had had connections. I asked them, in view of these types of stories, why they were still so adamant about sending their children to the off-reserve schools. Marleen explained: "Yeah, maybe at that time I didn't have a good experience personally, but educational-wise, I learned lots. In that way I did. I did do my homework when I had to, and I learned something." From Marleen's point of view, her academic progress and learning over the long term were more important than the impact of the negative experiences that she had faced. Nonetheless, Marleen did not downplay the negative effects of her schooling experience on her identity development. She was confident, however, that this would be different for her children, because, unlike her own grandparent caregivers, she was in a better position as a parent to help her children to deal with these personal struggles. On this topic Kristine reasoned, "A generation ago parents weren't in the position to talk about racism and unfair treatment with their children, but today they are, so that makes things easier for kids today." She was confident that as long as the school offered good academic programming, parents and extended family members would be able to offer the emotional and spiritual support that their children needed to make it through the system.

Marleen and all of the other parents with children in public schools wanted their children to be on par academically with their non-Native peers, and they charged that if their children attended a reserve school, this would not be possible. They were sending their children to off-reserve schools, often the same schools that they had attended themselves, because they genuinely believed that their children would have a better chance in life if they attended a public school. As Louise said, "Reserve schools lag academically."

Dakota understood that provincial schools "really do follow the curriculum," something that she thought does not happen in the reserve schools. For example:

> My niece . . . used to send her kids to the reserve school, and our children were in the same grade. My daughter was doing ten spelling words in Grade 1 and her daughter was doing two. She continued to send her kids to the reserve school because . . . it was cheaper for her to send them there. Then when her second one started on the reserve, she felt that "Maybe you are right. Maybe I will try and send them to another school." When she sent them to another school [a public school], they were put back [a grade level] because they couldn't do the work.

Stories such as Dakota's were common. Everyone shared examples that supported their views that the reserve schools are below the academic levels of the provincial schools. To these parents, providing their children with access to the same curriculum that other students in

Alberta were using was the most important criterion that guided their decisions about where to send their children to school. Bernice suggested:

> The emotional, physical, and cultural needs are the responsibility of the parents anyways. I know when I send my son off-reserve, there will be more homework for us to help ensure that he is proud of who he is and where he comes from and instill the cultural part.

Although the research question focused specifically on school choice, the participants wanted to and did share so much more information about the contexts of their decision making around schooling for their children. Every parent whom I interviewed expressed a high degree of frustration with the current local education system. Their stories clearly indicate the limitations of trying to address the formal question of school choice for First Nations parents outside the broader context of multiple personal and social issues and challenges within which the question was embedded. The stories clearly point to the fact that parental school choice, as applied to First Nations parents, cannot be discussed without due and unbiased consideration of the fact that Native parents are forced to make school choices based on factors that would receive minimal weighting, if any at all, in non-First Nations parents' school-choice decision making. Part of the reason for this lies within the broader social context of issues, but a more significant part, if the stories are heard clearly, seems to lie within the attitudes and practices carried out within the school walls, whether these schools be on- or off-reserve.

Of the 15 parents who participated in this study, 8 reported that their children were currently attending schools off-reserve, but all 15 parents had had experiences in the off-reserve public schools, either through their own schooling or because their children had once attended these schools. In this section I will share the participants' comments on and descriptions of their personal experiences in off-reserve schooling environments. As indicated above, most participants contended that public schools offer a better education, at least academically, because of their strict adherence to the Alberta curriculum; although the parents recognized that this was not all that a schooling experience should be, for them, academic achievement outweighed everything else for success in today's society. "So much emphasis is placed on academics, and I wanted to go on to postsecondary, so I decided I would never transfer to the reserve school," explained Simon, a youth participant who was completing his Grade 12 at a public high school.

Some of the participants used the term *tradeoff* to define the situation that they faced in having to give up the positive aspects normally expected from a school experience, such as caring, cultural acceptance, and valuing, to try to increase their children's academic achievement. However, they mentioned other tradeoffs in exchange for the academics of off-reserve schools; these were the negative experiences that First Nations children have to bear as a normal part of their schooling such as (a) unfair treatment, (b) low teacher expectations, (c) racism, and (d) the loss of opportunities for cultural learnings. I have chosen to present the participants' descriptions and comments on these topics in their own words to honor the voices and thinking of all those who spoke.

My elaboration on these issues clearly illustrates the fact that parental school choice for First Nations parents cannot be considered apart from the social context in which the schooling experiences of their children are embedded.

Unfair Treatment

The discussions with all participants revealed a general consensus that most Native children are not treated fairly within the public school systems. In their narratives both parents and youth referred to the following indicators of unfair treatment of Native students in the off-reserve public school systems: the special-needs categorization, the blame-the-Native-student syndrome, the time spent in detention, and the academic program streaming of Native students. In the following section I elaborate on and present these indicators as issues.

The Special-Needs Categorization

Special-education categorizations seemed to be a concern for many of the participants, and the topic of special education or special needs came up repeatedly. The participants shared stories about receiving notes and telephone calls from school personnel asking for signed permission to test their children. Although these procedures in themselves were not a problem, the stories revealed "hidden" practices that could easily be termed unprofessional and unethical, or even illegal, particularly if they had been formally challenged on the basis of standard and legislated school protocols around special-needs identification and categorization of public school students. The participants also shared their own schooling experiences in relation to this issue. One parent (Marleen) talked about being placed in a special-education class in her junior high years and admitted that her grandparents, who were raising her, had never questioned that placement. Of course, she herself had simply accepted that this was where she belonged:

> I don't know if it was a self-esteem issue or something that was blanketed with racism. There were some teachers that I felt lesser when around, and there was a point in junior high that I was put into special ed. I didn't know, but I assumed that I wasn't smart enough. . . . So I went to special ed. in junior high, up to 7, 8, and 9. . . . And then in high school I didn't go anymore. I didn't feel good [about going into special ed.], but I didn't say anything. I assumed [it was] because of being Native. . . . I always felt that White people were always smarter than I was, and it was something that I needed to accept, and I just did.

"Placing children in special-needs classes is not a thing of the past," according to Nadine. "The only difference between now and then is that the schools now need signed permission forms. They still always want to test Native kids." She recalled the time when her boys came home with these "disgusting forms!" She said, "When . . . they sent me those forms for me to sign, I just ripped them up! There was no way they were going to make money off my kids. They did not have special needs." Claire, another parent, recalled a similar incident that occurred the year that she decided to send her daughter off-reserve to attend a public school in the town of St. Paul:

> Right away they wanted to test her. Something was wrong with her. I said, "What!" "Oh, she is not talking properly. Her fine motor skills aren't what they should be." I am like, "Are you crazy?" I wouldn't let them. I wouldn't give them my permission, and they kept on bugging me and phoning me, and "Come in, we need to talk to you." So I would go in, trying to be an active parent, and "Okay, whatever. If you really feel that this is

necessary." So they did all their tests and stuff. There wasn't any problem after I got this fancy paper from whoever assessed her. There was nothing wrong with her!

Several of the parents gave examples of requests at one time or another to test their children. Most reported that they would not sign the forms because they knew that their children did not have special needs. In fact, some parents who thought that their child might be coded as such if they went to a public school chose not to send the child to that school. They feared that the label of "special needs" would have negative long-term implications for the child. George explained that this was a determining factor in his decision to send his son to the reserve school: "I didn't want him being labeled as learning disabled." Furthermore,

> I didn't want him to go there [off-reserve school] because the kid is intelligent. He had a bit of a reading disability when he first started, but he worked with the resource room teacher, . . . and he is fine now. He is reading at grade level. If I would have allowed him to go off reserve, he would have been placed in a special-needs class and probably would be still there today.

In Marleen's assessment, "The number of Aboriginal children in special-needs programs in the provincial schools is high; I just don't know how high. All I know is the old system of coding Native students as special needs is still there." She added:

> I know that. I learned it . . . working within a system. I see. Because once they get [a student] coded, you get these extra dollars. . . . With on-reserve schools, they only get federal funding, whereas off-reserve schools get provincial and federal funding.

The participants recognized that "like other children, some Native children do in fact need special education" (Marleen), but the point of concern for them was the effect that the labeling, which they deemed was often inaccurate, would have on their children over the long term. Marleen could attest to that because for years she had felt that she was academically inferior to the "White man," and it was not until she was in postsecondary (nearly 30 years later) that she realized, "Yes, I am as smart as them."

In Makokis's (2000) study on high school dropout rates in First Nations communities, she revealed similar concerns. A community leader in her study expressed his concern about the school-system practices around special-needs categorization:

> I was sort of discouraged about it. Like how our Native students were categorized, you know, in the outside schools, in the area of special ed. programs. . . . I was never aware of that till I got involved in the process [board member]. Then I find out that the majority of our Native students are categorized as special ed. students automatically, regardless if they need it or not. (p. 146)

All of the parents who addressed the issue of special education expressed their frustration with this type of labeling, and, like Makokis (2000), they contended that Native children are unnecessarily being placed in special-education classes. Many of the participants thought that the motivational factor for this type of classification had to be money; Makokis supported this theory: "Schools currently receive more funding for students diagnosed as requiring special education" (p. 146). The provincial schools with which Saddle Lake and Goodfish Lake reserves have tuition agreements end up with considerably more funding because they receive both federal and provincial funding for First Nations children who are classified as special-education students.

In a review of First Nations special-education policies, Hurton (2002) concluded that there are in fact major discrepancies in special-education funding between the two different school systems. He pointed out that, "unlike provincial jurisdictions [that receive funding from both federal and provincial sources], First Nations schools are funded through one source only, Indian and Northern Affairs (INAC)" (p. 17). Furthermore, "INAC regions do not have formal policies on special education" (p. 21); each region is responsible for negotiating individual agreements with INAC. Overall (at least in Alberta), it appears that most reserve schools receive an average of $219 per special-needs student at a low-cost rate. Although both high-cost and low-cost students attend First Nations schools, the low-cost rate is the one commonly allotted to those schools.

Securing funds and other resources for special-education needs on-reserve can be a very costly endeavor, and one that may not be worth pursuing, considering that most First Nations schools are allotted only a very small amount of funding per special-needs child. Perhaps this is one explanation for the low numbers of children in special-needs classes in both the Saddle Lake and Goodfish Lake Schools. Although the reserve schools were unable to provide exact percentages in this area, one parent who had worked in both on-reserve and off-reserve schools indicated that "up to 50% of our children that go off-reserve are labeled as having some type of learning deficiencies, whereas in the reserve schools this number is well below 12%" (Florence). Williams (2000) supported the claims of these parents that a high percentage of Native children are classified as special needs in off-reserve public schools. She explained that these discrepancies may be attributed to the fact that "additional funds for which First Nations students are eligible are usually based on disability, deficiency and deprivation" (p. 144), which suggests that making a case for special-needs funding for these children would mean "amplifying the negative aspects of some First Nations students and thus further entrenching the negative stereotypes" (p. 144).

At the same time, this lack of funding for special needs in First Nations schools may be a partial explanation for the fact that many "First Nations students have been and some are still forced to attend provincial schools to receive services because special education services appear to not be adequately funded in First Nations schools" (Hurton, 2002, p. 13).

From my own experiences as an elementary student in a provincial school, I often feared that I might end up in "that class," particularly after learning what a teacher had said about me when my father attended a parent-teacher night: "Your daughter could do better than just Cs, but she doesn't participate." I did not even know what *participate* meant, but I thought that this might mean I was on my way to "the class"—the class that was overflowing with Native kids. I remember thinking, "Oh no, now everyone will know I am a 'true Indian' because only Indian kids go to that class!"

Williams (2000) reported that the public school system has a history of assessing and labeling Aboriginal students for special placement not only because there is a substantial amount of funding that follows that child, but also because the child is often mistakenly labeled as having limited ability. This is so primarily because teachers do not understand and value the child's skills and knowledge and because it is easier to pass off the child to someone else. She suggested that "one of our greatest challenges has been to help teachers and administrators to curb their first impulse to push First Nations students out of the school as quickly as possible and to direct them towards other resources" (p. 143).

Williams (2000) cited an example of a study that was conducted with 500 Grade 5 teachers in which the teachers were given a profile of a 10-year old boy "that describe[d] him as being sometimes disruptive in class but not behavior-disordered. He was two to three years behind in language and mathematics, but he was not learning-disabled" (p. 143). The researchers told 25% of the teachers that the child was Caucasian; 25% that he was Asian, 25% that he was East Indian, and the remaining 25% that he was Native Indian. They were asked to answer nine questions, one of which was, "Will this child graduate?" "Of the returned questionnaires, the majority of the responses were positive when ethnicity was given as Caucasian or Asian, while the majority of responses were negative when ethnicity was given as Native Indian" (p. 143).

It is unfortunate that our children are still so misunderstood, because ultimately it is the child who suffers and loses. Grouping this 10-year old boy with children who may genuinely require special education and expecting less of him quickly becomes a self-fulfilling prophecy. If he is not being challenged at the level he should be, he will begin to behave like a child with special needs. Watt-Cloutier (2000) suggested that

> if education does not genuinely empower children, then pretending that it does will only confuse them further. And it may even break their spirits because they will think it is their fault that they can find so little meaning in it. If education is done poorly, then it can do more harm than good. . . . If programs are designed and delivered without respecting and challenging the full creative potential and intelligence of children, then they will crush rather than liberate. (p. 118)

During her interview Leah shared with me:

> The way I see it, Native children get penalized just for being Native. Sometimes I think the school really does believe that Native kids are not capable of much, and that their coming to school is just a waste of everyone's time. I believe we are an inconvenience to them. Maybe this is why they place so many negative labels on us. They don't expect much from us.

The discussions in this study show that irresponsible special-needs categorization has been and continues to be unfair treatment for children and parents. A wide and indiscriminant practice of negative educational labeling of First Nations children will diminish the special intellectual gifts and strengths of First Nations peoples and communities.

The Blame-the-Native-Student Syndrome

A second practice of unfair treatment with which parents have to be prepared to deal in sending their children to a provincial school off-reserve is what I will call the "blame-the-native-student syndrome." "Native children often get labeled as shit disturbers," Leah remarked in speaking about the unfair treatment of Native students that she often witnessed in the school. "Native kids get blamed for everything." In an effort to help me better understand what she meant by this remark, she provided the following example:

I remember every time there was a fight, . . . it was an automatic in-school suspension. Well, I remember one year, this was a really large fight that happened up town, and in fact there were three fights at the same time. The Indian kids got a home suspension, and the White kids only got half a day in school. I remember asking about it, because . . . I wanted to know for myself, because I saw that as unfair, so I asked, "What is the fairness in that? Why does that person have to have an at-home suspension (or whatever they call it), and this person has only a half day in-school suspension?" The Native kid had a three-day suspension out of school, and all they said was, "Because they started the fight."

"I knew that they didn't start the fight," she added, "but that was just the way things were at that school. Native kids got blamed for everything." She shared another story about unfair treatment directed at her as a student and the perceptions that teachers have of Native children:

I remember our math class. I always heard of this one specific teacher who was a really hard marker, but he was a good teacher. So I remember our first exam I studied really, really hard, and I ended up getting 100% on it. Well, then the next day, when he wrote down all the marks on the board, he didn't write names or anything; he just put, This is how many got this percentage and this percentage, and he made it a point of saying, "Of all the years I have been teaching, no one has ever aced my exam. I don't believe this. I still don't believe it. I looked over this exam over ten times, and I just can't get over it." Well, it turns out the person that got 100% was me, and it didn't feel good to get it because I felt really demeaned, because it was as if it was impossible, and still wasn't good enough for him.

When he was making those comments, all I could think was, "He expected me to fail," and I thought to myself, "If I had been non-Native, would he have made the same fuss?" I didn't think so.

Although the teacher had never formally accused her of cheating, she said, "He may as well have, because this is exactly how it felt." She had many other examples to share about unfair treatment that she had often been subjected to in this school as a student. However, she said, at that time she did not give it much thought. "In hindsight now, when I think back, I wonder if this unfair treatment was intentional, a way of keeping Native children in their place. I guess I will never know for sure," she concluded.

As I reflected back on what Leah had shared with me, I began to think about the public school experiences of my own children. When my youngest daughter was in Grade 11, I spent a great deal of time at her school trying to resolve a conflict that she was having with another student. The arguments with this student had escalated from name calling to fist fighting, and we spent a significant amount of time in the principal's office or in a mediation room trying to resolve the conflict.

During the many times that I was in the school, when announcements were made on the intercom, it was almost always for a Native child who was being called into the office. I asked the principal one day, "Is it just Native students who get called to the office? I can't help but come to that conclusion, because every time I am here, 99% of the students being asked to report are Native students." My comment seemed to shock him, and his response was, "Are you accusing me of being racist?" I said, "No, I am not, but it seems odd that so many of them are Native children. Are they being called because they are in trouble?" He responded, "What are you doing, accusing me of being racist? I have worked for approximately 13 years with Native children." My reaction to that was, "Working 13 years with Native children does not exclude you from having a racist attitude." We became angrier and more emotional, and perhaps the conversation ended only because we decided to return to the reason for my being there.

This discussion with the principal frustrated me immensely, and I walked out of that school thinking, "What is the use? Why am I spending so much time trying to reason with a person who does not expect anything more from Native students anyway? Why am I trying to talk him into believing that the behavior that my daughter is exhibiting is not normal for her?" My daughter had attended this same school since Grade 1. The principal was new to the school and the students. Before passing judgment on her and other Native children, he might have talked to the staff who were there throughout her schooling. After that incident I never went back to the school, even though my stepson was still a student there. If I as a parent had felt so powerless and defeated after talking with the principal, how must our youth feel about having to live and work in that environment every day? "We feel the same," insisted my daughter, when I asked her this question. "We feel the same, and the thing is, even if we are not guilty as accused, which most of the time we are not, we feel guilty, we look guilty, and we act guilty, so we get blamed." I knew exactly what she meant because I remembered an incident in which I, as an adult, had been falsely accused, and I too had ended up feeling guilty.

In her study Makokis (2000) interviewed several youth who had dropped out of school and found that most of them had dropped out because they felt that they were not welcome in the school and that they were being picked on; when they did not understand a lesson, the teachers made them feel inadequate by the way they responded to their students' lack of understanding. When something negative happened in school, they were consistently blamed. All of the students whom Makokis interviewed cited examples of unfair treatment, and many concluded that what they were experiencing was racism. Makokis shared Asiny's story:

> Although Asiniy identified the fact that he was "different" as his reason for leaving school, he shared the following story of why he left. He stated, "I just didn't like the teachers. . . . Some of them were racist; some of them would make fun of a person." When asked to give an example of what he thought was racist, Asiniy shared the following, "When all the White people were around me, he [the teacher] started calling me 'Chief.'" When he was asked which teacher, he identified his physical education teacher, noting, "The reason why I left from there was, I went to school one day and I had physical education and then all of a sudden, they all blamed me for stealing two hundred and fifty bucks from all those kids and then the teacher went along with them and he said, 'Did you do it?' I told him, 'I was right with you guys all this time.'" Asiny felt he was being picked on. He stated, "I was the only Native in that class." Whether that is, in fact, the case, from his perception, he was separated out as the victim because of his ancestry. Asiny got mad and wanted to leave Nobleton High. He stated, "I told him, 'I quit.'" I was trying to get a transfer letter and they wouldn't transfer me so I left Mahihkan and went home to [city]. (pp. 119-120)

Asiny quit school because he could no longer cope. He felt picked on and beaten up, and he felt that he was a victim of racism. As Makokis (2000) put it, "Whether that is, in fact, the case, from his [Asiny's] perception, he was separated out as the victim because of his ancestry" (p. 120). This unfair treatment, whether intentional or unintentional, is very harmful to Aboriginal students. In many cases these students react against these expressions of unfair treatment by fighting or by developing unruly and uncooperative attitudes. Inevitably, they come to be seen as trouble makers, with all of the many negative consequences that follow from that label; or, as in the case of the young man whom Makokis described, they simply exist. They drop out of school knowing the consequences of that action but wanting to hang on to whatever little personal pride and dignity they have left.

Time Spent in Detention

Students must often deal with the effects of labeling in their personal lives. Native children can be labeled in ways that impact them for the rest of their school years. My younger brother and my stepson have both experienced the consequences of labeling. Both coped with the pressures of school by becoming "class clowns," and both spent many days sitting in the detention hall. My brother fell far behind in his school work, and although he tried hard, he never completed his high school requirements. He very likely spent more time in detention than he did in class, and his academic achievement suffered.

Hampton (1995) shared a story about how a young man's experiences with detention were instrumental in his decision to conduct research on Indian students' self-esteem:

> A young white man told me he wanted to do a research project on the effect of group counselling on Indian students' self-esteem. He wanted to do his master's thesis on this topic, and I asked, "Why . . . ?" We talked and went round and round talking about the problems of the assessment for self-esteem, problems of what self-esteem means in the Eurocentric, physiological theory, and what self-esteem might mean in a traditional society. We talked about all kinds of things, and finally one day he said, "Well, the reason is I teach at this school over there, and I've got a whole bunch of Native students and they keep getting sent to detention, and in detention all they do is sit there. And I think that if we could get some group counselors in, we would at least give them something to do while they are in detention, instead of detention. And maybe that will be better." I said, "That makes sense to me. How come you're interested in that?" We talked some more and he told me of a memory. He said he was sent to detention all the time when he was in school; and he said it hurt. "It hurts my heart when I see those kids go down to detention and sit there." (p. 51)

Spending time in detention hurt this young man, and he was concerned about the effect of this experience on Native students who already face self-esteem issues. He was certain that detention would have a detrimental effect if they continued to spend most of their days in the detention halls. Makokis (2000) interviewed a student who had dropped out of school for this reason. When Makokis asked the student what might have helped her to stay in school, she responded that she would have stayed in school "if the teacher wouldn't have kept hassling me about detention and talking." This student referred to "a sense of being pressured by the teacher, detentions, teacher favoritism, and a sense of the teacher disliking her" (p. 108) as reasons for her exit from high school.

"Non-academic classes, special-needs classes, and detention rooms seem to be where most of the Native kids spent their days in my son's schools," Pamela reported when I asked her to tell me about her son's school experience at a public school. "My son never talks about it, but I guarantee he does see it." So what is happening? With regard to Native students who are seeing this day after day, Silver, Mallett, Greene, and Simard (2002) hypothesized that "many Aboriginal students . . . quite naturally disengage from the school system, and some, perhaps many, carry on the tradition of active resistance to white-controlled school system with its colonial assumptions of Euro-Canadian cultural superiority" (p. 40). In Leah's words:

> Many Native children just throw their arms up and surrender, thinking, "Why should I go to school?" You know there is a lot of that attitude, and actually, I remember some of my friends dropping out, and they had that attitude: "I don't need it; I don't want to go. And when I look back at some of the people that dropped out, well, yeah, they weren't liked; . . . they weren't favored by the teacher. They were treated like they weren't important. They felt like they didn't matter to anyone, and they thought, "Why bother? I'll always be the bad guy anyway."

Streaming Native Students

Another example of unfair treatment that many participants described is streaming students into the nonacademic route when they reach Grade 10. Although many Aboriginal students are capable of taking the academic route, the participants felt that their children were almost always steered away from that direction: Simon informed me:

> On the rare occasion, Native students go this route, but they are the ones with the very high grades. In most cases, especially when you get into Grade 11, 12, it is rare to see any Native students in these classes.

Pamela explained, "I think it is because Native students are discouraged from going that route. At least, this is what it was like in my own experience."

George recalled his own experiences with streaming when he registered in the academic courses in high school: "I applied to go the advanced route in Grade 10, but the teacher said no, I was not ready for it." Because of his fear of authority, he accepted the decision, trusting that the teacher knew best. It was not until one week later when his mother saw his timetable that she realized what had happened. She took immediate action and had him moved the next school day. "If she hadn't done that, I would have just stayed where I was and probably would not have gone on to college or university," George added. This student accepted the decision, but his mother did not. She knew that her son was capable of taking the academic route, and she was not going to allow the school to determine her son's fate, so she asked to have him moved.

From my own experience, what this parent did was an exception because many Native parents "do not know that their children are enrolled in terminal programs" (Wilson, 1992, p. 53). In her study Wilson found that being pushed into low-level courses seems to be the norm for Aboriginal students, because the school assumes that they are incapable of handling the advanced courses and that they do not aspire to attending university anyway. Wilson gave an example of what often happens to Native children in the public school system:

> A classic example came from a student who wanted to enroll in a computer class. A teacher advisor suggested that he take a mechanics course instead because "there will always be broken down cars to repair on the reserve but I doubt that there will be computers to work with." (p. 52)

Dakota indicated that this was the case for her as well. She too had been discouraged from taking any academic courses, and like many other Native students, she never questioned it:

"I didn't think about going to college or university, because I just felt it was for the rich kids, and no one ever suggested that it might be a possibility." Pamela, who had also been streamed into the nonacademic route, wondered

> how many Native children have been wrongly streamed this way. . . . The thing is, this continues to happen to our children. Without my knowing it, my son, who is in Grade 10 this year, was forced to go this way. He wants to go into the welding trade when he completes high school, and knowing this, I wanted him to get the best math possible, so I registered him in Pure Math 10 [and other academic courses]. But just last week I found him with Applied Math 10 books. When I asked him why he had switched, he told me that the school counselor had switched his classes because she didn't think he was capable of doing them, particularly Pure Math 10. When I went to the school to talk to the school counselor, I walked past his math class, and you know what? All the students there were Native! I was mad! I asked her why she had done this and why there were only Indian kids in that class, and her response was something like, "Because their marks were not high enough for Pure Math."

In the end, Pamela allowed her son to stay in the Applied Math 10 class, but gave in only because she had done some research and found that this stream is sufficient for the trade that he had chosen. Still, she was very angry knowing that the school counselor had undermined her authority. Although she had already registered him in specific courses, the registration form had been completely altered. She said:

> I really do believe that this school does not have much faith in the Native kids, and this became even more obvious to me when I walked by [sons'] class and saw only Native children sitting there. Yeah, maybe their marks are low when they go into Grade 10, but that is because they had already got left behind in junior high. No one encouraged them and told them that they were capable of doing more. Instead now they are told they are not capable.

The following story demonstrates the impact of streaming:

> You will make a great secretary," they told her. "If you take the typing courses, a little bit of accounting, and some occupational courses, you will always be able to find work in your reserve. You will be good at this." Why did they keep saying that to her as she was reviewing the list of courses she might want to take in Grade 10? She always hoped that she might be able to go into law, but she never said anything to them. This was an outlandish thought, a secret shared with no one, because she was afraid she might get laughed at. After all, she wasn't the sharpest tool in the shed, and least that's how she always felt. All of her grades were just in the high 50's and low 60's, and realistically, how could she ever become a lawyer? They were right. She was not university bound anyway, so she may as well take what they were proposing to her. The courses would be a breeze, and she would complete her high school in record time. She wanted to get out of this school anyway, where she felt so inferior. She would become the best secretary she could be. Maybe after high school she would take a secretarial program, to solidify the skills she would attain in high schools, but university, no way! She was not smart enough!

This young lady worked in a clerical field for many years before gathering the courage to enroll in some university courses. The messages that she had received in school left a permanent imprint on her mind, and like the teachers in grade school and high school, she had doubts about her ability to compete in the academic world. "You will make a great secretary" was permanently etched on her mind. And although she excelled in her undergraduate degree, most of the time she still had doubts and often wondered how she had ever accomplished that. When she enrolled in graduate school, she was certain that she would be turned away:

> In my first day of classes they are going to know I am a fraud. I know nothing. How can I compete with those scholars? Did I merely get accepted because there is an Aboriginal quota that has to be fulfilled?

Her transcripts contained all the proof she needed, but still she doubted. Why is this? Even to this day, as she writes her doctoral dissertation, that nagging little voice makes its way back in: "You are not capable of such a huge undertaking; you will never complete this task." The difference is, today she is able to push those thoughts away, but she understands that the self-doubts will always creep back into her life because of the permanency of the scars and because she understands that she lives in a society in which stereotypes about Native people still prevail. Mihesuah (1996) agreed that stereotypes discourage many Native students from attempting to pursue higher education and shared a story that a Native graduate student had told her:

> Recently, an Indian graduate student complained to me about a comment she had heard about herself. One professor had remarked to another that the only reason Indians were in graduate school was because the school needed to fill its minority quota. I could sympathize because I had heard the same thing about myself throughout graduate school. I was also told by a Euro-American professor the year I arrived as Assistant Professor that there was no need for Indian history on the graduate level because "Indians can't handle graduate work." Because some Indians have not been properly prepared for their university tenures, professors still believe most Indian students are mentally deficient and feel that they must "give them a passing grade" out of sympathy. (p. 93)

Casual remarks such as the one that this professor made affect students' self-image, and, as a result, many Native students do not pursue higher education. Their experiences in primary and secondary school were enough to deter them.

"It is hard to get up after being knocked down so many times," explained Dakota. Kristine suggested:

> Educators are always trying to find ways to increase high school graduation rates among Native students, but it's a simple answer. Just respect us, encourage us, listen to us, learn a little about us. Then maybe you will begin seeing more Native students graduating from high school.

Statistics Canada (2001a) revealed that very few Native youths pursue postsecondary education, and it is probably safe to assume that this is directly related to the fact that most Aboriginal students also do not prepare for postsecondary education while they are in high school: "The school personnel's preconceived idea that the situation is hopeless is played out. Low expectations become a self-fulfilling prophecy" (Wilson, 1992, p. 53).

I did not do well academically in junior high school, but I also did not try very hard. I did as much as I needed to "get by," which is likely the reason that I was steered toward the nonacademic route. Entering Grade 10, I knew that the expectations were minimal, because otherwise I would have been encouraged to take the academic route. Although I heard other students talking about what they needed to get into university, I did not see that as an option for me. University was out of reach for me. In hindsight, I wonder whether I would have tried harder and done better in school if someone had pushed me, motivated me, and told me that I was capable of much more; if I had been pushed toward an advanced diploma. I wonder if that is why so many Native students do not graduate with the courses that are required for university and/or college entry and why so many Native students have to upgrade after completing high school (Makokis, 2000; Silver et al., 2002).

Low Teacher Expectations

Research has revealed that, generally, non-Native teaching staff have lower expectations of Aboriginal students than they do of non-Aboriginal students (Makokis, 2000; Silver et al., 2002; Wilson, 1992; Wilson, 1992). From my observations and my discussions with the participants in this study as well as with other Aboriginal parents and youths, there appears to be a general consensus that academic expectations of Native children are low within the public school system. However, there was also agreement that if children do well academically, they are not subjected to unfair treatment. The parents whom I interviewed had this hope for their own children. Veronica reported that her oldest daughter fit this category, and she concluded:

> Encouragement is there for the Native students if they are good students, if their attitude is "right," and if their attendance is good. Unlike the rest of my children, my oldest daughter possessed and met all of these criteria. She was encouraged in her studies by the teachers, while my other children were discouraged. This is probably why she was the only one of my children to graduate high school and the only one to obtain a university degree. Teachers liked her. She was the model Native student.

Surely, even without an in-depth analysis, all educators will understand this powerful but subtle indictment of public schooling for First Nations students!

Public schools encourage competition and individual gain (Goulet, 2001; Makokis, 2000; Wilson, 1992), and students who attend these schools not knowing how to play the game are often left behind: "Those Native children that prove they can be just as competitive as their non-Native counterparts may not be subjected to the same unfair treatment the other Native students receive," Simon asserted.

Bazylak (2002) revealed that low teacher expectations can affect Aboriginal students' educational success. All of the participants whom I interviewed concurred with this statement, and many felt that their children, and even they themselves, might have done better in school if the teachers had supported and encouraged them. As Dakota suggested, "Even if one teacher would have showed care, concern, and encouragement, it might have made a difference in my schooling experience. But I never received any of that." Marleen agreed: "Even one teacher can make a world of difference." She shared a story about a physical education teacher who had had a positive effect on her in Grade 10. What he did for Marleen remained in her mind, and she carried his teachings into her postsecondary studies:

> There was only one time that I really felt good about what I was doing in school, and that was in Grade 10. I did a report in school, and I worked hard on it. It was in Phys. Ed class, and in fact I still have that report, and I used it in my own educational journey as part of a portfolio that I did [for a postsecondary course]. I got 24 out of 25, and at that time I felt really good because I worked really hard on it, and I always asked the teacher, "Is it ready? Did you mark them?" And he wrote on there, "No wonder you wanted it back because you worked so hard on it." I was told if I did this in all my work, I would be an A student, but I had this desire that I wanted to do it. It was something that I was interested in.

When I asked Marleen what made the difference for her, she replied,

> I felt he really cared. I can say that I really wanted to show him that I could do it, because he was one of my favorite teachers, and he treated me with respect. I never felt "lesser than." I think if I had all teachers like him who treated me like he did, I think I would have done a lot better in high school; that I was worth something. And if for every little thing I did, someone would have said, "Right on! That was a good try!" it would have made a difference. Yes, because when I think about this phys. ed. teacher and then a math teacher who never spent any time with me, and where I struggled with math all my life—so in going back to university I had this fear of math. It was different in university because that math instructor took time and spent time with me, and I went for extra tutoring until I understood and then, wow! I excelled in MATH, and it was stats. And it was like, holy! And yet I couldn't do Pure Math 10 in high school because I never got that attention. He picked his favorites, and he made it clear who his favorites were, and they were all non-Native. And if you weren't in the favorites, you didn't pass.

In his study Goulet (2001) discovered that many non-Native teachers have low prejudicial beliefs about the Aboriginal students they teach. Referring to Wilson's (1991) study and the work of Wax, Wax, and Dumont (1972), Goulet concluded that many non-Native teachers believe that Native students are unable to compete with their non-Aboriginal peers. The teachers in these studies believed that "[Native] students had inadequate home life and so did not possess the skills necessary for success in school" (p. 69). Wilson (1992) found that Native students are often prejudged, even before the teachers know them: "Many could not imagine these students could ever have been successful. Students were classed as unable to cope with a heavy academic load" (p. 53).

Kristine, a youth participant, agreed that teachers' expectations have everything to do with how well Native students perform in school. She elaborated:

> I think some teachers knew that I was capable of doing the work, but they didn't push me. They probably thought that I would not ever complete high school anyway, so why bother? Therefore I didn't really bother to work hard; therefore I always just squeaked by. I think they had low expectations of me not only academically, but socially as well. These messages came out loud and clear when I was having problems with a Native girl from another reserve. It was like they didn't care whether we resolved our dispute or not. They just wanted us to quit bothering them. Maybe that is why I didn't complete school right away, because they didn't think I could do it. I think I surprised them in June when I

called them to ask if I could write my departmental exams there. They probably thought I would never do it; just another statistic.

The students in Makokis's (2000) study dropped out of school for various reasons, but one prominent factor that contributed to their withdrawal was their belief that their teachers did not care and that they had very low expectations of them. This was evident in many ways, including the unfair treatment that they received. A young lady told her, "I did almost all my work and everything, but it seemed like the teacher didn't like me and my cousins. She always seemed to give us bad marks. She would always give me detention. I don't know why." Like several of the participants in this study, this young lady believed that non-Native teachers do in fact have low expectations of Native children.

Although the general consensus amongst the parents and youth was that Native students are often treated unfairly in public school systems, there also seemed to be complete agreement that children who do well academically are generally not subjected to the same unfair treatment that other Native children receive. Thus the significance of teachers' expectations must be highlighted in relationship or direct linkage with academic achievement and unfair treatment.

Revisiting her own childhood experiences, Bernice agreed and recognized that she had been treated better than other Native children had been for this reason. She described her situation: "It's probably because I was able to adjust and integrate readily enough. I had my brains to bear when I went in there [the public school]." This participant and her sister had received a tremendous amount of encouragement from their parents to excel in school, and when they began to attend the town school, they were "well prepared to compete in this individualistic and competitive system."

From his own schooling experiences, Bernice's father was very much aware that Native children are often "lost" in the system, and he was determined that this would not happen to his children when he and his wife decided to enroll them in the neighboring town's public school. He was prepared to put up a fight if he had to. When he dropped his children off for their first day of school, he immediately noticed that all of the Native children had already been assigned to the C classes. The B classes were made up of predominantly White children, with a few Native children in each. The A classrooms were filled with the town's French children. Further investigation revealed that no Native children ever occupied seats in the A classes, and he knew that he was about to make history when he insisted that his daughters be placed in those classes. With their impeccable school records, they could not be denied entry into these classes. Their father kept very close watch on their progress, and when he saw injustices, he did not hesitate to inform the school of his views. Bernice recalled an incident that proved their father's commitment to their education:

> I remember when I was going to school in [town], the whole class for some reason got detention, and we all had to do lines. I remember taking those lines home and my Dad asking me, "What are you doing these for?" "The whole class got in trouble, and we had to do these." I remember him taking those lines from me. He sat down and he wrote this letter on the bottom of my lines, and it said, "If you are going to give her something to do like this, I'd prefer if you give her extra homework or something constructive." He said "You take that back." I was scared. I didn't finish my lines, but I took this back and showed it to my teacher. She looked red, and she had this kind of look on her face that was like she got told. I never had lines again after that. It was just those little things, I guess, just really stood out for me.

I asked this participant whether she had ever experienced racism in the school, and she responded, "There's nothing that stands out in my mind. It's probably because I was able to adjust and integrate readily enough, or perhaps it was because I didn't let it get to me." She did not deny that it happened because she recalled incidents when she would join her Native friends in the playground at recess when racial comments were made, such as "There are all the squaws hanging together." She explained that she always knew that she was different, not only because of the subtle reminders, but also because of the curriculum. An incident in one of her classes reminded her of how "Indian" she really was. "It was at those times that I was reminded of just how different I was":

> I remember . . . this . . . word we were looking at in phonics class. The word *beverage* came to my attention, and I was like, What is this? I tried to reread the sentence and the context, and I was thinking, Boy, I must be a dumb Indian; I don't know what this means. And I didn't want to go and ask a teacher, because she had singled me out that one time with another sentence having to do with the capitalization of the word *Indian*, even as far as something in reference to Indians used to live in teepees. I remember having a discussion afterwards where all my classmates were asking me if we still lived in teepees. I was like, "Duh! We live in houses now."

After rereading this interview several times, I thought to myself, "That is where I went wrong in school." Unlike this participant, I had not known how to integrate; I did not have the same worldly experiences that Bernice had had when I was growing up. Her parents had been very involved in business outside of the Native community, and the children often took business trips with their parents. They already felt comfortable around other peoples and cultures, whereas in my family we did not. We lived in a very sheltered world, and only very rarely did we visit a metropolis such as Edmonton. In fact, going to the town of St. Paul from Saddle Lake was like visiting a different world. Therefore, because I was not familiar with the protocol of integration, I often embarrassed myself if I tried to fit in with children who were not of my people. Furthermore, because I did not have the same grasp of the English language that Bernice did, I think that this resulted in a very different schooling experience for me. According to Wells and Crain (1992):

> When parents of the dominant class are able to transmit high status culture that is greatly valued and generously rewarded in the educational system to their children, the children of lower-status groups are at an extreme disadvantage in a competitive educational market. (pp. 76-77)

Although Wells and Crain (1992) spoke of the dominant culture as White upper middle class, this situation of difference applies even in First Nations communities. When children have broadened experiences—experiences outside of their own culture—they are going to have a better chance of "fitting into" these school systems because they and their parents will know the "protocols," the expected and accepted behaviors. Thus, these children will tend to do better in school because they have greater personal resources that 'fit' with their teacher's expectations, including particular types of information, educational background, and social connections.

Racism

> The fear washes through my veins
> Contaminating the deep red blood.
> It travels through my body,
> Further, deeper.
> The rage heats my skin
> Igniting a blazing fire. It burns my brown skin,
> Heating, hurting
> The sadness flows through me
> Touching my heart in the most sensitive places
> It brings tears to my eyes
> As the wall of racism,
> Slams against my face. (Canadian Race Relations
> Foundation, 2007, p. 16)

It was not surprising to find that all participants identified the theme of racism as one of the most serious points of consideration in making school choices for their children. All parents expected that their children would be on the receiving end of racism, and, in fact, at least two of the parents wanted to actively prepare their children to face this issue. These two parents wanted their children to grow up experiencing racism, believing that it would better prepare them for the "real world." Dakota explained that this was the very reason that she chose to send her children off-reserve:

> The reason [that I sent my children off the reserve] was that they need to be prepared for the racism outside of our small home, outside of our community, because they are going to experience that when they go to college or university. I need them to get a taste of that. That is the purpose of me wanting them to attend a bigger school with different races. . . . I think if we as parents shelter our children, then we are not really doing them any good when we do that, whether it comes to our education, whether it comes to anything in that outside world. The first experience I had with racism, nothing prepared me for it. My parents never taught me about it. I experienced some of it in school, but I knew that was going to happen. But when you go to college or university knowing that you have to work three or four times harder than the next student, I think my kids need to be prepared for that.

Louise agreed that there is no better way to prepare her children for racism than to send them to off-reserve schools:

> I think they are strong enough [now as a result of going to off-reserve schools] to be able to cope with stuff like that [racism]. I always tell them, "You are going to experience racism, prejudice, whatever," but it is up to them how they are going to cope with it.

It seems outrageous that Native students have to learn to accept racism but this is a "fact of life. Learning to cope becomes the means of survival" reported Steinhauer (1999) in her master's thesis.

In my own off-reserve school experience, beginning in Grade three, I remember children often being quite vicious and often engaging in games at the expense of Indian children. On particular game was known as "Indian germs." It was a game of tag which began with a white student touching an Indian kid then playing tag with those germs for the entire recess. Of course Indian children were not included in the game. Although it was hurtful at the time we learned to cope by playing in other parts of the playground or school. Gradually learning how to cope became the means of survival, and . . . sometimes some of the poor white children would play with us, since they too were outcasts. Like the participants in this study I grew to accept racism as a fact of life. (p. 51)

Children cope with racism in many ways. Some Native students simply ignore or shrug off the comments, but many react by physically fighting back or resisting authority. They fall back into the 'blame-the-native-student syndrome and come to be seen as "troublemakers," suffering severe consequences, sometimes for the rest of their lives. In fighting back against racism, children will face detentions and expulsions and invariably become very dissatisfied with school. Evidence suggests (Makokis, 2000; St. Denis & Hampton, 2002; Silver et al., 2002) that students who are negatively affected by racism are less likely to attend school regularly and are likely to drop out of school earlier than other groups of students. Untangling the silken threads of the web of interconnected malignant forces that work against the academic success of Native students is only one part of the work to understand the context of parental school choice for First Nations parents.

In her study Makokis (2000) found from the Native students whom she interviewed that racism was a major contributing factor to their decision to drop out of provincial high schools. The students described being unfairly treated when they tried to defend themselves. When she asked one of her participants why he had left school early, he told her that he had left because "there was discrimination and he often got into fights over that. Whenever there were fights, the teacher would side with the White students and kick the Indian students out of school" (p. 127). These students recognized that most Native students were not treated well and that Native children were constantly subjected to racial harassment. As a result of such harassment, many of the participants in Makokis's study fought their way through school. The participants shared their thoughts on how racism is internalized and spoke at length about how racism affects self-esteem and identity development. A discussion of these concerns follows.

Internalized Racism

Leah lamented:

I found a lot of the Native kids to be more negative, but rightly so, because they were treated wrong. When you are treated wrong, when you are oppressed, you are automatically going to be defensive toward things. Racism, experienced on a consistent basis, becomes internalized, and we [the Native students] begin to hate one another. It can have very damaging effects.

What Leah meant by this became evident when another youth whom I interviewed told me that it is true that Native children are not treated well. However, unlike Leah, Yvonne argued that these Native children deserve it. As a result, she deliberately separated herself from other Native students at her school. She did not want to be placed in the same category as the rest of the

Native children: "I noticed that the kids that were troublemakers in class were usually Native kids, and I didn't really hang out with a lot of Native kids because I always tried to do well in school."

The second youth seems to have concluded that Native children deserve the treatment they receive and that they bring such treatment upon themselves. The second youth, however, attributed the negative behavior of the children to their unfair treatment. Why did Leah see the students as victims, whereas Yvonne saw them as troublemakers? Was Yvonne trying to prove to the school personnel that Native children are capable of handling the academic course load? Perhaps this was her way of protecting herself and other Native students. Perhaps she was proving that Native students do not all have to be failures. Perhaps this is an example of what Silver et al. (2002) referred to as *internalized racism*. Racist attitudes toward Native students were very prevalent in the school that Yvonne attended. Perhaps she had come to believe that Native students were, in fact, troublemakers and incapable of competing in the public school system.

"The institutions, the public schools, are responsible for this internalized racism," Sheila accused. Leah expanded on this idea:

> They teach us that Native students are anything but good, so we internalize this. We begin to believe that we are in fact no good, trouble makers, incapable of 'real work,' and in order to survive, we begin rejecting, and beating up each other. I hate to admit this, but I was guilty of rejecting my own Native peers as well. I am so ashamed of myself now that I recognize this.

Leah and I continued on this topic of internalized racism, and I too had to admit guilt. I told her about an incident in which I had inflicted physical and emotional pain on a young boy in my Grade 5 class:

> Grade 5 was a very difficult year for me. I don't know if I was subjected to more racism this year, or if it because I was becoming more aware of how "ugly" my Indianness really was, but I think this was the year that I decided I was going to try to be less Indian and maybe more "White," if that was possible. But something in my 10-year-old mind must have clicked off, and I felt a greater need to be accepted; I don't know. But this one day, Samuel, we will call him, a Native boy from my reserve, peed his pants, and the children in the class were laughing at him. They were pushing him, calling him names. He was crying, obviously very embarrassed, and then someone called him a stinking Indian. He huddled himself in the corner, and before I knew it, I was standing next to him, along with many other students in the class. Some kids started kicking him, telling him to get up, and I found myself doing the same. I too was kicking him and laughing at him. When he got up to leave the classroom, I pushed him. I pushed him and I laughed at him. I felt a sense of power sweep over me as I watched him walk out of the classroom with his head hung down. I turned around and noted the looks of approval that I was receiving from my non-Native peers. For a fleeting moment I felt big and tall, and possibly even acceptance; but that feeling was short lived, because as soon as I sat down, I felt a sense of guilt and shame. I never apologized to Samuel for what I had done, and even to this day I feel guilt over it, but I think Samuel understood.

Although I recognized immediately that the treatment I had inflicted on this young man was unacceptable, the discomfort and shame that I felt about my own Native origins overpowered me. I hated being Indian, and throughout my schooling I continued to wish that I could be less Native. I think somewhere along the way I even managed to convince myself that I was not as "Indian" as some of my Native peers. I began to make mental categories in my mind: This group was very Indian; that group was somewhere in the middle; my family was even "less Indian." Why does a 10-year-old mind have to conjure up such categories? I did this because I felt that I needed to qualify my place within this school system. I needed to convince myself and others that there was a space for me in this school and that I met the criteria for being in that space. One of those criteria was to be "less Indian."

Like the two youth in this study, as a child I was coerced and pressured to agree with the distortions of racism—and I came to believe that Native people are unimportant and inferior. Having been a target of racism since my early childhood, it was hard to maintain a sense of myself as good, smart, and important. I began internalizing the messages of racism, and eventually I began to mistreat other members of my group in the same ways that I had been mistreated. When I kicked Samuel that day, I was kicking myself. When I created those mental categories of "Indianness," I was turning upon myself, my family, and my people. I was authorizing and validating the behaviors of my non-Native peers but thinking that I was validating myself!

Within the context of my own life experience and this work, I found it interesting that in a study that Mackay and Myles (1995) conducted on Aboriginal retention and dropout rates amongst Aboriginal youth in Ontario schools, they did not mention racism as a contributing factor to the students' behaviors. Although some students referred to being discriminated against by others in the school, it was near the bottom of the list of contributing factors. Language skills, parental support, and home-school communication topped the list. In contrast, in a study on the same issue, Makokis (2000) identified racism as a major contributing factor. This discrepancy in findings takes on significant import when I consider the responses that I have gathered in my own work. Mackay and Myles did not provide details on the complete research processes (such as data-collection methods, for example) that they utilized, so it is hard to determine whether racism was intentionally downplayed, ignored, or not recognized or whether the opportunity was simply not there for their Native participants to explore it as a choice of factors. Perhaps they intentionally omitted them because, as Calliou (1995) suggested, racism is an issue that many people would rather not have to deal with, even Native people. Racism creates imbalance and disharmony, and discussing the issue can be emotionally, physically, spiritually, and mentally challenging and exhausting. Most people would rather not face the issue because it would require that they

> dismantle oppressive structures that give them an unjust power over people of color and to learn to live in this county and the world as nothing more or less than a part of the whole. This is long hard work. (Bivens, 1995, p. 1)

However, again as Calliou (1995) asserted, racism has to be named. Although she recognized that, in doing so, "emotion will emerge from the underground of denial within individuals, lunch rooms, classrooms, textbooks, media, or school grounds," she contended that it is important to do so if we want to have the "public, affirmative spaces" (p. 58) that we like to think our Canadian classrooms are. Silver et al. (2002) agreed that "the cultural/class divide that separates so many schools and teachers from so many Aboriginal students" is wide and that the "'blame the victim' response—a form of institutional racism" (p. 26) is flourishing. The problem, they suggested, is that this institutional racism in not even recognized (p. 26):

> But it is there, and it is a significant part of the explanation for why so many Aboriginal students are not thriving in the school system. And we believe that if non-Aboriginal teachers and administrators were to grapple openly with the problem—name it, describe it, come to accept and to understand its prevalence—they would eliminate much of it. But racism is such an ugly word that when an Aboriginal person says something is racist, the tendency is to retreat, to go on the defensive, to deny the racism. (p. 26)

When I asked Suzanne how racism affected her, she responded:

> It pissed me off! I hated being put down all the time, and I got to the point where I hated being Indian! You can say that my schooling experience had a major impact on my identity and self-esteem. I hated myself because others hated me.

Our schooling experiences can and do shape the persons we become, and because so many Native children have had negative experiences in school, we can expect that many Native children, youth, and adults have wounded spirits and low self-esteem because of their internalized belief that they are inadequate, flawed, defective, and unimportant. These negative beliefs and experiences have long-term effects on their personal and social beliefs, attitudes, and behaviors.

Racism and Its Effect on Self-Esteem and Identity Development

> People are "empowered" when they have learned to control the development and maintenance of their own powers—when they know what to do to continue their learning and development without being told what to do. Educators call this lifelong learning. Our Elders call this wisdom, and it is what we all want for our children so that they may control their lives rather then being overly controlled by external forces. (Watt-Cloutier, 2000, p. 118)

All parents want their children to have a healthy sense of self-esteem. They want their children to feel good about themselves. They want their children to be cared for and to be accepted by their peers. Parents want their children to feel that they belong in their school, but many of the parents I interviewed for this study reported that this is not true, nor do these things happen for their children. Native children still do not have equal educational advantages, particularly those who attend public schools (RCAP, 1996). They often encounter prejudice from teachers and other children, and thus the healthy sense of self-esteem with which they might have started school quickly dissipates. This was the case for me.

Prior to starting Grade 1 in a public school system, I was confident and very sure of myself. I thought I could do anything and become anything. After just one day in a public school, I began to doubt my abilities. I realized on that first day that I looked different, talked different, and according to the non-Native children, I even smelled different. I quickly learned that I did not belong with this group of people, and the sad thing is that I grew up believing that I was never quite as good as the White children. Many participants grew up feeling the same way, and as Marleen explained, she too felt that White people are better than she is: "Well, I didn't feel good with my self-esteem. I didn't feel good, but I didn't say anything. I assumed . . . White people were always smarter than I was, and it was something that I needed to accept, and I just did."

Both Saddle Lake Cree Nation and Whitefish Lake (Goodfish Lake) First Nation are in very close proximity to the non-Native towns that surround the reserve, and yet the non-Native population knows very little about who we really are. They make generalizations and draw erroneous conclusions, and racist attitudes are rampant. Such attitudes are often harsh, pervasive, and very damaging to young children and other vulnerable persons. With schooling experiences such as those that the participants reported and with a wider social environment of racist attitudes and practices, many First Nations children come to believe that they are in fact inferior, and any feeling of self-worth that they may have begins to dwindle. Feelings of insecurity often result in shame, and this is evident in Native students' wanting to become someone else. Suzanne remembered wanting to be White: "I started dying my hair and trying to be more White."

George, another participant, concluded that this internalized racism has been very damaging to us as a people: "We try to become little brown White men. We got screwed out of so much, and yet we are still trying to change ourselves into something we are not." Why is that? Sixkiller Clarke (1994) suggested that it is because many Native children have "suffered from an identity crisis. They wished they had not been born an Indian" (p. 118).

I recall wishing that same thing many times. Why did I have to be born into a culture that is viewed as substandard? Everything about being Indian was humiliating. I tried so hard to keep a low profile because I did not want to be singled out and noticed. Yet it was next to impossible in so many situations. One good example was the distribution of school supplies. As a First Nations child living on a reserve, the Department of Indian Affairs paid for my tuition, books, transportation, and school supplies. Every year my non-Native peers reminded me of just how lucky I was and that their parents were "taxpaying citizens." I had no idea what that meant, but from the tone of their voices, I knew that I was guilty of something. My interviews revealed that almost every participant had felt as I did at school-supply time. They had dreaded that time because they knew that when they returned to their classrooms with supplies in hand, they were going to be targets for abuse. Claire talked about how that felt:

> You would get comments all over the place: "Well, you are an Indian; you get everything for free; you don't have to pay for anything yourself." And you are not really armed with the knowledge, and you know that somehow along the lines this is true, but you don't know why, and you have no defense, so you are just left to feel bad about it.

Leah shared her feelings and memories of this dreaded moment as well:

> When they would announce it [to pick up your supplies], you would be in class. So all the kids that are from this First Nation or this First Nation—I don't even remember the announcement, but you knew when you had to go. And then, of course, there would be comments: "Oh, it must be nice to get your stuff paid for." . . . And the stuff that they gave you was so cheap. Your binder fell apart in a month. I remember I still went to go get it, but I was embarrassed, and I remember at the beginning of each school year I'd always want to get supplies. I remember my dad saying, "No, you get supplies." And I would say, "No, I do not want to go and get supplies," but I didn't want to tell him why I was embarrassed.

Having experienced this type of humiliation year after year was very difficult. Alexis revealed, "As a result of my experience, I get my daughter her own set of supplies. I remember that. That was so humiliating." Like this parent, I did the same thing with my children. I knew that there would be a package of school supplies ready for them during the first week of school, but I would discourage them from retrieving the package. I wanted to protect them from the humiliation that I had experienced at the beginning of every school year. These concerns may seem trivial to someone who has never had to endure the feelings of shame and guilt—or perhaps I should say this abuse in an environment that claimed legislated protection for every child. However, this simple event of picking up school supplies—a legal and constitutional right through international treaty for First Nations children—in combination with a multitude of other negative experiences of abuse can eventually break a child's spirit. In fact, we know that this often happens. Unfortunately, the impact of these experiences of abuse on our emotional and spiritual lives follows us until the day we die. First Nations parents know from personal experience that without strong support systems, their children's experiences in the public school systems are a threat to their spirits.

A few years ago, while I was working at the Office of Native Student Services at the University of Alberta, now the Aboriginal Student Services Centre, a young man poked his head into my office and asked if I had a minute. It was not unusual for students to do this, but it was strange that this young man would even come into the office since he is non-Native. He was, however, a minority student, and I did not give it a second thought. He introduced himself and proceeded to tell me that he was a recent immigrant to Canada, and he was puzzled about why Native people in Canada got everything for nothing. He indicated that he been in a class where this topic was being discussed, and he was angry and wanted to know why Native people were treated differently and why he did not get that type of treatment since he was part of a minority group as well. He was especially concerned because while he was paying a great deal of money to be in school, Indian people were getting their education free. I began by telling him that what he had learned was not true: Not all Native people get free education. I told him a little about the Treaties that were signed in Canada between the Nations and the federal government and talked about the fiduciary responsibility that this government has for First Nations people. I provided him with a shortened version of the different Aboriginal groups in Canada—First Nations, Métis, Inuit, and nonstatus. In the end I do not think that my short lesson convinced him of anything. I am sure that he walked out of my office with very little change to the picture that had already been painted for him about Canada's First Peoples. I wonder whether this was a case similar to Yvonne's, in which she was trying very hard to fit in with her nonminority peers and 'kick' the Indians as they did to gain their acceptance.

> All First Nations students, including myself have heard the resentful accusations that our education is paid for at the public expense (i.e. their pocketbook); the accuser is seemingly oblivious of the fiduciary responsibly of treaties and agreements between the nations within and the colonial government of the settler Nations. (Calliou, 1995, p. 49)

As adults, some of us do have the knowledge to understand why this arrangement exists, but as Claire stated, as a young child, "You have no defense, so you are just left to feel bad about it; just one more thing to feel bad about."

The school can have a major impact on the identity development of Aboriginal students. Although school should be a place where students are afforded opportunities for mental, emotional, physical, and spiritual growth, the participants in this study have illustrated from many perspectives that this has not really been true in their own or their children's experiences within public school systems. In the processes of identity development, the participants' stories point out, Native children even as young as five or six rapidly learn in school that there is something not quite right about them. They may not be able to articulate what is happening when other children are looking at them in a strange way or calling them names, and they may not understand why they are the last ones being picked for the teams in gym class, but they quickly learn that they are not wanted. In terms of identity development, these children may regress and become very shy and nonresponsive when a teacher asks them questions, or they may not want to go to school (Friedel, 1999; Silver et al., 2002; Wilson, 1992) as a result of these experiences. The school culture communicates to them the school's attitudes toward a range of issues and problems, including how the school views them as human beings (even if it is not always verbalized). It does not take long for a Native child to figure out that he or she does not belong in that school.

Unless children grow up in a home where their culture is valued or where they at least receive reassurance that their culture is good, they may begin to resent their cultural identity. My study has revealed that some children are not bothered by the cultural tensions that they experience in school, whereas others are so ashamed of who they are that they do whatever they can to try to hide their identity.

One of my participants, Veronica, grew up in a Christian home, and even at a young age she knew that she was "a child of God." Although her skin is darker, and she is often reminded of this, she knew that God loved her just as she was. Knowing this helped her to get through her primary and secondary years: "I don't know what it was, but there was racism big time. . . . They used to call us squaws, and I didn't think anything of it." I asked whether this bothered her, even a little bit, and her response was, "I am trying to think . . . if it bothered me; I can't remember it bothering me." She went on to explain why:

> I was always taught as a kid and in God's Word . . . I am no different from anybody. God made me. . . . I was just brought up to think that way, that God made you special, He made you different, and that we were all special in His eyes; that nobody is more important. He made us all and He loves us all, the same kind of thing. That kind of teaching was in my mind right from when I was a kid. So if these kids were saying "Squaw" to me, it didn't bother me.

Veronica was an exception. She was comfortable with herself. She was a "child of God," and she had learned at a very young age that she was just as good as the rest of the children. She believed this, and the Word of God confirmed that belief. In addition to these teachings, she had a very strong and supportive mother who always put everything into perspective for her—both from a religious and a traditional Cree perspective.

Leah attributed much of who she is today to her experiences in the provincial school system: "It shaped my personality in the way of wanting to be accepted." She explained that she always tried so hard to fit in. She worked hard academically and did what she could to please the teachers. Leah said that her Native peers knew exactly what she was doing, and as another youth reported, Native children saw her as "Miss Goody Two-Shoes." It was hard trying to fit into a world where there were such tough messages: "I wasn't accepted by some Native people . . . because I am not seen as Native enough. . . . But then, on the other hand, from the White kids I was always an Indian kid; I could never be accepted into their bunch."

According to the United to End Racism Group (2001), it is not uncommon for people of the same race to "beat each other up" like this:

> Racism has made us place higher value on members of our group who appear more white, and denigrate those who have darker skin, kinkier hair, or other "less white" features. We also do the reverse—we target those with lighter skin as not being "black enough" [or not Native enough as in Leah's case], not legitimate persons of color. (p. 2)

Leah admitted that, in the end, she was very confused about how she should act:

> In the phys. ed. class one side of the wall would be Native, one side of the wall would be White, and I found that hard because I just didn't seem to fit in anywhere because I felt as if I wasn't accepted by the Native kids. . . . But I wasn't fully accepted by the White kids because I didn't look white. So I remember that year it made it more challenging because I didn't know where to sit. I remember in social class, same thing: I didn't know where to sit, so I just kind of sat in the middle.

The separation for Leah between the White and the Native students conveyed a very strong message: She belonged on the Native side. Even though she wanted to stay in the middle and remain neutral, she knew in her heart that she had to take a position. Unfortunately, she did not favor the Native side because of the message she had received for so many years: that Native children are lesser-than: "Right through all of my school years I received this message. This message came from both students and teachers, and if teachers believed this, then it must be true." Aboriginal children have been taught that they must respect their Elders, and for Leah, Elders meant anyone older than she was; this included her teachers: If her teachers believed that she was lesser-than, then it must be true; if teachers considered it acceptable to segregate students in their classes, obviously that had to be fine. At least, this is what she had reasoned. She said, "It is almost sad to know that all these teachers play such an important role, and they instill their values in you, and they almost shape who you are."

Teachers do have a tremendous impact on their students, and Taylor (1995) worried about this because so many Native children are being taught by persons outside of their culture:

> Ninety percent of Native children in this country will, at one time or another, be taught by a non-Native teacher, and many of these children will receive most of their education from non-Native teachers. The Native student's self-image, perception of Native/non-Native interactions, and chance of graduating will all be influenced by their non-Native teachers. (p. 224)

Leah's statement that "they almost shape who you are" is very troubling:

> I admired the knowledge and wisdom of my teachers; therefore, what teachers imparted on me had a major affect on how I wanted to live my life. I would have to say, most of the time, it was positive, but there were many times as well that I would have to say their influence was negative. Overall, I think what I learned from them, even if they didn't say it, is that the White, middle-class life was what we should aspire to obtain.

Leah shared another story with me about something that a teacher had taught her that had had long-term negative implications for her. In their social studies class the teacher was giving a history lesson on residential schools. Most people remember with deep pain the experiences that they suffered during their time in residential schools. Unfortunately, many Native youth know very little about these experiences of their parents, grandparents, and ancestors until they take a course in college or university. This was the case for Leah. She recalled that this teacher painted a very beautiful picture of residential schools for her and that, finally, in university, when she actually heard the truth about some of the things that went on in residential schools, she was angry—angry because for so many years she had been fooled into believing that those who attended these schools were very fortunate. She shared her story:

> I remember—I think it was Grade 8 or Grade 9; it was in junior high—I remember learning about residential school, and from my teacher's perspective it was a good thing that Native kids went to residential school. He really played it up because you got to wear uniforms, and how cool was that? Back then people didn't make a lot of money, so then you got free clothes and you got to go to school to learn this and to learn that. So I thought residential school was a good thing. And I remember going home and asking my mom and dad, "Did you guys get to go to residential school?" My dad was the only one that did, and he said, "Yeah, I did," and "Oh, that is so cool that you went!" I had no idea what was all entailed in residential school.

After Leah shared this story with me, I wondered how her comments had affected her father. When she asked her parents whether they had attended residential school, did this question evoke some negative memories for her father? What would have happened if her father had told her that what she had learned was untrue? Would she have believed her father or her teacher? After all, he was "the teacher," and "teachers are smarter than your parents," she told me.

Coming to the realization that much of who she is today was influenced by the non-Aboriginal teachers in her life has been very overwhelming for Leah:

> It is scary that strangers with their own perceptions, their own viewpoints, and their own values and beliefs instill these into you, especially if it is two completely different cultures, and particularly if they are saying that mine is more important than yours, and they are instilling that in you. That is really scary.

Children react to the negative messages that they receive about their culture in very different ways. Like Yvonne, some turn against their Aboriginal peers because they do not want to be placed in the same category; they have learned that teachers see Aboriginal students as inferior. Wilson (1992) substantiated this. In her study of Native students who had just transferred to a public high school after leaving a reserve school, she learned that "even before the teachers knew the students, they had prejudged them. They could not imagine that these students could ever be successful" (p. 53).

Patterns of internalized racism lead to individual disconnection from other members of the cultural group, and this disconnection impacts heavily on identity-development processes. One participant (Yvonne) referred to troublemakers who are of her own people:

> I was usually a good kid, pled to the teachers, never back talked to the teachers like other kids who shall remain nameless. Because I noticed that the kids that were troublemakers in class were usually Native kids, and I didn't really hang out with a lot of Native kids

because I always tried to do good in school. That didn't really look good with these other kids because they thought, "Oh she is a goody two-shoes; she is sort of smart," and always trying to bring me down. And I am like, "Whatever. . . . If you want to think that way, fine." But the only negative experiences I had in school were with other Native kids, not really with the White kids.

The isolation that results from internalized oppression can become so severe that a Native person may feel safer with and more trustful of White people than other Native people, as seems to have been the case for this participant. Hampton (1995) suggested that this illusion can be very harmful because, as Native people, we need one another. Being with 'your own' "frees people to be themselves":

It is best to admit that in general Indians and whites have not worked well together. Certainly there have been many occasions of goodwill, but despite the friendliness and good intentions on both sides we have not done very well in most of the everyday business of life for most of our people. Part of the problem may be that there are some things that can only be said from an Indian place. (p. 40)

Kristine concurred with Hampton: "I went to a provincial school from kindergarten to Grade 11, and it wasn't until I went to school in Saddle Lake that I realized just how much I needed my own people." She elaborated:

To be honest, I think it really affected me negatively. Going to school with mostly non-Native kids, I always tried so hard to be like them. After a while it was so tiring. I don't know; I guess I was ashamed of being Indian, that I did everything I could to be accepted by them. I played on their teams, went to their homes, invited them to my home. But you know what? Even after all those years, probably 11 years for sure, I still was never comfortable being around them. I don't think I even realized how hard it was trying to fit in until I learned what fitting in meant when I went to Saddle Lake School. There I could be myself; there I could be an Indian.

I knew exactly what this young lady meant when she said, "There I could be an Indian." I suppose this is what I was trying to say when I told someone one day that I would rather go to a function where there are mostly Native people than to one where I would be a minority, because there, I could be an Indian. We are different, and that is okay. Our "sense of time, of space, of energy, of humanity, are all different. Truth, beauty, and justice are evaluated differently. Epistemology, ontology, and cosmology are all different" (Hampton, 1995, p. 41). What a liberating feeling for me to finally be able to say this out loud: "I just want to be Indian! I just want to be comfortable in who I am!" (Daes, 2000; Steinhauer, 2001).

In her chapter *Peacekeeping Actions at Home: A Medicine Wheel Model for a Peacekeeping Pedagogy*, Calliou (1995) wrote, "Teachers and learners need to confront unspoken feelings of internal or external racism, need to confront denial" (p. 58). She continued:

One text which might begin the dialogue is Howard Adam's (1995) *Prison of Grass*. Adams, who grew up in a Métis colony in Saskatchewan, links racism to Euro-imperialism and economic factors where "Indian stereotypes created by the exploiters had reduced native people in the eyes of the public to animal like creatures." In order to remove himself from his 'Indian' roots, Adams "made a complete break with" his parents, home, and community because he perceived his identity as "ugly and shameful." He understood that in a "white-supremacist society, more opportunities and privileges exist for Indians and halfbreeds who can pass." However, he came to realize how badly be needed his cultural heritage, but not before he began to internalize feelings that he was "stupid, dirty, drunken and irresponsible," which 'stripped [him] of all humanity and decency.' (pp. 57-58)

Calliou added, "Racism abounds in Canada, . . . and classrooms cannot be public affirmative spaces unless teachers model these types of classrooms" (p. 58). Using the works of D'Oyley and Stanley (1990), she warned that "teachers must demonstrate and model 'the right of all those present to be there and to participate' in curricular experiences which do not victimize, delegitimate, or denigrate some members with words and images" (pp. 58-59). Curwen Doige (2003) echoed Calliou's sentiments and added that making a positive change is urgent because

> when an Aboriginal student suffers the pains of racial slurs that are inherent in the stereotyping and discrimination that still exists in our schools, he or she is stigmatized. When a student is stigmatized, that student's personhood is devalued and he or she disconnects from the attributes that assist in the development of self-respect, confidence, and the ability to trust oneself and others. This rift is the insidious tool of disenfranchisement because not only is the student told that he or she is unacceptable, the student now feels inferior and rejected. The affective, spiritual part of the student has been jeopardized. . . . Not respecting, cherishing, valuing the spirit of the Aboriginal student deeply affects the process of the individual's being in becoming a unique person responsible for his/her own life and actions in the context of significant group situation. (pp. 153-154)

Loss of Opportunity for Cultural Learnings

A regret that several parents had about sending their children off-reserve to a public school was that their children were rarely, if ever, exposed to anything that had to do with their Cree culture. Even when schools had Cree classes, the exposure was still very limited. The perceptions of the youth who participated in this study were that neither faculty nor students attached much value to these classes, and therefore none of them had ever enrolled in the courses, which were designed for students who were pursuing the nonacademic route. By this point in their education, the youth had been conditioned to believe that "Native stuff isn't as good as" (Haig-Brown, 1995, p. 280). According to Haig-Brown and the personal experiences of Native people, students' not wanting to be attached to anything Native is a normal reaction for those who have been subjected to racism. Haig-Brown related a story of a young lady who had

> mentioned that she would attend a non-Native broadcasting program rather than the First Nations one available in another institution because 'it had a higher credibility and higher chance of employment in the mainstream.' As this is probably an accurate perception, it is a disturbing reflection of persisting racism. It exemplifies an attitude which occasionally surfaces in relation to various other First Nations programs. (p. 280)

Many Aboriginal postsecondary students, such as those in the Indigenous Peoples Education specialization at the University of Alberta, know firsthand about this phenomenon or byproduct of societal and institutional racism.

Leah's arguments in relation to the Cree courses in high school are logical and well reasoned:

> I didn't take the courses for two reasons: firstly, because these classes were always scheduled when I had my core courses; and secondly, because I believed these classes were not very beneficial. Learning Cree words is not the same as learning the Cree language. No one can learn to speak Cree that way; and besides, learning Cree was not my priority at that time. My priority was getting a high school diploma.

Yvonne's and Simon's reasons for not taking the courses were similar to Leah's. They did not see any reason to take the courses, and, in fact, Yvonne took French instead. Goddard (2002) explained that students' reluctance to take Aboriginal languages and culture courses can be attributed to what he referred to as the "binary of mainstreaming versus cultural relevance" (p. 126). The locally developed curricula are considered different from, and also often less intellectually significant than, the "regular curricula" (p. 126). Native students quickly get this message when they see their teachers using their language and cultural classes as preparatory classes. Goddard suggested that "tuck[ing language classes] away behind stages or in the farthest reaches of the schools" (p. 130) confirms this to students. Another indicator is the meager resources that are allocated to these classes or the timetabling conflicts with core courses.

Although several of the public schools celebrate an Aboriginal Day when the school hosts a mini powwow and displays different aspects of the Cree culture, many parents felt that this is not enough, especially in public schools where the Native population is nearly 100%. A few participants also worried that the cultural elements on display might be misinterpreted because, as Pamela stated, "This is only a small part of our culture and who we are as Cree people." Curwen Doige (2003) agreed:

> Traditions are only one aspect of the ever-changing dynamic within a culture. So to focus on traditional dress, food music, ceremonies, and artifacts freezes a culture in time and perpetuates stereotypes. Artifacts are static. People and their values, beliefs, feelings, and thoughts are dynamic, and these define the culture. Spiritual ideas and traditions like sweetgrass and sweatlodge must be understood from the perspective of Aboriginal epistemology. Otherwise, the identifying values of Aboriginal people are treated as fixed as well. (pp. 150-151)

This is exactly what Yvonne was talking about when she said, "Ceremonies are sacred, and the school is not the place for them." Not only was she afraid that those who did not understand the culture would misunderstand the ceremonies, but she also did not want people to make generalizations. Pamela pointed out that "not all Aboriginal people practice Native spirituality, and I don't want people to make that assumption, and I think they would if they started having ceremony in school."

Now that Yvonne has finished school and is looking at her schooling experience in hindsight, the one thing that she regrets is not ever having had the opportunity to take Native studies courses at school. "I feel cheated as a result," which she explained:

> Going off reserve did cost me. They were just starting to go into the multicultural theme in Grade 7, . . . but [it was] not soon enough. So basically for me to learn anything about my history, my people's history; treaties or anything like that, I had to go and learn that in university. That is where I suffered when it came to learning about my people. I knew nothing about that. I didn't know anything about Native health concerns, why we are suffering from cancer. . . . You don't hear about that in school. That's the drawback of going to a provincially run school.

"Although it might appear that our culture is being put on display, you have to give some credit to the school, because they are trying," Louise acknowledged. Dakota agreed and admitted that even having the one Aboriginal Day and allowing the children to dress in their traditional regalia and perform their dances for the school community is a good start and a good opportunity for all other children to experience even a small part of the Cree culture:

> They have a little mini powwow, and some of these kids, regardless of whether they have regalia on or not, they want to go in that circle and be a part of that. I go and watch every year because I am very, very proud of them, about what they do, and they are so proud in themselves. You can just see the empowerment in them.

As the foregoing discussion has revealed, the participants had mixed feelings about what parts of the Cree culture should be brought into the school. However, overall, everyone agreed, as Pamela affirmed, that "there has to be a place for Aboriginal content in the curriculum."

Concluding Reflections

Despite the formidable array of negative public-school experiences, more parents in the communities of Saddle Lake and Goodfish Lake chose to send their children off-reserve than to enroll them in on-reserve schools. One might ask then, Why do these First Nations parents, who are fully aware of the unfair treatment to which their children are subjected within these public school systems, continue to make the decision to educate their children off-reserve? Do they not love them? If they sincerely care about their children's future and well-being, why do they subject them to the unfair treatment that they know continues to exist in these schools?

As a child who was sent to one of these schools and a parent who sent her children to one of these schools, I can respond with full confidence that they send their children to these schools because they love them, and they want the best for them. This is the basic and simplistic answer based on my own personal history and connections within my own and other Aboriginal communities. In this study the parent participants wanted their children to graduate from high school and become self-supporting, and, as Pamela asserted, the "White education is the best education" because it would get their children to college or university or . . . land them the higher-paying jobs." According to Wells and Crain (1992), "The whiter and wealthier a school, the better. . . . This is a deep-seated altruism that nearly every parent and educator is aware of, although few will admit it" (p. 67). They saw this truism as buttressed by two central themes:

> White . . . students, on the average, score higher on standardized tests and are more likely to go to college then non-white and low-income students. Hence the two most frequently applied measures of a "good" school—standardized test scores and college going rates—are constantly employed to reinforce the belief that whiter, wealthier schools do a better

job of teaching students than schools servicing darker, lower-income students.

The social climate or "moral atmosphere" of a school—the achievement ideology of the students, their educational and occupational aspirations, their cultural capital, and so on—is yet another way in which the large society defined good and bad schools (see Maddaus, 1988).... "Good" schools are those that enroll students who are quiet in the hallways and able to stay awake in class, students who see a direct link between a high school diploma and their futures, and students who value a traditional Eurocentered curriculum. "Bad" schools, on the other hand, are those enrolling students who carry weapons, have little hope of going to college or getting high paying jobs. (p. 68)

All of the parents who participated in this study want what is best for their children, and those parents who send their children off-reserve truly believe that public schools offer their children the best chance of success. They measure school quality by factors that are inherently biased toward White, middle-class standards. "This is the result of internalized racism," suggested a friend when I talked to her about the results of this study. "We have succumbed to the conditioning that Whiter is better without even realizing it," she added. I wondered whether she was right that we *had* succumbed. Do we think that White is better? Although only a handful of parents suggested this, it became apparent that, even without those particular words, many of them believe that we will never be quite as good as White people, at least in an academic sense. Although most of us know that that is not true, it is hard to abandon the thought after years of being bombarded with that message. We want our children to be able to compete in the outside world, which means competing with non-Native peers. Within the social context of the racism against Aboriginal persons and peoples that is evident in schools as well as the institutions and agencies in Canadian society, we recognize through direct experience that if we are to be deemed successful, we must be as good as, if not better than, our White peers.

Veronica talked about her decision to send her children off-reserve:

> I wanted to integrate them into the "White" kind of society. I had always told them that: "In the workplace you'll eventually have to work side by side with White people, so you may as well get used to it while you are there [in the public system]." This was my thinking.

The parents in this study felt that, to fit into the outside world, their children had to be able to compete and fit into the individualistic goal structures that society has imposed. We are consistently being compared to the rest of society. Statistics tell us that 58% of on-reserve Aboriginal people between the ages of 20 and 24 have not graduated from high school compared to 16% for the rest of the population (Statistics Canada, 2001b), and we can be certain that Aboriginal parents have heard the message. Aboriginal parents continue to hope that by sending their children to off-reserve schools, their children will somehow help to turn those statistics around and that if their children compete with their White peers, the future will be better for them.

After having interviewed the parents and analyzing the data, I believe that these parents made the choices that they did because they love their children. They wanted their children to be well-educated because that leads to everything else that is required to live in the contemporary world. They wanted their children to be accepted as human beings. Like all parents, maybe they just wanted their children to be able to love themselves and to be accepted and loved by others.

The parents who participated in this study clearly knew that, without an education, their children would struggle merely to survive. For these parents, educational choices were about basic survival. Although they were very much aware of what their children had to endure in attending the public school systems, the parents felt that they had no choice if their children were to have even a minimal quality of life in their adult years. They believed that their children needed to graduate from high school, and all available information, including numbers, seem to say that the only place where this graduation could be achieved was within the public school system. Ultimately, these parents felt that they had no school choice; they were making decisions based on the need to prepare their children to survive in a non-Native world.

CHAPTER 5:
THE ON-RESERVE SCHOOLING EXPERIENCE: FINDINGS

In the preceding chapter I presented the findings related to the participants' discussions of their public school experiences. The parents suggested that they had sent their children off-reserve because they believed that public schools provide a better education. They recognized that their decisions came with a price tag and that they were making a tradeoff. Their stories identified and exemplified the fact that parental school choice for First Nations parents cannot be considered apart from the significant issues that arise from the schooling experiences of their children.

Like the parents who sent their children to public schools, those who sent their children to on-reserve or band schools felt that they too were making some tradeoffs. However, unlike the situation for the public school parents, their tradeoffs did not appear to be as extreme, negative, or harsh in their immediate impacts on the students. Many of the parents whom I interviewed spoke to the problems and issues that they identified in relation to the on-reserve schools. In this chapter I will present the challenges and the positives that the participants discussed in sharing their views with me about on-reserve schooling.

From informal discussions with others in both Saddle Lake and Goodfish Lake, I knew before the interviews that many parents had concerns about curriculum and safety in First Nations schools. To better understand this particular area of parental concern, I invited Brian Wildcat to an interview to share with me his thoughts about these particular concerns because he had regular contact with First Nations parents and school personnel. Mr. Wildcat is a formally trained and certified educator with years of experience in working within First Nations communities and First Nations education as a school and systems administrator. He was serving at that time as the Director of Treaty 6 Education,[14] and I felt that his contribution would be a good introduction for me to the discussions about on-reserve schooling. I asked him directly what parents, teachers, principals, and Elders were saying about these three areas of concern with on-reserve schools. Perhaps it is not surprising that his responses were very similar to those of the parents whom I interviewed. He indicated that there were many reasons that parents choose to school their children off-reserve, but, overall, the top three reasons that he had heard were "curriculum, safety, and discipline, with safety topping the list." Furthermore, "Public perceptions about band schools are that they are not safe schools." Although he had heard this repeatedly from members of the Treaty 6 communities, he was not convinced that safety in the schools was as large a concern as was commonly portrayed:

> Now the question is, is that reality? I don't think so. I think a lot of the band schools are good schools. But that is the perception that people have: "I won't send my kid there because he's going to get beat up." The parents' duty is to protect their kids. I don't blame anybody. That's why I don't think you could force anybody to go to band schools. But that's where the duty is—on the band schools and for us at Treaty 6—to somehow get the community in there so we can improve the schools, so that schools attract the

---

[14] In my interview with Brian Wildcat, I learned that Treaty 6 Education works with 27 First Nations schools in Alberta in 17 First Nations communities that include Alexander First Nation, Alexis First Nation, Beaver Lake First Nation, Cold Lake First Nation, Enoch Cree Nation, Erminenskin First Nation, Frog Lake First Nation, Heart Lake First Nation, Kehewin Cree Nation, Louis Bull Tribe First Nation, Montana First Nation, O'Chiese First Nation, Paul First Nation, Saddle Lake Cree Nation, Samson First Nation, Sunchild First Nation, Whitefish Lake (Goodfish Lake) First Nation.

students, not trying to make people go to them without addressing that perception or that situation.

Mr. Wildcat was convinced that the comments about First Nations schools are often based on inaccurate perceptions and that those who make these statements often have never entered a reserve school:

> You talk to parents that do send their children there, and they will confirm that safety and discipline are not as out of control as some people think. Yes, there are issues around safety, but it isn't at a point of crisis.

Many of the parent participants who had sent their children to an on-reserve school would agree with Brian Wildcat's assessments. Marleen echoed Mr. Wildcat's views: "Much of what is said about the reserve schools is perception." She added, however, "Safety is an issue to some extent, particularly when it comes to bullying. There are quite a few bullies in our schools." Other parents agreed with this, and as Claire stated, "I didn't even know how bad it was until I watched my daughter get knocked to the ground one day. Maybe it isn't that bad, but when you watch your own child get picked on, you begin to worry."

The participants in this study spoke clearly to the challenges as well as the positives of having their children attend an on-reserve school, and I will elaborate on them in the following sections.

The Challenges of Attending an On-Reserve School

Curriculum and Teaching Concerns (Low Teacher Expectations)

Although all of the parents who had sent their children to the reserve schools knew that the approved curriculum for both the public and reserve schools is the same, many felt that their children might not be receiving the same level or standard (quality) of instruction, particularly at the junior/senior high levels. However, not one of the parents seemed overly concerned about this. They were more concerned about the unfair assessments that people in general were making of the reserve schools without any insider knowledge. Pamela suggested, "Outsiders and even community members think the reserve schools are not up to par, and this may be why most of our children are being sent to the public schools these days."

Carrie cautioned that

> the perception out there is that children that attend reserve schools are slower, and this becomes a self-fulfilling prophecy. If parents feel that their children are in fact academically slower, then they are more likely to send them here. [But] it is absolutely not true that they are all slower. There are many very bright students that attend this school as well.

"It is too bad that so many people have this perception," added Sheila, another parent who sends her children to an on-reserve school. She concurred with Carrie that this particular perception contributes to the types of students that the reserve school attracts. "This is too bad," she adds, "because what you put into it is what you get out of it. . . . That's how I see it." She was satisfied that her children were receiving a quality education. Claire, another parent, suggested that "this school could be a top-notch school if more people would change their attitude and if more parents would get involved. If we believe that the school is substandard, then it will be."

Like the parents above, Veronica was convinced that individual and public attitudes had a huge impact on the various educational aspects of the school: She pointed out, "If even our own Boards of Education don't believe in our schools, then we are going to get mostly those kids that might otherwise have difficulties in the provincial schools."

"Teachers that come to teach in our schools are also responsible for these perceptions. They come with a set of preconceived notions, and they think that Native children really do not want to learn," added Leah. Most participants agreed that low teacher expectations contribute significantly to academic outcomes for students. Pamela reported, "This became very obvious when my son was here [in the reserve school] in Grade 9":

> My son didn't do well because the teacher he had was very slack, where I thought, . . . because there were only 10 students in the class— . . . Grade 9 was crucial to me when I was in the provincial school, and I thought he would have a lot of one-on-one. And . . . I remember in March, just looking at math, they were only in chapter two, and . . . they only had a couple more chapters left [in the public school]; they were on Chapter 10. And he [the public school math teacher] said, "The text only goes to Chapter 13, and we are done." What a difference! So I begged for my son to be allowed back [into the public school]. He had fallen back a lot, but they [the off-reserve school] helped him catch up.

Veronica similarly was appalled the day that she discovered that the Grade 9 students were so far behind in one of their classes: "This is February, or January, and some of the children are on the 2nd module of 15. . . . How can they pass the course? How can they pass Grade 9 if they haven't done the core courses?" She asked the principal what he was going to do about that; his response was merely, "The kids just refuse to do it." "This tells me just how seriously our teachers take the students," she added. Another parent agreed: "They do become complacent. They just take it for granted that teaching in reserve schools is easy and that they don't have to teach the way they would in the provincial schools." Suzanne, a Saddle Lake participant, suggested:

> We have to turn this mentality around. Otherwise our children are not going to make it. If you have teachers who come into the school who don't have faith in their students, they [the students] are not going to make it.

Pamela asserted:

> We have to be on top of things if our children are going to succeed. Perhaps if we outwardly showed we cared about our children's progress, then they [the teachers] would care too. It is just that some teachers are just laid back, and it is not the child's fault, it is not the parents fault; but if the parents would just come in and just be on task and say, "Okay, where are you guys at today?" or "What are you learning today?" Or if they would just help their child by coming in daily, weekly, you know what? The kids would just excel. However, the blame can't just be laid on the teachers or the parents, because it is true that we do have many students that are not at grade level, and teachers have to teach accordingly, which means sometimes the more advanced children fall behind.

Thinking that her son would do better in a smaller classroom environment, Pamela moved him to the reserve school in Grade 9, but this did not work. By the middle of year he had fallen so far behind academically that she moved him back to the public school:

> Although at first I thought it was not necessarily the teacher's fault, now when I think about it, the teacher has to take some of the blame—not that I am trying to lay blame, but she was teaching to the level of the majority of the students in that classroom and forgot to teach those that were more advanced.

I asked this parent:

> Were most of the children really at a lower level, or did the teacher assume this was the case? Were the other children behind because they were not academically capable, or did the teacher assume that they were not and therefore do nothing to help them move forward?

After some thought, Pamela replied:

> I haven't really thought about that before, but come to think of it now, I think a lot of the teachers, especially the non-Native teachers, don't have much faith in our kids. They don't push them, because I think they think the kids are not capable of handling any more than that.

Veronica's expressed her view:

> If a child is not pushed, if any child is not pushed, not encouraged, chances are they will not perform to the level they are capable of, and I think that was what was happening with these Grade 9 students. They were several modules behind because no one pushed them. The students cannot take all the blame for that.

These parents agreed with Veronica's statement that "blaming the students takes the responsibility off the teachers."

According to Mackay and Myles (1995), "Such an apparently cogent explanation can enormously comfort educators because it places responsibility for a student's behavior firmly with the [student] and releases the school system from both blame and remedial action" (p. 166). Veronica and Pamela also agreed that, generally, it is non-Native teachers who have "low expectations of our children" (Veronica), but Pamela was quick to point out that "not all non-Native teachers could be put in the same category, because many, many non-Native teachers that come to teach in our communities really do care about the kids that they teach." In fact, both parents stressed that Native teachers can also have low teacher expectations. However, as Pamela explained, "I guess what I am saying here is that non-Native teachers are more likely to make these assumptions because they don't know us."

Taylor (1995) agreed that most non-Native teachers know very little about the Native communities in which they are teaching: "Indeed, the vast majority of teachers . . . had never visited the reserves" (p. 166). Without any prior knowledge, all that teachers have to rely on to formulate opinions about Aboriginal children is their own lived experience, what the media have fed them, or what they have heard from colleagues with previous on-reserve school experience.

Marleen spoke to the issue:

But we cannot completely exclude non-Native teachers from coming to teach in our schools. We don't have enough trained teachers, and even if we did, I don't think we can exclude all of them, especially those that fit into our communities, and many do. Many just fit right in.

Barman et al. (1987) supported the views of the parents:

> Successful teachers of Indian children, whether or not they are Indian are characterized by their ability to create a climate of emotional warmth and to demand a high quality of academic work. They often take the role of personal friend rather than that of impersonal professional, and use many nonverbal messages, frequently maintaining close body distance, touching to communicate warmth, and engaging in gentle teasing. After establishing positive impersonal relationships at the beginning of the year, these teachers become demanding, as an aspect of their personal concern in a reciprocal obligation to further learning. Highly supportive of any attempt students make, these teachers avoid even minor forms of direct criticism. Thus these teachers are effective because of their instructional and interactional style, and not because of their ethnic or racial group membership. (p. 13)

They also pointed out that "Most Native children will be taught by non-Native teachers" (p. 241); therefore, more attention must be paid

> to improving training for the large non-Native teaching force which will continue to exist for a long time. When this issue is addressed by teacher education faculties, band school administrations, and by the teachers themselves, the results should benefit Native students immensely. (p. 241)

Most of the participants in this study took it for granted that their children would be taught by non-Native teachers even on the reserve, and most did not object to that. However, Claire clearly expressed what they did object to: "Many white teachers take jobs on the reserve, without any real commitment to the community and to the children. To many this is a temporary stop until something better comes up." Taylor (1995) concurred: "The reserve school is a temporary station to achieve or begin to achieve personal goals" (p. 225). Because many teachers may go to First Nations communities with the intention of staying for only a short time, often these teachers will not go out of their way to develop relationships with the children and/or the community. They have a goal when they arrive at a school, and that is mainly to do their job. Taylor postulated that many of these teachers feel that, "if I do my job well, that is sufficient; I have satisfied my employer and myself and I have given the child good, caring instruction" (p. 225).

My data collection revealed that the students, parents, and community would like to develop some type of relationship with their teachers. They want to know that the teachers value their children and have a genuine interest in getting to know them. When teachers go to the reserve only to do their job, relationship building does not occur. Without any relationship-building activities or any attempt to get to know the community, teachers can become disheartened; as a result, they never have or make the opportunity to learn anything about the First Nations communities or their students. "They don't know what is important to us, what we value, or where our priorities are, so everything we do looks backward to them," Bernice said.

Because the people and the community are so frustratingly different, teachers find it easier to just go in and do their jobs and then return to the comfort of their own homes at the end of the school day. Taylor (1995) cautioned that even those teachers who reside in the First Nations communities rather than living in the nearby non-Native towns fall into the same patterns of thought and actions. They exist in their own little worlds, finding fault with everything that the community does:

> A non-Native couple who had been living on reserve for many years continually found fault in the community around them. They would often verbalize their complaints to other non-Native teachers, expecting and usually receiving, affirmation that certain things in the community were inadequate. These complaint sessions are what Berger and Luckman ... describe as "Legitimation or Universe-maintenance." Legitimation is a process which people justify their reality or their concepts of 'the way things should be.' Simply put, it is a method by which individuals convince themselves that their way is the right way. This process is necessary for people to protect their symbolic universe, which is a socially produced set of realities within which a group of people exist. (p. 228)

Hampton (1995) spoke about the differences between Natives and non-Natives:

> At the historical level, Native and non-Native look at the world from opposed positions. Not only must they contend with personal differences in viewpoint, language, and experiences; not only must they contend with cultural differences in value, understanding of human relationship and modes of communication; but they must contend with world shattering differences between the conquered and the conqueror, the exploited and the exploiter, the racist and the victim of racism. (p. 41)

What non-Native people see as important may not necessarily take priority in a Native world. Halee suggested:

> People judge us before even knowing us, and most of the time the judgments that they have about us are completely off. Just because we don't do things the same way as White people or we don't attach the same value to material things, we are thought of as backward.

The following story demonstrates what Halee was saying about being misunderstood. In the story the non-Native person can see things only through her "White experience," and as result, she sees everything in a Native world as "backward":

> Recently I was at a spa, and after learning what my doctoral research was about, the proprietor/technician proceeded to tell me that her daughter-in-law was a teacher in a northern First Nations community. This was now year two of the northern experience, and so far it appeared everything about it was negative. I asked why her daughter-in-law went back to teach there for a second year if everything was so bad, and the response was, "Well, she couldn't find a job locally." I indicated that I had a hard time believing that she could not find a job elsewhere, because I knew many of the surrounding First Nations communities were looking for teachers at all grade levels. She went on to say that her daughter-in-law only had to pay $238 for rent and utilities over there since

teachers were provided with on-site housing. That last bit of information revealed a lot. Like many other teachers that go to First Nations communities, their stay is only temporary, long enough to get their certification (Taylor, 1995), and in this case it was a great way to save money as well—get certified and accumulate some savings. The complaints about this "backward community" continued, and a very colorful picture was painted for me. I learned that in this community sibling disputes ended with one stabbing the other, and I learned about the corrupt leadership. I learned about the misuse of funds and about how this community got everything for nothing, particularly "free education." Apparently the school is a beautiful facility with "top-of-the-line computer equipment" that no one knows how to use. I heard how the White teachers worked so hard and went out of their way for the children, and about how, even if they wanted to, they weren't allowed to develop relationships with the children and the community. I also learned that it was a good thing that the daughter-in-law had taken her dog along. I listened with disgust, and I could not wait to get away from this woman. I felt like I couldn't breathe as the anger welled up inside me. I tried desperately to educate this woman. I talked to her about culture differences and tried to educate her about the effects of colonization and residential schools. I spoke about perceptions and preconceived stereotyping and White privilege, and let her know that I had a hard time believing that people were stabbing each other on a consistent basis to settle disputes. If that was the case, there would be no one left in the community. I talked to her about worldviews and how her daughter in-law was seeing and interpreting things based on her own lived experience. My words fell on deaf years, and the response to what I was saying was, "We all have choices, and these people choose to live that way." She added, "Look at me. I grew up poor and oppressed, but I chose not to stay there." I asked her, "Do we really have a choice? Do you really believe that 'those people' that have now become addicted to drugs and alcohol have a choice about whether they take a job tomorrow? Do they have the 'free will' to make this decision? I don't think so!" I said. I needed to end this conversation, so I concluded by suggesting that she instruct her daughter-in-law to leave that community, because if she continued to work there with that attitude, it would do more harm than good to both her and the children she was responsible for.

Daes (2000) discussed free will:

Let me begin with the philosophical concept of "free will," which, we should all realize, is something of an illusion. None of us is ever completely free to do as we wish. We are guided, albeit often without our conscious knowledge, by the past—our memories, the values that we have been taught, the actions of our ancestors. We are also limited by the circumstances of the present, including a great variety of physical elements and forced that exist beyond human control. (pp. 4-5)

Being a member of a First Nation myself, I was offended by what the spa owner had said about another First Nations community. She was talking about "these" people in much the same way that government officials did over 100 years ago. From her daughter-in-law's complaining, this woman had concluded that the "Indians" up north are backward, and although she did not say it, I kept hearing the word "savages" (her statement about siblings stabbing one another to resolve disputes evoked that image). The woman was describing and demonstrating the familiar pattern that we interpret things and events based on our own lived experiences, that we come to believe that our way is the right way, and that we continue the cycle of repressing others' views. Because other people talk differently, live differently, and have different priorities, we assume that they are wrong and we are right. If outsiders continue to go to Aboriginal communities only to find fault, then the cycle of oppression will never be broken. They will continue to perpetuate the common-people stereotypes of Aboriginal people, seeing us as backward, useless, lazy freeloaders. We will continue to be known as "those people" on whom the tax-paying public consistently wastes good money.

In his study Taylor (1995) found that it is not uncommon for non-Native teachers to react the way that this lady's daughter-in-law had because "some non-Native teachers enjoy feeling superior to the world around them" (p. 231). He explained this phenomenon as the teacher's experiencing culture shock and reacting to this shock with confrontation, which he described as an absorber of the shock and as necessary to "confirm the non-Native teacher's subjective reality. Subjective reality is personal understanding of and confidence in the reality of one's life and way of living." (p. 231). He elaborated on confrontation:

> Confrontation may take the form of 'complaint sessions' in the evening at non-Native teachers' homes or may be directed openly at the community such as that by the teacher who asked the students "What is wrong with your parents?" Whether conversational confrontation is direct or indirect, it is the non-Native teachers' main method of protecting their reality. (p. 231)

Several parents in my study were not convinced that teachers or the academic focus in school had a great deal of impact on their First Nations students. Halee pointed out:

> We spend too much time worrying about all these things—what our teachers are teaching our children, the effects non-Native teachers have on our children, everything. We get so hung up on academics. Academics are not even an issue for me. How they score on a provincial exam does not determine whether a child will go on to university or college. They will go because they want to go, and once they reach high school, they will make sure they get the grades they need to get there.

Leah concurred: "I went to university even without super-high grades. I got in. If you are passionate about doing something, you will find a way to do it." Carrie noted that her life had also followed that pattern: She had graduated with a teaching degree without ever having completed Grade 12:

> I think the difference between me and some of the other Native students is that I had support, support from so many people. Being a straight A student in high school really is meaningless without support, guidance, and encouragement. I completed a degree because people believed in me.

Safety and Discipline

As the introduction suggested, all of the parents who participated in this study revealed that safety is an issue of concern to parents with children in First Nations schools. Some of the parents who were sending their children off-reserve admitted that safety at school was definitely a factor of consideration when they made the decision to school their children off-reserve. The parents of children attending on-reserve schools were concerned about this issue as well, but obviously not to the same extent.

I talked with an administrator at one of the schools who confirmed that the school had received several calls from concerned parents about bullying. They want the reassurance that their children will be safe and that appropriate measures are being taken to prevent their children from being victims of bullying. Florence reported:

> Like other schools, bullying is a problem, but it is an issue that is constantly being addressed. The teachers and administrators are always strategizing to find ways to deal with bullies. At the beginning of every year, each teacher reviews the rules of effective behavior, and children are encouraged to participate in these discussions.

Florence affirmed that asking students to help write the rules and take part in the process of deciding upon the rules and consequences makes it more likely that they will feel a sense of ownership.

According to Clarisse:

> There are different expectations for students when they are in a feast setting, or when they are in the washroom, or in the library.... They learn when to be quiet, when they have to listen, and so forth. Although some students might need a few reminders initially in these various settings, it doesn't take long for these rules to become habit, especially when they [the students] are at feasts or other traditional events.

Sheila acknowledged:

> I send my kids to this school [reserve school], and although I am not overly concerned about their safety, I am concerned sometimes because of the social problems on the reserve. The problems have to make their way into the school.

Florence agreed and put this thought into perspective for me:

> Sometimes I feel and I often say that, "Our kids live in a war zone." Let's say our kids are dodging bullets sometimes—and I am not saying that metaphorically; it's literal. They are witnessing violent acts every day, and yet we expect them to come and be ready to learn. And some of that might come into our school. A child who has been hurt, who's been bullied will express that, and they will hurt others and they will bully others. Now that is a battle that we have to acknowledge and say, "Yes, this happens here in [in the community]."

"Our school is a reflection of what is going on in our community," added another parent, and Marleen observed:

> Children that witness violent acts are more inclined to repeat those acts, and, unfortunately, these are the children who get sent to the reserve schools. These children become the school bullies. They are the ones that are walking the hallways and basically running the school.

Bullying is an old and widespread problem in schools. Most of us can recall episodes of bullying to which we or our classmates were subjected during our school years. Research estimates indicate that the problem affects far more students than teachers or parents are aware of. In a recent study of 1,041 students in four Toronto-area schools (Grades K-8), Pepler, Craig, Ziegler, and Charach (1994) showed that between 12% and 15% of the children reported being victimized more than once or twice over the term and that between 7% and 9% reported having bullied others more than once or twice over the term. These statistics refer only to those incidents that are reported, which means that a significant consideration is that children who are bullied will often not report the incident out of fear of reprisal.

A few of the parents were concerned about the unreported incidents. When Claire saw her daughter being pushed to the ground, she panicked, knowing that this must have happened many times before. She was sure of it when her daughter quickly got up and said to her, "That's okay, Mom, it didn't hurt." Claire suggested that, although her daughter had a look of fear on her face, it appeared that the girl was only trying to prevent the other child from getting into trouble. Knowing that this was a typical reaction of children who have been victims of bullying, she became even more convinced that her daughter was a victim; her daughter, however, merely wanted to leave things alone. Was her daughter afraid of the other child? Was she fearful that things might get worse for her if she told? Halee explained that children

> don't want anyone to raise a fuss over the harassment they are receiving because they are fearful that it will escalate if they complain. Children are getting picked on, and they are terrified, but they don't want their parents to get involved because they don't want to be seen as 'rats.' My daughter was picked on a couple of times—really, really picked on—and she came home crying and being really, really depressed, and I told her, "I'll go talk to the school to make sure nothing happens. We just really have to do something about it." She said, "No, Mom, the kids will find out, and nobody likes a rat." So for this reason I chose not to interfere. I also decided not to interfere because I didn't want my daughter to stop talking. I was afraid that if I reported the incident, the bullying might get worse. And I also did not want to jeopardize that line of communication between my daughter and me.

Claire thought similarly:

> I am afraid she is being bullied, but because she won't admit it, I just have to make sure she is being watched more closely. All I can do for now is make it clear to her that under no circumstances is mistreating another person either physically or verbally ever acceptable.

Nadine reported:

> Bullying is bad here [in the reserve school]. You feel sorry for the kids that get picked on, . . . and many of the children that are bullied have special needs and have behavioral problems, and this bullying sparks a lot of anger for these children.

She knew that the school was making every effort to put a stop to the bullying that they knew about, but she wanted the school administration to pay closer attention because she was convinced that they did not know about most of the bullying that was going on. She was afraid that this bullying "can have serious consequences for children who do not have the tools to defend themselves," particularly the special-needs students.

 Nadine understood that bullying occurs everywhere, and when I asked her to comment on this, she responded, "Bullying exists all the time, everywhere. . . . But [in the public school], at least they are able to stand up for themselves and not be afraid to voice their opinions." I asked her to elaborate:

> Well, in [the public school] when there are fights, everyone that is involved has to answer to what happened. Everyone is given a chance to give their side of the story, and a penalty is paid by all those involved.

In further discussions with her, she told me that she had worked within the reserve school system and had seen how incidents such as this played themselves out. According to what she had witnessed, children in reserve schools are often not given the same opportunity to tell their side of the story. They are called into the principal's office, but the principal will just talk to them—both will receive a little lecture—but it goes no further than that. She argued that this leaves children feeling voiceless, because even if they do not initiate the incident, they receive the same lecture that the other student does. I asked her why this was, and she said, "Because the staff is afraid of the parents. If someone is given a suspension or some kind of time out, then the parents will come and raise hell."

 Other participants spoke of "parental interference" as well. I asked Dakota whether she thought parental inference had anything to do with discipline issues in First Nations schools:

> It has to make a difference. Some parents continually pick up for their children. They just cannot believe that their child could be so mean to another child. . . . If parents continually stick up for a child that has behavioral issues, then that child is going to think they are doing nothing wrong. They are being rewarded instead for their bad behavior. The reward is their parents' attention.

 Parental interference, or "overinvolvement of parents," as George called it, poses a problem for teachers and administrators. Many of the participants were concerned about the affect that it was having on their children. As Pamela stated, "These discipline problems are taking up a lot of the teacher's time, and teachers are finding that they are not only cheating the other students of quality education, but they are also cheating the behavioral students." Although everyone had his or her own theory about how this situation could be rectified, all recognized that their hands were tied when it came to reserve politics. According to Sheila, who voiced what many of the parents felt, "This is a community issue, not just a school issue."

 The job of the principal is both extremely demanding and critical to the success of a school in a First Nations community. In addition to leading the school, maintaining discipline, managing the budget, assisting staff, responding to parental inquiries, and reporting to the local education school boards, a principal in a First Nations community may also be asked to sit on a variety of out-of-school committees, help with programs for youth, participate in community planning, and often act as school carpenter and plumber. A principal on the First Nations reserve might have endless responsibilities, but what he or she does not have is power. From the outside it may look as though principals have a great deal of power, but the reality is that in First Nations communities the Chief and Council have the power of veto over every decision that the principal(s) or any program manager on the reserve makes. If the Chief and Council object to a school suspension because the parent is a friend, they have the power to end that suspension and allow the child back into the school. The Chief and Council can veto a principal's decisions even though they are in strict accordance with his or her assigned responsibilities.

Everyone in a First Nations community is very aware of the power structure that exists on the reserve, and this may be why, as Dakota suggested and other parents agreed,

> a parent feels they can come into the school and freely raise hell—something they wouldn't do in a public school. If parents don't like something about a teacher, an administrator, or another student in the school, they feel they have every right to say whatever it is they want to say to that particular person, even if it is hurtful, because they know there will be no consequences for them to deal with, especially if they have some political clout with the Chief and Council.

Noella Steinhauer (2007) explained why and how these power relationships play themselves out:

> The right to veto decisions can include school-based decisions made by the principal. The principal's power in a First Nations community is not governed by the School Act because it is provincial legislation and because First Nations are a federal responsibility. The principal on the reserve has no power under this act. The Indian Act assigns sections 114–122 to cover schools. These sections cover issues like the ability of the minister to enter into agreements on behalf on Indian children, attendance, who does not have to attend, who can be a truant officer and his powers, even the use of force, denomination of the teachers, right to have a Protestant or Catholic school, and some definitions. Nowhere in the Act is there mention of the authority of the principal. As a result First Nations usually develop their own policies and procedures of the operation of the school, but the final power still rests with the Chief and Council. (p. 63)

"The only way we are ever going to get to the bottom of these behavior problems, these bullying issues, is if we [the community members] work together," Louise asserted. "We need to find ways of creating unity." The participants from both Saddle Lake and Goodfish Lake spoke extensively about this "lack of unity." Pamela elaborated:

> I think one of the biggest problems on our reserves is that we can't seem to work with one another. When one person gets ahead, others try to bring them down. Unless we address this, nothing is going to improve in our communities and our schools. It is our children that are going to lose out in the end. Why can't we understand that?

Veronica agreed: "Our attitude [the whole community's] has to change about each other and respect each other and realize that we all have strengths. We can't continue to pull one another down." Florence suggested, "This will only happen if we have a vision of where we want to take this place [the reserve school]." I asked her how she thought this might be possible: How could we begin the process of involving everyone? She noted that it would be a slow process but that the best place to start might be with the teachers:

> They can't work in isolation and they can't have divisions. . . . They have to come together and have to be able to talk. They have to feel free to express their concerns, and when they do so, it can't be held against them. They can't be afraid.

But other parents such as Sheila countered that this is difficult to achieve without the support of the Chief and Council:

> They [Chief and Council] are busy on a daily basis dealing with a number of community and political issues, so they may not have the time to spend on school issues. This is why they need to be able to hand over some of that power to the principal. They need to be able to say to community members, "We leave that decision to the principal."

The participants agreed that, unless this happens, parents will continue to undermine the school principal and staff, and behavioral and discipline issues will continue to be a problem.

All of the participants whose children were attending the reserve school agreed that creating a perfect school system would not happen overnight, but all were optimistic that things would turn around. Pamela pointed out:

> We just have to believe, because we do have good things happening in the school. Our schools provide our children with so much more, but I want to say our children are not all behind academically. Many, many of them are strong academic students. But a school has to be more than about academics anyway, and I know our local school does provide more than that. When I look at our Native schools, there are a lot of good things happening. If parents would only come in and be a part of it— . . . The way I see it, it is our Native schools where we bring their [children's] self-esteem up. We try to get them into everything that is out there. We nurture them. We want them exposed to everything. We encourage them big time. Just go out and see the world! Go and do everything that you can think of doing. You can be anything you want to be.

The Positives of Attending an On-Reserve School

Knowing that the majority of the people in our community do not have good things to say about our reserve schools, I came back to the question of why parents choose those particular schools for their children, and I saw again in the interviews that these parents were choosing for their children's best future. Some argued that their children need stronger academic programming and were convinced that the off-reserve provincial schools offer this. Others chose the on-reserve school because they wanted their children to be in a place where being a "Cree Indian" is honored. Although academic achievement is important, they did not feel that they were giving this up, and they chose a school where that their children would be able to develop strong cultural identities and grow up being proud of the ancestry into which they had been born. The parents were adamant that this level of comfort with self could not be achieved in a school system where "being White and fair-skinned is the picture of beauty and success," as Suzanne declared.

Regardless of where their children were being schooled, all parents had one thing in common: They wanted their children to feel happy and secure as they went through the schooling process. They wanted their children to be proud of who they are, and they hoped that throughout their schooling, the children would embrace their Native heritage. The interviews revealed a belief and an awareness based on personal experiences that attaining these goals for their children would be very difficult in a system that "creates advantages and benefits for whites, and discrimination, oppression, and disadvantages for people from targeted groups [Native students in this case]" (Wijeyesinghe, Griffin, & Love, 1997, p. 93).

Compared to the parents who had chosen to send their children to off-reserve provincial public schools, the parents who chose to send their children to on-reserve schools identified many more positives in support of their decisions. Comfort and familiarity were the key reasons. They wanted their children to be in a place where they felt comfortable in and with themselves. Halee explained:

> I want my daughter to know that being Indian is something to be proud of, and I know this can only be achieved if she is with her own, because in the world outside of our reserve, being Indian is devalued.

Other parents shared the same sentiments.

Comfort and Familiarity

As I previously reported, 47% of the parents who participated in this study were sending their children to on-reserve schools. Their children were comfortable attending these schools, and the parents chose their comfort over any concerns that they might have had with academics, safety, and discipline. Wells and Crain (1992) supported this rationale: "Maximizing on the comfort, familiarity, and convenience of a same-race school" is a perfectly rationale choice for a Native child (p. 72). In researching school choice, these authors found that Black families, like Native families, often choose a school for this reason alone. They explained why:

> All parents—rich and poor, black and white—want what is best for their children. But some parents are faced with more difficult choices than others—choices that are mired in the reality of discrimination and domination. Black parents who have sent their children to desegregated schools often tell of the tradeoff between the pain of exposing their sons or daughters to racism and thereby possibly crushing their self-esteem and the desire to enroll them in a higher-status school. White parents, in their search for whiter, wealthier schools, do not have to make such tradeoffs. In a society steeped in status group conflict and stratified according to race and class, a decision to keep a black child in a low-status black school to spare him the pain of racism is a perfectly rational choice. But it is not maximizing—it is sacrificing. (p. 80)

The Cree parents whom I interviewed in this study faced the same situation that the Black parents in Wells and Crain's (1992) did: They were very much aware of the perceptions that others hold of their reserve schools. However, these parents cannot give their views and judgments too much weight in their decision-making processes. They felt strongly that the advantages of choosing the reserve school for their children outweighed any disadvantages. Their children were happy in the reserve school, and as Sheila explained, "They can't see themselves anywhere else. They can't see themselves in Ashmont; they can't see themselves in St. Paul." The reserve school has always been a very comfortable place for these parents, and when their children said that they "don't want to be any place else," the parents fully understood. The context of such understanding is clear in the following quotation in which a parent reminisces about returning to the reserve school after being in a public school for a few years:

> When I got there [the reserve school] in Grade 5, to me it was like a dream come true. It was like I finally came to a place—and it was new to me—but I felt this was my school, this was my classroom, and I belonged here. I could put up my hand and I could say my opinion. You know, it was just like freedom, and—I don't know—I think I must have walked around with a smile on my face for I don't know how long. I thought, "Everybody must be just happy to be here," as happy as I was.

Hearing this parent tell me about walking around with a smile on her face reminded me of the time that I was at one of these schools collecting data for a course I was taking. I went to the school every day for two weeks, and every day I would receive warm hugs from the children. They appeared to be happy, and, like this parent, they walked around with smiles on their faces. I was envious, and I wondered whether this would have been the case if they had been in a public school. I knew that I had not had such a smile when I was in school and that today my memories of school are clouded by a great sadness.

Sheila had never had much experience in a public school, but she had attended one in a nearby town for a very short period of time. All she remembered about this experience was that she did not fit in. Even after the first day she realized that she had absolutely nothing in common with her new peers, and she left the school a few days later. Remembering her own experience in a public school, Sheila could not understand why at the start of this school year she had told her daughter that she would attend an off-reserve school:

> I was saying at the beginning of this year to my daughter, "My girl, you are going to Racette next year," and she was like, "No way! . . . No way! I am not going there!" And I was just thinking, "Yes, you are," kind of forcing that on her. I was just thinking about it, and I thought, "Why am I saying that?"

After realizing what she had said to her daughter, Sheila stopped herself and thought about how important it is to feel that a sense of belonging, to be in a place where it is possible to be happy and comfortable, to be truly understood by friends. She too had attended the reserve school, and she knew how important this feeling of belonging was. She recollected:

> We all shared a common interest. We all shared being able to sit together and could relate to one another. Even to this day, of all the ones I graduated with or even went to school with, we all share a special bond still as adults.

Another parent reported, "There is no prejudice here, and she is a lot more settled, a lot more grounded." When I asked her whether her child liked to attend the reserve school, she responded, "Oh, she loves it!" Unfortunately, not all children enjoy their schooling experiences, as the words of another parent show:

> I was just debating with a good friend of mine recently. She . . . put her children in a non-Native school in St. Paul, and [before she did] I said, "Well, that is your choice, but you will find out. But me, you know, I am going to keep my kids here." Sure enough, a month went by, and her oldest daughter that is in Grade 5 did not want to be there. She got to the point where she didn't want to get up and go to school, and I was like, "Hello! Bring her back here!" And sure enough she is back and doing fine, and she is good.

All that this child needed was to come back to the place where she was comfortable, and her old self was restored. Unfortunately, some children are forced to stay in a school that wounds their spirits. Morrisseau (1998) recalled that his own spirit had been wounded when he was a child attending a public school:

> School was supposed to be a place of learning, growth, and development, but for me, it only presented a different set of problems. . . . My clothes usually had patches, my lunch consisted of mustard sandwiches, and my body usually was dirty. Being called a "dirty Indian" brought forth anger and hatred for a system that was supposed to teach me. Because of this, I never developed a commitment to education. (p. 64)

Noella Steinhauer (1999) reported that the students in her study felt fortunate that they had the option of coming back to the reserve school to complete their high school education, especially after having "encountered racism in their early years of school" (p. 50). The youths needed to be in a place of comfort and familiarity, and they found that in the reserve school:

> Leanne copes by staying in the comfortable surroundings of [the reserve]. She speaks of how much she enjoys the comfort and familiarity of the reserve school. When she speaks of her home community, her face brightens with a smile as she says, "Then when I am here, everyone just gives you a smile or something." (p. 56)

All parents want their children to feel comfortable at school, and those parents who chose to send their children to the reserve schools were confident that their children did in fact feel comfortable, secure, and at home in these community schools. "I know my daughter feels right at home in this [reserve] school. This is her home away from home. Being in her own community must make it even more so," Halee remarked.

The peace of mind that the parents gained by knowing that their children were in a comfortable and familiar place outweighed any doubts they may have had initially about their school-choice decisions, as Claire confirmed: "My daughter is happy here. She is learning so much about who she is culturally. She has so many cousins, aunties, and even *kokums* in this school, and she finds this so exciting."

The parents explained that their children felt more comfortable in the reserve schools because they were immersed in their culture, they heard their own language, and they had the opportunity to pray. Further, they noted that their children seemed to be able to develop better relationships with their teachers. The parents attributed great significance to a schooling environment that promotes and supports the development of cultural understandings and expressions and positive student-teacher relationships, which they deemed very important to the child's learning and future success as an adult.

Culture

> In the broadest sense, culture is everything—material and nonmaterial, learned and shared by people as they come to terms with their environment. It includes the totality of a group's shared procedures, belief systems, worldview, values, attitudes, and percepts of life. (McCaskill, 1987, p. 155)

Culture came up many times in my discussions with the participants, but the question seemed to center on how culture is defined. When the participants spoke of culture, some referred to ceremonies—smudging, sweats, and others—whereas others thought that it meant schools' incorporation of the natural laws of love, honesty, sharing, caring, and determination. Some spoke about the Cree values of respect, humility, tradition, and honor, and other parents considered language and culture inseparable.

Whichever way they interpreted culture, it was a topic that was very important to every participant. At the Saddle Lake Elementary School, Cree cultural expression is visible everywhere: "I like that Saddle Lake [Elementary] has a strong cultural component to it," Clarisse responded. She appreciated that her daughters have had the privilege of being immersed in the Cree culture on a daily basis and that this immersion fosters a sense of pride in her children for their spiritual heritage. In their school, "there are Native themes everywhere, all the time, and there are people talking Cree in the hallways."

Knowing that her daughters were hearing their language on a consistent basis reassured Clarisse, particularly because she wanted her children to know their language. Her oldest daughter is "pretty good talking Cree," which she attributed to the fact that "there are good Cree teachers in the school." Because her daughter feels so comfortable speaking the Cree language, she has competed in a Cree language competition every year, a rewarding and empowering experience. Clarisse reported that her children were very happy in their school because they are "being exposed to their culture." She commented in the interview that her daughters looked forward to all the cultural events that the school hosts, but most of all, they looked forward to the quarterly feasts:

> They have four feasts a year, and I know my girls really look forward to it when it comes to feast time because they learn proper protocol—how to sit, how to behave, what to expect, what is going to happen. I think that is such a good thing. My kids were exposed to that . . . right from birth, but a lot other kids aren't. I think it is a good thing for them to learn that this is . . . part of our culture.

Food and feasting involve more than a community's getting together to share food. A feast defines a community by establishing and renewing relations between those who eat and those who are hosting. When people come together for a feast, strict protocols must be adhered to, and preparing to eat may take several hours or even days. According to Clarisse, children quickly learn "the basic principles of patience and respect."

The child is the centre of the community, and when parents, grandparents, and other community members gather in the school gymnasium for the school feast, this event becomes one of celebration of the youth. By watching and listening, children learn the cultural norms and rules of behavior. The parents recognized that many traditional values, aspects of cultural identity, and pride have been lost over the years and suggested that events such as the quarterly feasts are the opportune time to reintroduce these Native activities and practices. The goal of every parent is to raise "healthy, happy children," and by "teaching them and exposing them to all those positive aspects of our culture, we will be contributing to their emotional, mental, emotional, and spiritual wellness," Marleen stated.

In these formal ceremonial settings, the children learn not only the practical knowledge about a particular ceremony, but also, as the parents suggested, proper behavior and protocol pertaining to particular ceremonies and events, and they can extend that knowledge into their daily lives. As Clarisse said, "It shows them self-control. You have to sit still, you have to be quiet, and you have to wait your turn. You have no choice." Self-control and patience are attributes in our lives, and teaching our children these very important rules of behavior assists them as they move along their learning journey. When we teach them about self-control and patience, we are contributing to the strength of our children. As Rogers (2001) put it, we are "helping our children grow to be independent, responsible, loving adults . . . [and are making an] important contribution to a lasting native legacy" (p. 1513).

Language

Language is at the core of cultural identity. It links people to their land, it protects history through story and song, and it holds the key to kinship systems and the intricacies of tribal law, including spirituality and secret/sacred objects and rites. Language is a major factor in retaining cultural identity, and many have said that "if the Language is strong, then Culture is strong" (ATSIC, 2000, p. 4).

With the European invasion, Aboriginal languages and cultures suffered enormous erosion, partly a result of the reduction in the population who speak the languages. Makokis (2001) estimated that only 15% of the people in Saddle Lake still speak the Cree Language:

> A Statistics Canada national language survey done in 1992 revealed that in most Aboriginal communities only 11 per cent of the people spoke their language fluently and that 30 per cent of Aboriginal communities had an Aboriginal language that was endangered.
>
> Less than 50 per cent of the adults spoke their language fluently, and a very few, if any, were younger speakers. (Alberta Sweetgrass, 2002, p. 2)

All of the parents who were sending their children to the reserve schools recognized the importance of language to the revival and maintenance of their cultural identities and the impact that it could have on every child in developing a strong sense of self-esteem and self-worth. For these parents, language is an expression of the wholeness of the people. They recognized that "Aboriginal languages are spiritually interconnected with the land; that they embody values and relationships; that survival and forgiveness, love and laughter are all intertwined with the authentic language of a place and people" (Fettes & Norton, 2000, p. 29).

"Learning our language is so important," Sheila emphasized. Bernice concurred, and, although she is not a Cree speaker, she saw the value of learning the Cree language and hoped that her children would one day become fluent speakers. Her mother, a teacher of the language, once told her that "students who speak their language are always well-behaved, and they are always so kind and respectful. If a child is misbehaving and you speak to him or her in their language, their attitude, their behavior will change instantly." Many parents agreed that children who know their language are better behaved, so I asked a parent to speak to this point. She told me that this "is because of the intonation in the language—the stress, the tone, the pitch. Kids listen when they hear the language; even if they don't understand, they listen." Why is it that children's attitude and behavior change if you speak to them in their language when they misbehave? Makokis (2001) explained that the reason is that hearing the language evokes a feeling: "You can almost feel the movement, the feeling" (p. 118) that the spirit in the language evokes. "The language of feeling is expressed in the evolving relationship" (p. 118) between the listener and the speaker. Her participant, Skywoman, described this interaction between the listener and the speaker:

"It is your own thought/mind that you will use, that is how you develop. And that was our way. There was not any written text; you sat there until you understood. You will understand in the mind, but you will have to put it here in your heart. . . ." She was explaining the importance of listening intently to what the speaker was imparting. The relationship between the speaker and the listener was intense. If the listener could feel the intent of the speaker, the interaction was purposeful. However, if the listener only partially understood in the intellectual sense, then the relationship was not validated. Then the speaker's intent was not fully brought to heart. (p. 118)

The late Lionel Kinunwa addressed the notion that a child's negative behavior can be altered just by hearing the language, and he referred to blood memory or cellular memory as the source of connection with the ancestors and therefore with the language of the ancestors. His teachings imply that the child hears the language of his/her ancestors and is moved by the power that he or she experiences as a result of the unexpected but natural and powerful connection that is made in the moment of recognition of an ancestral but 'strange' language. Knowing that "selfhoods are constructed, identities are forged, and social processes are enacted through the medium of language makes one wonder why more emphasis is not placed in the teaching of language, particularly in our First Nations schools" (Steinhauer, 2002, p. 7).

Like many other schools, both Goodfish Lake and Saddle Lake Schools teach Cree in very short blocks, maybe two to three times a week. The parents expressed concern about this and proposed that more time be allotted to Cree-language programming. At the same time, everyone was very aware of the limited funding that First Nations schools receive for language programming: "If the school puts more resources into the language, then something else has to be given up," one parent argued, and Pamela agreed: "Without additional monies, not much more can be done about the programming." All parents regretted that more time and resources could not be put into language programming at this time, but for now, they were "grateful for what our children that attend the reserve schools have." Language instruction is not confined to 20 or 40 minutes of class time; as an administrator pointed out, the children hear "the Cree language . . . in the hallways, on the playground—just about everywhere in the school. Staff are encouraged to speak their language as much as possible."

Clarisse emphasized that "we must do what we can to ensure that the schools believe in the language as much as we [parents] do, because language is our culture. Our language is what is going to sustain our culture." According to Ermine (1995):

> We need to experience the life force from which creativity flows, and our Aboriginal resources such as language and culture are our touchstones for achieving this. It is imperative that our children take up the cause of our languages and cultures because therein lies Aboriginal epistemology, which speaks of holism. With holism, an environmental ethic is possible. (p. 110)

Prayer

Prayer is a practice that has core value among the Native people, and most, if not all, peoples have therefore practiced it for generations (Cajete, 2000b; Ermine, 1995; Graveline, 1998; Makokis, 2001). It is a way of communicating with our Creator. When the principal of one of the Saddle Lake schools talked about prayer as part of a regular school day, it seemed natural and logical: "I feel lucky to be here where we could . . . pray to a greater power every day. We are not a denominations school. It is a . . . school for our community and all members' needs should be met in that school." In an attempt to honor all of the different denominations in the community, the school principal invited different spiritual leaders from the community to come to the school to lead in prayer:

> We had an event not long ago, . . . and we invited a traditional man to do a prayer for us, as well as the drums to do the honor song. That's who we are—is to pray like that and to honor people with the drum. But we also had our local parish priest . . . come in, not just to pray, but to say a few words, as well as [the] reverend from the United Church. We invited the spiritual leaders from the community to come in and do some prayers and say a few words to our kids, because I see in that class a mixture, and that's where the kids pray. I did invite also . . . [another] . . . spiritual leader in the community . . . just so the kids will see that our people from the four corners of Saddle Lake should be represented in that school. We hope to invite others too, because that is where the kids pray, and they will see that we support them by asking their leaders to come and pray in our school.

Even within our communities there is diversity, and by honoring these differences, Florence hoped that the children would see that diversity is "just one basic aspect of being human; that we come together, not that we have to be the same, but just to be able to say, 'I accept you for who and what you are.'"

Although the students in Goodfish Lake School do not come together to pray as they do at Saddle Lake, a parent told me that the students had the opportunity this last year to participate in Bible studies one evening a week. However, this parent, George, also felt that this was not fair to the other religious denominations in the school because "in order for one religion to be accepted in a school, I think they should all be accepted in a school, not just one." Another parent observed that "children do need some foundation of spirituality" and that, at the least, "we need a school that has morals and values taught." She added, "If we have this, then we have [children with] happy souls; then we have healthy behaviors."

Prayer is an everyday part of our lives, and as I was writing this section, I realized that I pray constantly. By incorporating prayer into everything that I do, including my dissertation writing, I have seen the process become less like work. Hampton (1993) quoted a graduate student on prayer:

> It is sort of a clue to what might be a solution to hard work. I used to realize that a lot of what Indian people did was a lot of hard work to make everything so much from scratch. What [this has] taught me was the way spirituality lightens the load. By praying over every step of the process, . . . then the impact of that work becomes less because everything has so much meaning. (p. 293)

A colleague once told me:

> When Elders open up a meeting, they start by giving thanks for the beautiful day and for all the wonderful things that the Creator has provided. They ask that the meeting will progress in a healthy, productive fashion. They ask that the words that are spoken will not be offensive and that good results will come as a result of gathering. They ask that the

Creator will have compassion over all as they come together for the same cause. That's why those meetings feel so good. That's why they go so well.

Prayer is an essential part of our being. It sustains us, and it gives us hope. At the Saddle Lake Onchaminahos School, every day begins with prayer. Claire explained that "standing in a circle and praying with your friends provides one with a sense of security and feelings of belonging." "Why is it that prayer has been taken out of the schools?" asked another parent. By taking prayer out of the schools, we are taking away [the Creator's] powerful protection." Clarisse thought that "we are lucky on the reserve, because we do have the opportunity to pray in our schools if we want." "It is too bad that we don't do enough of that in our school [Goodfish Lake]." Veronica responded, "But we could, and we should." Makokis (2001) commented, "Life is sacred," and for everything we must give thanks. Praying with our children will strengthen them:

> If you do not [pray], you are actually refusing these essentials to your Cree life.... It is simple to understand. It [prayer] is the first thing you [should do] when you get up and the last thing to [do] at night. Greet the Creator and give thanks for the chance to live. If all of us did this simple thing, we would get stronger. (p. 102)

Student-Teacher Relationships

> Relationships are the core of the Cree worldview. Our relationships with the natural world and with each other are paramount in guiding our behavior. In the Cree language the words that describe education (teaching and learning) express it as a relationship that is formed from giving and receiving, that is focused on growing together, and that emphasizes the process rather than the content. (Chisan, 2001, p. 17)

To develop positive self-identity, First Nations students need to perceive value in schooling, and to achieve this, they need to feel that they belong. They need support and encouragement from family, peers, and community; and they need teachers who are warm and supportive and have positive expectations. While they are in the school, they need to be able to establish positive relationships with their teachers: "These are the people they spend most of their days with," Pamela pointed out.

"Strong healthy relationships built on trust and mutual respect contribute to the educational success of Aboriginal students. The strength of the student-teacher relationship often dictates the level of success the student achieves in school" (Bazylak, 2002, p. 144). In this study the parents identified healthy student-teacher relationships as a factor that they were sure would contribute to the success of their children. One participant reminisced about a very special teacher in a reserve school who had influenced her life and instilled in her a desire to learn:

> Oh I had all kinds of teachers, but . . . one teacher . . . had an influence on my education and . . . had a real impact on me and really challenged me. . . . I don't know why she had that special interest in me, and I really believe in my mind now that the relationships that teachers have with their students can make a difference in their learning, because now I wanted to do work for her; I wanted to do my best. It was like I was doing it for her, and she would put my work on the bulletin board in the hallway. [In Cree]: She would put my

handwriting in the hallway, so I tried even harder to write really well. I would take my time and make sure I did my best, and she would hang my writing on the wall.

Knowing that a teacher cares can change a child's life, and that is why "teachers need to win that child," Florence suggested. She maintained that student-teacher relationships have everything to do with whether or not a child will come to school. She spoke about some of the attendance problems that reserve schools often face, but she was convinced that attendance would not even be an issue if teachers formed strong personal relationships with the children whom they teach: "If that kid wants to come to school, he will come to school, no matter what," if that child feels validated and loved.

A lot of times it is up to that child to say, "Today I want to go to school. Today I am going to school. My teacher wants to see me," so he will get up and come. A lot of kids are getting up in the morning and bringing themselves to school . . . because they want to be there.

It was the end of the school day, and Florence looked into one of the classrooms, and what she saw touched her heart. As the children were lining up to leave, she heard them saying, "I love you, Teacher," and the teacher said, "I love you too." This was a special moment for her, and she asked herself, "Where else could you get that?" I learned from her that teachers who have good relationships with the children in their classrooms tend to have the highest attendance. Florence reported that this particular teacher had a 90% attendance rate, which is extremely high considering that the overall rate is about 74%.

"I know today many teachers will not make physical contact with the children, but I think it is very important," Bernice stressed:

> I know it was important to me. . . . When I say this, I am thinking about a particular teacher who used to work in the reserve school. She was a caring teacher. She'd walk through the class while you were doing an exam, and she'd rub your back and ask you how you were doing. This little touch was so reassuring. Most teachers didn't do that, but it was so comforting and encouraging at the same time. It felt good to know that this teacher really did care about me and the others in the class. As a result, I worked really hard in school.

"[Teachers] need to . . . show the students they care," Claire suggested. She noted that this care is very noticeable in her daughter's reserve school, and she shared a story of a creative teacher who always found ways to encourage her students to become active participants in their learning. "This compassionate, caring teacher had a great relationship with her students as a result":

> As a way of maintaining a good relationship with her students, this teacher encourages her students to be active participants. She does this by allowing them to evaluate her. She will give them a little evaluation form that asks them, "Do you like what was happening there? Circle the little happy face if you liked it. If you think, "No, don't ever make me do it again," circle that really mad face.

In remembering their own schooling, the participants tended to recall the best and worst of their teachers, and they talked about the impact that these teachers had on their lives. Teachers who had the ability to motivate, encourage, and be understanding and caring and who provided a positive school experience inspired students and contributed to their successes in their later lives. Evidence of the importance of student-teacher relationships is shown in the following story that one of the parents shared:

> I was at a workshop lately, and one of the speakers was talking about an exceptional teacher he had worked with. In her class there were many troubled boys. They gave the teacher a hard time, but this teacher just kept showing them that she cared, that she loved them, and showed by her actions that she really cared for these students. Years later they saw her; she was old now, and they knew her. The teacher was glad to see them, and the thing was, although many of their peers were in jail, none of these kids went to jail. These guys, they were adults now, and they told her, "Your love kept us out of jail. You showed us you cared."

How rewarding it must have been for that teacher to hear the words "Your love kept us out of jail"! Other teachers who are unable to do these things can make school a negative and unproductive experience for their students. Much of the research has identified student-teacher relationships as a critical variable in students' school experiences and learning (Mackay & Myles, 1995; Makokis, 2000; Wilson, 1992). It is possible that a negative experience with just one teacher is enough for a student to enter a conflict cycle and eventually leave school. Makokis saw evidence of this when she interviewed a young man for her study:

> Although Asiny identified the fact that he was "different" as his reason for leaving school, he shared the following story of why he left. He states, "I just didn't like the teachers. . . . Some of them were racist; some of them would make fun of a person." When asked to give an example of what he thought was racist, Asiny shared the following: "When all the White people were around me, he [the teacher] started calling me Chief." When asked which teacher, he identified his physical education teacher, noting, "The reason why I left from there was I went to school one day and had physical education and then all of a sudden they all blame me for stealing two hundred and fifty bucks from all those kids and then the teacher went along with them." . . . He boldly shouted, "I was mad, really mad, I couldn't stay there, I would have did something. . . . They just all pointed their fingers at me."

"Students want to feel connected personally to their teachers. . . . They want to know that teachers have thoughts, feeling, and experiences that both enliven and go beyond the academic content of the classroom" (Bazylak, 2002, p. 146). Claire affirmed, "I will be first to say I know that most of the teachers that work in our schools have great relationships with their students."

Summary Statements

In this chapter I presented the findings from the participants' discussions of their on-reserve school experiences. The parents revealed some of the challenges and struggles that their children have faced within this system, and all parents recognized that any school-choice decision has a price tag. In contrast to the parents who had sent their children to off-reserve schools, the parents who chose the on-reserve schools were able to identify more positives about their schools of choice.

Like the Black parents in Wells and Crain's (1992) study, it is evident that First Nations school-choice decision making always involves tradeoffs. Those parents who sent their children to off-reserve schools made the tradeoff between "the pain of exposing their sons or daughters to racism and thereby crushing their self-esteem and desire to enroll them in a higher-status school" (p. 80), whereas the parents who sent their children to the on-reserve schools felt that, overall, they were making a tradeoff and choosing comfort and familiarity over academics.

Generally, in analyzing the literature on school choice amongst non-Native parents, I found that in their search for "better" schools, these parents generally do not have to make such tradeoffs. Therefore, to talk about this concept in relation to First Nations parents on reserve, the term *parental school choice* is probably not the most accurate way to describe the situation. This study suggests quite clearly that First Nations parents in fact have no possibility of school choice in that they have no positive educational alternatives from which to choose; the schools that are available to them are not offering alternatives within a range of positive educational physical settings and environments, nor are they offering schooling choices based on alternative formally recognized educational philosophies and methodologies.

CHAPTER 6:
THE SIGNIFICANCE OF RELATIONALITY, PARENTAL INVOLVEMENT, AND NATIVE TEACHERS

Whether their children are attending schools on-reserve or off-reserve, all of the parent participants in this study maintained that relationship building (or relationality, as I refer to it in this section), parental involvement, and more Aboriginal teachers are three key prerequisites for the successful school achievement of their children. From the interviews it also became obvious that the parents believe strongly that educators and parents must work together to accommodate and accentuate these factors. Florence advised, "Relationship-building has to occur in all areas. We need to find ways to develop positive student-teacher relationships, as well as positive parent-teacher relationships. In addition, I believe Native teachers are also key to the success of students."

This chapter focuses on a discussion of these three factors—relationship building, parental involvement, and the presence of Native teachers in the schools—through the words of the participants and pertinent references to educational literature that speaks directly to these points. Part 1 addresses the concept of relationality, including student-teacher relationships, peer relationships, family relationships, and relationships to place; part 2 speaks to parental involvement in schools generally; and part 3 looks at the importance of having more Native teachers involved in the education of First Nations students.

Relationality

Positive relationships formed through warm, sensitive, and responsive care help children to feel valued and gain more from their learning experiences. Relationships between teachers, families, peers, and even to place are important and help to build environments that nurture children's growth and development. Leah thought that "establishing positive relationships with all students is important, but I think this is even more important for Native students. Native students have been subjected to so much hurt, racism, and pain, and as a result, they carry with them feelings of insecurity." She was speaking from experience. For her, having positive relationships with teachers and peers gave her the validation that she needed to survive in a school system where she "never felt quite at ease":

> Some of my experiences in school were negative, but I also had positive experiences as well. I have to attribute those positive experiences to teachers that saw me for who I was as a person, and they built relationships with me. They genuinely cared about me, and they validated me. This is my own perception, but I think many Native students spend much time in school just trying to survive the racial prejudice they are subjected to at school. This is why I think it is so important to be validated by teachers and even your friends. We need to feel like we matter.

Whether their children attended school on-reserve or off-reserve, all parents wanted their children to have an affirmative school experience and asserted that this could be accomplished only if their children were given the opportunity to develop and build positive relationships with all those around them—"teachers, staff, relatives, and peers" (Leah). They realized that education has been a destructive force for many Native people, and they wanted their children's schooling experience to be different. They felt that positive relationships with others, particularly teachers, could provide their children with the powerful forces needed to break free from the feeling of insecurity that Leah spoke about earlier.

"If a teacher shows a child she truly cares, that child is going to thrive," Leah suggested. "I have seen too many students broken because the teacher did not like that student, and the student knew it." "Education is the most powerful institution in any society, and teachers are its most powerful agents" (Williams, 2000, p. 129). Teachers have the power to make or break a student. If the student-teacher relationship is weak, then "the students are less likely to respond to this type of teacher. There is little basis for trust between teacher and student and therefore a weak basis for teaching" (Taylor, 1995, p. 235).

The parents who participated in this study talked about student-teacher relationships, peer relationships, family relationships, and relationships to place. The following section expands on their words and speaks to how and why these relationships reinforce and contribute to positive schooling experiences for Aboriginal children.

Student-Teacher Relationships

All of the participants felt that positive student-teacher relationships would provide their children with a steady footing to support them through the numerous challenges that they would encounter within the school system. Whether their children attended school off-reserve or on-reserve, the parents recognized the impact that teachers have on their children: "Teachers can really make or break you," said Leah. "What they do and what they say can impact you for the rest of your life." This triggered a very painful memory of an incident that occurred in Leah's Grade 12 year in high school that had nearly broken her spirit, and she explained the consequences:

> The unfortunate thing is that not many Native students survive these kinds of incidences. Once the school crushes their spirit, they quit school or move on to another school where they think they might better fit in. But with such wounds, most of them will simply just give up.

Leah shared her heartbreaking story of this incident:

> In Grade 12 Chemistry I was accused of cheating. I was the only Native person in that class. I was accused of cheating. I was the second one done the exam, and I remember two girls . . . thought I was cheating, and then I remember getting a zero. After . . . the exams were marked . . . I remember him [the teacher] handing me my exam, and his face was all red—and he is now the principal. And he didn't say anything except, "I'll want to talk to you after class." And I looked at it and thought, What! It had a zero on it, and he goes, "You know why you got a zero, right?" And I said, "No, I don't!" He goes, "Because you cheated." And I said, "What do you mean, I cheated?" He goes, "Well, sources tell me that they caught you cheating, so I have to give you a zero."

Leah recalled the pain and humiliation that she felt, and she repeated:

> A teacher can make or break you! It is for this reason that I think student-teacher relationships are so important. If he would have taken the time to get to know me and to see me for who I was, this would have never happened. Even on *Oprah*, sometimes you

hear stories about "Oh, it was this teacher that shaped me or that changed my life," but most of those stories are good stories. And yeah, they can change your life, but unfortunately it is not always good. Since that day I was so petrified of science, and even in university I was petrified.

During our interview, Leah shared several other stories about injustices inflicted on her and her Native peers. She reported that many of the students simply give up "because they don't have the will to fight anymore and probably also because many don't have the support of their families." Curwen Doige (2003) warned that if children are to thrive in their schooling experiences, then positive student-teacher relationships must be developed: "The relationships between students and teachers create and maintain the learning dynamic that comes from open honest discussion and negotiations" (p. 152). Furthermore, "teachers must make a determined, conscious effort to create and maintain a nonmanipulative, trusting environment that fosters meaningful relationships and learning" (p. 152).

Students want to establish relationships with their teachers, and often teachers will find students reaching out and trying to develop these relationships. However, as Taylor (1995) suggested, teachers are sometimes afraid of these relationships because of the "elements of risk" (p. 236) that they carry with them. "However, a student who reaches out should not be denied" (p. 236), because

> this is an opportunity to help a student and build a relationship in which a teacher as a friend can ask the student to achieve and excel. Obviously life is not always so simple and straight forward, but this is an effective approach which, while it may not ensure success, will enhance the chances of it. (p. 236)

Peer Relationships

Several participants suggested that positive peer relationships are equally as important to student success as teacher-student relationships are. Pamela commented:

> It is so important for kids to be accepted by their friends. Kids want to belong, they want to feel included, and probably many kids go to school simply because they have that need to socialize. I know my son goes to school mostly for that.

Her son was attending a public school and reported that he enjoyed being there. "He doesn't ever want to miss school," and he is "liked by all the students," which has had a positive effect on him. This, however, was not always the case for Pamela's son. At one time he was a loner, and "getting him to go to school was a challenge." His mother reported that now that he has found a place for himself at this school, he is thriving. "He doesn't even want me to schedule his appointments for school days because he does not want to miss. I think he is scared he is going to miss out on something." Although her son is only an average student, Pamela attributed his desire to be in school to his friendships: "We are so lucky because his close friends are good kids, and their influence is positive. He wants to succeed because he doesn't want his friends to leave him behind." In McInerney, McInerney, Ardington, and De Rachewiltz's (1997) study, Navajo students identified peer relationships as having a direct influence on their success in school: "In general, it was thought that students who were located within a peer group which espoused the importance of learning at school were advantaged in their own motivation to learn and to succeed in school" (p. 10).

Yvonne agreed that friendships are very important to students: "If you have one good friend and that friend is interested in school and really wants to do well, you are more inclined to want to do the same." Simon too stressed the importance of friendships: "I love hanging out with my friends, especially with my Native friends, because we understand each other." However, "I did have non-Native friends as well. It is the friendships I had with the Native kids that have lasted."

"We often misinterpret their hanging out together as a way of keeping themselves separate, but really it is an informal support system," Brian explained. Claire commented, "Although I was in the A class with mostly White kids, my Native friends were my support system. The Indians just stuck together. At recess it was just my cousins, and at lunch we just hung together." This support system was their saving grace, especially when they faced racial taunts: "We all understood one another, and although we never really talked about it, we were protecting each other's sanity."

When Claire moved to the public school system and was placed in a classroom with only non-Native children, she felt isolated and often excluded; but when another Native student transferred into her class, she was elated. She described how she had felt at the time as well as the teacher's response to her elation:

> There was a girl that came and transferred into our class for about two months, and she was Native. And I guess I must have been too enthusiastic, or I don't know what, but I remember my teacher saying, "Well, don't overdo it." You know, just being so happy that she was there and wanting to talk with her and just to be with her, because I just thought, "She'll understand me."

Even at a very young age Claire already understood the value of relationships. She had wanted to be with a peer whom she felt would understand her. Although as a parent I can look back at my children's relationships, I do not know whether I ever fully understood what peer relationships meant to them; however, I was recently reminded of how important these relationships were to them. As I was editing my daughter's paper one night, a quotation that she used reminded me of the important role of her friends in her life. For this assignment she had been asked to interview a woman who was different from her in at least two ways, and she had chosen to interview someone with whom she had been best friends in high school, but had lost touch with over the past few years. The friend's statement caught my attention:

> I remember spending a long summer with you and just being awesome friends. That was really one of the greatest times in my life. Yeah, you and me, . . . we were inseparable. . . . You helped me and I helped you, and together we made it through, even the bad times. I loved hanging out with you. You were my confidant, and you helped make my difficult times bearable.

When I read this young lady's statement, I was reminded of the two Métis girls with whom I had been friends in high school. Although we met only in high school, these two young ladies had been my saving grace as well. They had understood me, and in their presence I could just be me. Suzanne affirmed that everyone wants to "fit in, and most people want to be with those who share attitudes, interests, and circumstances that resemble their own." People choose friends who accept and like them and see them in a favorable light. "We want to belong, so we pick those that accept us unconditionally," Kristine remarked. "We want to be with those friends." As a result, some parents reported that their children often sought permission to attend the school that their peers were attending, and many parents made their school choices with this in mind, which reveals how significant they felt that peer relationships are to their children.

Education is about liberating a student's mind, but for many Aboriginal students, the schooling experience can be a debilitating experience, and they may need liberation from racial taunts and other forms of oppression that Claire mentioned. Native students find comfort and support in one another to face these challenges.

Family Relationships

Children's friendships have inevitable ups and downs. As Claire explained:

> Even though peer relationships are important to them during their school years, nothing could replace the security the children feel when they are in the same class with their relatives. I know this is the experience of my daughter. She is meeting all these cousins, and this is her *kokum* and this is her uncle, and she's got so many relatives with her.

A youth participant reminisced about how she had felt when she was a student at the reserve school:

> Looking back, I loved going to school . . . on the reserve . . . because I knew everyone, and I was related to half the school it seemed. I grew up going to school with a lot of my cousins, so in a sense I felt secure and had a sense of community. When I was 12 or 13 my mom, brothers, and I moved to Edmonton. I hated going to school in Edmonton. There was something different about going to school in the big city than a small community. That sense of belonging was no longer there.

Families play an important role in a child's education. Although many studies have revealed that parental/family involvement is not valued and/or practiced in First Nations communities, my study reveals the contrary, as Florence observed:

> I can't imagine a person not wanting what is best for their child; no matter where they come from, they love that child and they want what's best—the best that they can give. I don't believe there are any parents that don't want that for their children. It is universal.

A youth suggested that

> the problem comes with the definition that we have assigned to the term *parental/family involvement*. Really, I think our families are more involved with our education than society seems to think. I know mine was, and I have to say that, without the support of my family—not only my immediate family, but my extended family included—I would have never completed my high school education.

"My family kept me out of trouble while I was a teenager in school," another participant reported:

You were like 14, 15, and you wanted to go out on weekends to dances. Well, I couldn't; . . . I didn't have a chance to go out a whole heck of a lot. I remember graduating from Grade 9 in Saddle Lake. There was a dance, and I think I was allowed to stay until like 10:00. My boyfriend . . . was willing to bring me home and everything, but my Dad wouldn't have anything to do with that. I had to go home with them. I was just slightly embarrassed over it, but now in hindsight, I realize my family was protecting me. They did not want anything to interfere with my completing high school.

Florence emphasized that "everyone has to be involved in that family—not just the parents, but also extended family." In her family, "the whole family is involved in our kids' trying to be successful at what they do, because it is so hard out there." Sheila acknowledged her parents:

My parents never went into the school, but they must be commended for their contribution. They continue to have that same impact on the lives of my children. I have told my parents that I commend them a lot for just who I am and where I am at today. I give them a lot of credit for that. Yes, they showed me this way because they have always maintained that stability. . . . I am grateful to be able to understand all of that and for me now to understand and to kind of learn from that too and to try to do the best I can. . . . And even now I look at these things they did a lot more than I did. I don't ever try to say to them, "Well, I did more than you did." I think that they did do a lot. They showed me a lot, and I attribute where I am at to them. I am thankful for that. . . . . I want my girls to understand where I am coming from, to try to justify for them somehow, and for them to know that I don't have all the answers myself.

Melnechenko and Horsman (1998) identified family influence as one of the major factors in the success of Aboriginal students at school: "Educators have come to know that there is a positive correlation between success at school and positive family influence, support, and relationships" (p. 13). Leah concurred: "Without my family's support, I don't know if I would have made it."

Relationships to Place

Everyone who participated in this study spoke about the importance of belonging and "having a place." I asked one mother how she had decided where her children would be schooled, and she responded, "I want my children to feel that they have a place in their school, where they feel like they belong." "I want them to feel like they are part of the school community—to feel like they are a part of that family," another stated.

Family and kinship have always been very important to the Cree people (Makokis, 2001). Our families are the backbone of our culture. Families sustain and nurture us, and, for us, kinship extends beyond our immediate family into our communities. Leah explained:

We are all related in our communities, and like families we have our fights; but in the end, our responsibility is to our own. This is why I care so much about my community, because, ultimately, the community is a reflection of who I am.

Even at a very young age Native children recognize and know about this connection to place, to space, to family, and to community. They may not be able to articulate it in the same way that adults can, but as the following story clearly illustrates, they are very much aware of the importance of family and community. They have already established a relationship to place, even when they are young.

> I wanted to share a little story. I thought, "Geez, this is so ironic," because my daughter told me this, and then you called me the next day to do this interview, and I thought I could share this story. . . . It just so happened I left the arena. My youngest daughter plays hockey, and my boy plays hockey. We were leaving my boy's practice, we were at the arena, and my daughter asked me, just out of the blue she said, "Mom, do you think Saddle Lake is going to look like this in 20 years?" And I was just really shocked. She just surprised me, and I thought, "Where is her thinking sometimes?" She is a real deep thinker. And I said, "Oh well, yeah, probably." I said, "Ten years ago I remember it looked like this; there were fewer buildings." I was just kind of giving her that. She goes, "Yeah, I am going to live here all of my life." And I went, "Oh. Oh, well, I am not," just to see what she would say, and she looked at me, and I said, "I'm not; I don't know about you." And then she said, "Well, Mom, this is where my heart is [touches her heart]. This is where my heart is, Mom! I am going to live here for the rest of my life!"

This young girl realized the importance of place in her life. She felt comfortable being in Saddle Lake, attending the Onchaminahos School, and being with people with whom she felt comfortable. To her, this community was her family, and in her mind, they would take care of her even if her mother decided to leave. Her saying "I am going to live here all my life" shows how connected she felt. When her mother said "I'm not," her daughter was quick to find a solution. Her mother asked her who she was going to live with then, and her response was, "Well, I am going to live with *Kokum* and *Mosum*." For children, life is just that simple. It is regrettable that as we grow older, and supposedly wiser, we lose that simplicity. Claire shared that sense of belonging and recognized the "relationship to place":

> When I got there [to Saddle Lake], . . . [it was] like a dream come true. It was like I finally came to a place, and it was new to me, but I felt this was my school, this was my classroom, and I belonged here. I could put up my hand, and I could say my opinion. It was just like freedom, and, I don't know, I think I must have walked around with a smile on my face for I don't know how long. I thought, "Everybody must be just happy to be here," as happy as I was.

Many other participants spoke about how good it felt to have this place, this space where they felt comfortable. Halee told me:

> My daughter just loves going to school on the reserve. She loves the school, she likes to go to school here, and she has a lot of friends, and she likes the teacher. She loves this place. She loves the community, she loves the school.

As other parents suggested, this young lady was attached to "this place." Halee was speaking not only about the physical place, but also about the spiritual space. Wildcat (2001) suggested that

"Indigenous people represent a culture emergent from a place, and they actively draw on the power of that place physically and spiritually" (p. 32).

Sheila said:

> Yes, there is a lot of dysfunction in our community, but this place is our home, and we can't just throw our hands up in the air and say, "*Kiyam*" ["That's okay"] because, really, it is a collective responsibility. We have to ensure that our children will continue to feel good about calling this place home.

Many participants spoke about the "dysfunction in our community" but recognized that they cannot give up, because, as Marleen stated, "This is our home. This community is where our children will grow up." "This is why you have to build trust with your community, and if you do your part, the community should be able to support you," Sheila advised. When she said this, I wondered why it was that when Aboriginal people speak about community, it sounds like we are referring to a living entity—as though the community is a being. Morrisseau (1998) explained this phenomenon as follows:

> A community has a life of its own. It is made up of many individuals tied together through a collective desire to live in a type of harmony. This harmony must be enforced by a set of rules regulating relationships among its members. These rules are in some sense the laws that governed members of the community. It wasn't until much later in life that I began to appreciate what my community meant to me, for my community is more than a place. It is part of my history. It is part of me, a part that I could not deny or run away from. It was my connection to Mother Earth and the Creator. (p. 48)

Perhaps this is what the little girl above was feeling when she said, "This is where my heart is, Mom."

Some people do not understand why Native people want to continue to live in First Nations communities that are plagued with high unemployment, low graduation rates, and a multitude of social problems; sometimes we even ask ourselves that question. From the little girl's point of view, the answer is simple: We stay in our communities because "this is where our hearts are." This response must be difficult to understand for people who measure the practices and values of Native people according to White, middle-class standards. There is no denying that poverty permeates our communities and that "apathy, internal squabbling, substance abuse, teen pregnancies, dysfunctional parenting, political power struggling, poor social skills, and perpetual grieving" (Wilson & Wilson, 1999, p. 137) continue to hang over our heads like dark clouds. However, we also continue to survive because we have that spiritual connection to or relationship with our communities, a connection that is a life energy that enfolds and sustains us as individuals. Cajete (2000b) explained:

> Relationship is the cornerstone of tribal community, and the nature and expression of community is the foundation of tribal identity. Through community, Indian people come to understand their "personhood" and their connection to the communal soul of their people. The community is the place where the "forming of the heart and face" of the individual as one of the people is most fully expressed; it is the context in which the person comes to know relationship, responsibility, and participation in the life of one's people. (p. 86)

He added, "It is the place of sharing life through everyday acts . . . and where each person can, metaphorically speaking, 'become complete.' [Community is] 'that place that Indian people talk about,' the place through which Indian people express their highest thought" (p. 86).

Parental Involvement

The research does not support the widely held assumption that Native families do not have the same goals for their children's education that non-Native families do (Abele et al., 2000; Auger, 2006; Kavanagh, 2002; Makokis, 2001). "Like their parents and grandparents, today's parents want their children to succeed" (Castellano, Davis, & Lahache, 2000, p. 253). They want their children to graduate from high school and become self-supporting individuals. As Halee stated, "Although all of my children didn't graduate, [that] doesn't mean that this wasn't what I wanted for them. I wanted them to finish school so they could go out on their own and be completely self-sufficient." Every other parent in this study concurred, and Pamela asserted, "I want to raise independent children." Clarisse reasoned:

> If parents got more involved with their children and asked what they are doing, how they are doing, I would guarantee there would be more high school graduates, but reality is, most Native parents are not visible in the school.

Research has shown a direct correlation between academic achievement and parental involvement (Friedel, 1999; Kavanagh, 2002; Mackay & Myles, 1995; RCAP, 1996), yet these same sources have also revealed that Aboriginal parent participation is decreasing. The parents who participated in this study recognized that parental involvement is an issue not only in the public schools, but also in the on-reserve schools. They concluded that most parents are not involved in their children's education, at least not to the extent that the schools say they want them to be involved. As Pamela suggested, "It is really too bad that parents don't get involved, because their involvement can make a world of a difference." Sheila concurred and wished that more parents were involved:

> It's really up to me, for me to go out there and make those contacts with the school and to be able to be involved with the school and to be involved in making sure, not only for my daughters but for the rest of the children, that the kids are getting what they need there. You know, making sure that you have that influence on your own child. You know that you can make a very big difference in the choices that they would make, . . . and as parents we have to know that the influence is there, but you can have an influence on your own child in helping them make better choices, to think for themselves and . . . to teach them to do the best that they can.

Sheila complained that "a lot of parents send their kids [to school] with the assumption . . . [that] it is [the school's] responsibility" to give them all they need to be successful in school. This is unfortunate, because, as she suggested, "we could make our schools a whole lot better if each of us went in to ask, 'How can we help; how can we make things a little better here?'" She contended that if more parents were involved, the result would be fewer discipline issues. Kristine, a youth participant asserted that children want their parent to be involved:

> I am glad my mom was involved to the extent she was, because when I look back now, I made some very bad choices, and I honestly believe that without her interference, as I used to call it back then, my path might have looked different.

Children want their parents to be actively involved in their schooling, and as Leah, another youth, pointed out, lack of parental involvement can have a detrimental effect on a student:

> I think for me I was very fortunate that I had the family to back me up and give me that extra kick. When I think back, all through junior high and high school, if anything were to happen, . . . I would tell my parents right away, knowing that if I couldn't deal with it, then the next step was for them to come into the school and talk to the teacher or whatnot. They played a vital role in my schooling. Many children unfortunately do not have that, and that, I think, is why they drop out.

Research has shown that the lack of parental involvement is a common concern, particularly within the public school system (Mackay & Myles, 1995; Silver et al., 2002). Kavanagh (2002) suggested that, although this a concern for on-reserve schools as well, it does not seem to be as pressing an issue. George agreed and gave reasons for the lower levels of parental involvement in on-reserve schools:

> Parental involvement is an issue on-reserve, but in a small community we usually know why they can't attend or why they chose not to attend. I don't think it is a real big deal on the reserve because of this.

George's remarks are insightful in that he recognized and might have been suggesting a different basis for the involvement of First Nations parents who live on-reserve and send their children to on-reserve schools. He said that on-reserve, no one is overconcerned when parents do not attend parent-teacher interviews or do volunteer work in the school: "Although many educational researchers have validated the relationship between parental involvement and student achievement, they have not investigated these issues from the perspective of Native parents."

This factor, the particularity of Native parents' perspectives on involvement in schools, is one that would require serious consideration in any analysis of the impact of parental involvement on Aboriginal student success in public schools. My experiences and those of the participants raise an important question along the lines of George's thinking: Would all the other challenges with which Native students have to contend in public schools override any benefits from parental involvement? It is hard to determine this without a comprehensive study.

Parental involvement is commonly cited in the literature and in government-sponsored studies and reviews as a huge concern for public schools, "but in all honesty, do they really want us to be involved?" Alexis asked. She wondered about this, because whenever she volunteered to assist the teacher in the classroom, she was always turned down or relegated to menial tasks. She would be told, "Oh, Mrs. So-and-So is volunteering this month. How would you like to come and assist us when the children go skating? You can help tie skate laces." Another parent had a similar response from school staff when she offered to assist in art classes. Instead of being invited to participate, she was asked to make play dough, a job that could be done at home. These parents interpreted the responses that they received as "You are not capable of assisting in the classroom because you're not bright enough, but you can tie shoes because even a child can do that." This paternalistic attitude from school personnel was enough to deter these parents from ever offering to assist or being involved at school again. Only two parents commented specifically on this discouragement, so it is difficult to generalize or determine, based on this study, whether or not schools do in fact want Aboriginal parental involvement. However, this is definitely an area that requires more formal analysis and particular focus on the perspectives of Aboriginal people, including parents and educators.

Defining Parental Involvement

As indicated above, all of the participants agreed that it is important for Aboriginal parents to be involved in their children's education, but what they did not agree upon, according to Halee, was the definition that schools "arbitrarily assigned for parental involvement." Some parents defined or understood parental involvement in much the same way that Ascher (1988) did:

> Parental involvement may easily mean quite different things to people. It can mean advocacy: parents sitting on councils and committees, participating in the decisions and operations of schools. It can mean parents serving as classroom aides, accompanying a class on an outing, or assisting teachers in a variety of other ways, either as volunteers or for wages. It can also conjure up images of teachers sending home notes to parents, or of parents working on bake sales and other projects that bring some much needed support. Increasingly, parent involvement means parents initiating learning activities at home to improve their children's performance in school: reading to them, helping them with homework, playing educational games, discussing current evens, and so on. (p. 109)

Others assigned a definition similar to Friedel's (1999): Parental involvement is about "teaching their children values, priorities, and how to make sense of things" (p. 139).

The interviews with parents revealed that some parents defined involvement as participation in formal ways, such as on the Parent Advisory Committees (PAC), fundraising committees, and sports committees. Other parents referred to the more informal activities at home such as ensuring that their children to do their homework or practice spelling words and reading to their children. Still others defined involvement as providing nurturance; ensuring that children are fed, bathed, and well rested; and instilling cultural values. It appears then that parental involvement can be defined much as Ascher (1988) described it, as the diverse activities, either at home or at school, that permit parents to share in the educational process of their children.

In their research Mackay and Myles (1995) found that educators often had a very narrow definition of parental involvement and as a result were always quick to conclude that Native parents were not interested in the education of their children:

> One indicator that educators use to judge parental interest is the extent to which parents participate in parent/teacher nights organized by the school. By and large, it was reported that Native parents do not attend these meetings. Both Native and non-Native educators recognized that many parents are uncomfortable coming to school. . . . Many educators used the presence or absence of parental support to explain a student's decision to remain at or drop out of school. . . . Such an apparently cogent explanation can enormously comfort educators because it placed responsibility for a student's behavior firmly with the parents and released the school system from blame and remedial action. (p. 168)

Nadine explained:

> I know that teachers think we are not interested in our children's education if we don't show up for parent-teacher interviews, but they are wrong. I don't go to these any more because, as far as I am concerned, they are just a waste of time.

When I asked her to elaborate, she complained that all that the interviews did was make her feel inadequate. In her view, the interviews were all one-sided, especially during a year when her children were having some academic difficulties: "It was like the difficulty that my children were having was all my fault." There was pain in her voice as she spoke about these interviews. It was clear in her case that when the interview becomes more about the parent and everything that he or she is doing wrong as a parent, it is easier to stay away.

Halee stated, "You do your best as a parent, but they don't see that. Instead, they tell you everything that you are doing wrong." Although she continued to attend the parent interviews, she admitted that she hated going because it meant hearing about all the things that she was not doing right: "It just bugs me when they [teachers] tell me, 'Well, you should be helping your children with their homework. You should read to them.' When the heck do I have time to read to them? What the heck do they think I am doing all day—nothing?" Even prior to Halee's formal interview, I sensed that this was a "hot topic" for her, so in the recorded interview I asked her about it. A portion of the interview follows:

> Interviewer: So you really do have a problem with that phrase *parental involvement*, don't you?
> Parent: Yeah, because of the way it is interpreted—with the teachers' interpretation. They need to be educated about what parental involvement is, and that's to provide a stable, nurturing home for the kids while *you* teach them! I hate it when they try to put a guilt trip on me and they say, "Well, how much of this did you do, and how much of that did you do?" when you go for the parent-teacher interviews. Or you will get a report once in a while; once in a great while they will ask you to work more with the student in this area or that area. I hate it when it reflects on you as a parent. It is not your job. Your job is already there for you.

I decided to include this portion because it clearly reveals Halee's frustration. Although the inflections in her voice cannot be heard, the resentment is apparent in her words.

Halee agreed with Nadine's assessment: "I don't know if it is their training, but teachers present themselves as almighty!" Both of these parents were very much aware that teachers had prejudged them, and they resented that. Mackay and Myles (1995) concurred that parents are often prejudged, and in very few cases were the judgments based on direct conversations between educators and Aboriginal parents. This happens even when "the vast majority of teachers . . . [had] never visited the reserves, and few had personal conversations with the parents of their Aboriginal students" (p. 166).

Parents are involved in their children's schooling. I used to tell people that my mother was not involved in my schooling because she never attended the parent-teacher interviews, never came to school events, never asked me what I was learning in school, never went through my books to see whether I had actually completed my homework, and never even looked at my report card when she signed it. It was only recently that I began to appreciate how much she was involved in other ways. She provided my siblings and me with the stability that we needed. She was there when we left for school in the morning and when we got off the bus in the afternoon. We always came home to a spotless house, our clothes neatly washed and ironed, and full-course meals complete with fresh bread awaited us daily. She was there to guide us. She told us when to get up, when to go to bed, and when to do our homework. We had a stable home in which she taught us the basics of hard work and the values of love, caring, sharing, honesty, and determination. Today I realize that this was parental involvement at its best. She had a Grade 7 education and knew very little about modern schools. She went to school in a one-room schoolhouse, where all the children from Grades 1 through 7 shared the same teacher. My mother did not attend parent-teacher interviews because she did not feel that there was a place for her there.

Although the parents in this study were noticeably more involved, which means that many of them attended parent-teacher nights and participated in many of the activities that Ascher (1988) mentioned, most of them described parental in-school involvement as limited in much the same way that mine had been. Halee explained:

> Our home was as stable as it could be. . . . We always had food, and we were given a lot of responsibility on our parts, but my mother never once went to the school. My mother believed that her job was to take care of our basic needs, while it was the school's responsibility to take care of our academic needs. I believe this, at least to a certain extent. . . .
>
> That's why I told that one teacher, "Okay, you come to my place and do some of my work for me, and I will do some of your work for you," because it is their job; they went to school for that, and they are being paid to teach your kids. It just bugs me when they told me, "Well, you should be helping your child with their homework. You should read to them" when they were younger.

"Even though the teachers think parents are not involved, that they don't care, I know they care. They care and support their children in many different ways," Veronica said in sharing her views. Pamela added, "Parents buy books for their kids from the Scholastic book club. They are encouraging them to read. This alone should prove their involvement." Although most educators do not usually consider these actions involvement, Veronica argued that they are. She shared a story about her mother's involvement in her learning:

> My mom, though she wasn't educated—she only had a Grade 8 education— . . . saw the importance of education. . . . I used to just love to read. I used to just pick up and read a novel, and I would pick real interesting and exciting ones, and I would read. I would say, "Oh, this is a good story," and then my Mom would say [in Cree], "Well, tell me about it." And you know what? I would have to tell the story in Cree to her. I didn't speak English because we just spoke to her in Cree all the time. . . . I must have really had to comprehend the story in order to relay the story in Cree to Mom, and she would just make me read. I would end at the exciting part because I knew that maybe I could get away from work a little bit if she makes me read on, so I would read to the exciting part, up to where I knew she would want me to read some more. [In Cree she would say,] "Go and read some more so you could come back and tell me more!" I think I used that a few times. [laughter] My mom didn't know it, but she helped me with reading and comprehending, even though, when I look back now, that was a big task to try and

translate what I read, because I really had to have a good understanding of what I was reading. My mom helped me a lot, and I don't think she knew that.

Florence perceived parental involvement as occurring along a spectrum:

I think involvement can be described in different ways, and there might even be spectrum of involvement from a person who hasn't even opened a report card to a person who is there practically every day checking up on their kids. So there are different ranges and kinds of involvement.

The participants' comments displayed a variety of views and activities related to parental involvement in their children's schooling. The following quotations reveal some of the different ways that they described involvement:

I help them with their homework, and if there are issues, I phone the school. . . . I am more aware. . . . Kids need structure, and I grew up with structure, so my kids have that too. It's homework time, and that's when they do homework; and when it is bedtime, they go to bed. (Marleen)

I used to do lot of volunteer work with the school because I am on the Parent Advisory Committee; that is where I sit too. They are always into sports too, so I help out with the school program. I do volunteer work like work bingos and stuff like that. (Louise)

Others explained their involvement: "I think it helps the child when they know they have supportive parents, . . . and that includes being [involved] with their after-school activities, with their sports" (Dakota); "I do everything I can to help her get along in this world that much better. Fundraising for hockey, that's all I did all year. Drive her to practice, drive her here, and drive her there" (Alexis); and "It starts at home, like . . . getting him involved in the Cree language, listening to music, taking him to events or ceremonies, just exposing him to that" (Bernice).

Challenges to Parental Involvement

"While almost all parents want to contribute to their children's positive experiences in school, levels of satisfaction with parental involvement are not yet perceived as adequate" (Kavanagh, 2002, p. 12) by formal educators. Most teachers believe that Native parents are not doing enough for their children, and this perceived lack of involvement is often misinterpreted as a lack of caring (Friedel, 1999; Mackay & Myles, 1995; Silver et al., 2002). However, my interviews revealed that parents do care very much about their children's education.

As Inger (1992) suggested:

Many school administrators and teachers misread the reserve, the non-confrontational manners and the non-involvement of . . . parents to mean that they are uncaring about their children's education—and this misperception has led to a cycle of mutual mistrust and suspicion between . . . parents and school personnel. (p. 1)

The participants in this study contended that parents do not go to the schools, even the reserve schools, because they are uncomfortable. They feel intimidated by school personnel, especially if they use a condescending tone in speaking to the parents. "I can see that intimidation might be a contributing factor, especially with our principal. He is very intimidating," one parent reported. Another participant agreed and explained that she had, in fact, taken it upon herself to talk to the principal:

> I said to him, "You are not listening to the people." "I listen and I give them time to talk," he said. "No," I said. "While they are talking, you are interrupting them. I heard the parents. You need to really, really start practicing effective listening, where you really listen to what they are saying, what they are feeling. Just listen. Don't say a word, and just hear them out. Once they finish, then you can speak, but don't try and interrupt them as they are talking because they get really angry. They don't want to be interrupted. They want their voices heard too. And the other thing, don't smile like what they are saying is funny." I know he does that, because he does that to me too. It is like he is laughing at someone. I said, "You know what? You make people feel, "Hey, he is laughing at me." And I said, "You can't do that." He will do that to me, and then he will explain, "I'm not laughing at you; I am thinking about this." And then he will repeat what he is thinking of right at that very minute. And I said, "I have no problem [with your] doing that to me because you will explain it to me and I will stop, and you will have to explain it to me. But don't do that with my people. You can't, because you make them feel like they are not valued, like the statements they are making are just not important, and you are just laughing at them. That is what they feel. Don't do that to them." He said, "Okay."

Not all parents will take the direct approach that this participant used in speaking with authority figures. Most parents will let things go unchallenged for a number of various and obvious reasons. "Parents will react to the paternalistic attitude of teachers or administrators in two ways. They will do nothing, or they will overreact by yelling and screaming," George suggested. Another participant had witnessed this latter extreme in his school and described it as "overinvolvement sometimes" as a result of the frustration that parents feel at not being heard or listened to. If overreaction and a display of anger occur, the schools then view these parents as too aggressive. I knew what George meant when he said that parents "will overreact by yelling and screaming," because, as a parent, I have reacted to the school principal on more than one occasion, as my journal entries reveal:

> *March 16, 2003*
> *[Daughter's name] always seems to be in trouble this year. I don't know what it is, but I dread having to go and talk to [the principal] again. I hate going to see him, because he frustrates me. He patronizes me and makes me feel inferior. When I go in there, I immediately regress. I am just a dumb Indian again. My power is sucked out of me immediately. I know when I go in there again, he is going to get to me.*

> *March 17, 2003*
> *Well, as expected, our meeting escalated to yelling again. He doesn't listen to me. When he says something, I automatically get defensive. He is so condescending. I walked in there today thinking I was going to try my best to be calm, but his voice just irritates me. I can't stand his "I am the authority" voice.*
>
> *Today when I walked into his office, I tried to be conscious of how and when this*

happens. I realized our discussions turn bad almost immediately. He starts off by telling me what he has to tell me, and I give him my opinion. He doesn't like to hear my opinion. He thinks I am trying to defend [my daughter], but I am not. I am only trying to get him to see something from my point of view. I am trying to tell him why I think these two girls are fighting. But he doesn't want to hear it, so he begins to elevate his voice, trying to prove to me that his theory is right. I elevate my voice. Next thing you know, we are screaming at each other. We are not hearing each other. I can't take this any more. I think I am just going to leave things from now on; I'm not going to go to the school any more.

Reflecting on these journal entries helped me to put things into perspective. When parents such as Nadine say, "I hate going to the school because I always walk out feeling inadequate," I can fully understand. However, as a researcher and an educator, I have to continuously question and critically assess the sources of these feelings of inadequacy that seem to consume us as First Nations people. I believe that we have allowed ourselves to be consumed by such feelings because we have unconsciously internalized the distorted images of racism. Even though we know better, we have internalized the stereotypical and racially derived image of "the Indian" that permeates Canadian society. We see ourselves as inadequate and inferior because the society in which we are immersed perpetuates that image in multiple and continuous ways. Our responses to those feelings of inferiority, which we know are not true, are aggression or silence. Freire (2001) suggested that when this happens we are suffering from the "duality which has established itself in [our] innermost being" (p. 56). We want to be free, but we cannot let go. When we react with aggression, we are trying to take on the role of oppressor, but we cannot fully succeed because this is not our way. Freire explained this phenomenon:

> They are at one and the same time themselves and the oppressor whose consciousness they have internalized. The conflict lies in the choice between being wholly themselves or being divided; between ejecting the oppressor within or not ejecting them; . . . between speaking out or being silent, castrated in their power to create and re-create, in their power to transform the world. This is the tragic dilemma of the oppressed. (p. 48)

We have been oppressed since birth, and we have had few, if any, opportunities to understand, articulate, own, and release these learned feelings of inadequacy. In our adult minds we know the truth, and we understand the sources of these feelings; however, the opportunities are few for most of us to address these feelings of inadequacy, and we therefore watch as our children and our grandchildren enter the same cycle, often with the school providing the initiation fire.

When I hear parents talking about their feelings of inadequacy in dealing with authority figures in schools, I see again how a lack of power contributes to their anger and defensiveness. As parents and as Indians, we accept responsibility for our children's education and, ultimately, their survival; but throughout our histories we have lived without any power or authority to act on that responsibility. Our power to act on our own behalf as peoples and/or societies was and is continually being stripped away from us. That is an undeniable Indigenous reality in Canada.

Some parents were reluctant to become more involved in their children's education for numerous reasons, particularly when it involved going into the schools. In addition to the feelings of intimidation and guilt, the participants suggested that parents do not engage with schools in the formal education of their children because their expectations of how the school will show them respect and offer them space as parents differ from those of the school; their personal educational attainment levels are not considered, and this is obvious in the manner by which school personnel relate to them; their own past experiences with schooling were negative and personally debilitating; social and familial issues and needs inhibit and/or determine their involvement. Each of these factors is discussed separately in the following section.

Differing Expectations Between Parents and Schools for School Involvement

Often public schools begin their school year by inviting Native parents to sit on the Parent Advisory Committee. Some parents will go to the first few meetings, but their attendance drops off quickly because they cannot find a place for themselves at these meetings. The parents reported feeling uncomfortable and silenced, and a few referred to themselves as "token." Pamela felt this way:

> You know that your presence there is not really needed or wanted, but they ask you to come so they can say they have Native participation. But this is not true because there is no room for you to participate. You feel like a token Indian taking up space.

She shared her own experience of attending these meetings:

> I went to a couple of PAC meetings. They had called me and invited me, so I thought, "Here is an opportunity." I did go, but you know, I felt uncomfortable. They didn't acknowledge me, and they didn't even connect me with my child, other than the one parent who knew me, . . . and she was the one who invited me and wanted me to be a part of it. But you know what? They went yakking away, they talked, and I just sat back and listened. They didn't ask me about my opinions, and I thought, "What is the sense of coming back to another meeting?"— . . . even if they would have said, "Who is your child here?" They must have just thought, "Who is this woman?" But you know what? They will never understand that [parents do not feel welcome]. They will never understand that . . . it is a waste of time. I have always said that: What for? They still think, bottom line, we are still spit onto the ground.

Public schools are always trying to find ways to bring Native people into these circles, and as Veronica told me, one of the schools called her one day and asked, "How can we get Native parents to come to the PAC meetings and be part of our PAC meetings?" I know Veronica as a very optimistic and open-minded person, but when she received this call, she admitted that the first thing that came to her mind was, "Why? You don't really want us there anyway!" She shoved those thoughts away and suggested to the caller that perhaps it would be best to ask the Native parents this question directly. She took the initiative to arrange a meeting with the school representatives, and the parents answered their questions. Her recollection of the meeting was as follows:

> They had a meeting and parents said, "You know, we need to be welcome. We need to be made to feel welcome at your meetings. We don't want to just sit there and listen, and even if we talk, no one is listening to us. Our voices are not heard; we are not valued, and we want you to make us feel welcome. We don't want to be stared at when we go into the meetings and we are thinking, "Should we be here?" kind of thing." And then the

principal said, "Well, should we not bring the Parent Advisory Committee here, and you have one spokesman to go there and speak on their behalf?" And they said, "No, that idea is no good; we need to go there, or you need to bring your people here. But everybody has to have a voice." Well, those parents even gave them suggestions on how to make them feel welcome. They told them, "You need to pick up the phone, and you tell us that you are having the PAC meeting tonight and that you would like us to come. You need to have that personal contact with parents. You shouldn't keep sending letters of invitation to come to this or to come to that. You should go directly to the people. That is our way. Have a cup of tea with us and say, 'You know, I'd like you to be a part of this.'"

This community is encouraging parents to become involved in the school, but it has to be a collaborative effort. Teachers and principals need to view parents as integral partners in the schooling of their children and try to create an environment in which parents feel welcome, even if it means sitting down to "have a cup of tea" with them.

Educational Attainment Levels and the Impact on Parental Involvement

Schools expect parents to help their children with their homework, but some parents find that they cannot because of their own lack of education. They become ashamed and try desperately to hide the secret from others, so they will avoid situations in which the truth might be revealed (Friedel, 1999; Makokis, 2000; Morrisseau, 1998). "I think that is why my parents weren't involved," Alexis suggested, because "my mom only had Grade 6, and I think my dad was higher than her, but not much more." Another participant acknowledged that this might have been why her parents were never involved either:

My mother and father had very low education, maybe Grade 7, so they could not really help us with our homework. I used to think that they didn't care, but now I know that I was wrong to even think that. Even if they wanted to help, they wouldn't have known how. This is probably why they never went to the school as well. They probably knew they would be asked questions which they wouldn't know how to respond to, so instead they just avoided it.

Inger (1992) suggested that many schools have unconsciously erected barriers for parents, even through the correspondence that is sent home with the children. In some cases parents cannot comprehend a letter that their children have brought home because of the level of the language used. Educators make the mistake of assuming that everyone reads at their level.

I asked my mother one day if she had ever attended a parent teacher-interview, and she told me, "I did once with your aunty, and the teacher kept asking me questions and telling me things about you guys that I didn't understand, so I didn't go again." She told me that she was not smart enough to attend these interviews and concluded, "You and Ronnie didn't need me there. You were smart enough." How many other Native parents feel that they are not smart enough and conclude that they have no role to play in the school? Kavanagh (2002) and Silver et al. (2002) proposed that there are endless numbers. Like our parents, we have turned the racism inward, and we continue to perpetuate the belief that Native parents do not care about their children's education. This is unfortunate because "our children will inherit the future we teach" (Calliou, 1995, p. 71).

Negative Schooling Experiences and Parental Involvement

The parents who had stressful schooling experiences of their own "may be reluctant to interact with their children's school.... For example, some First Nations parents, and Elders in particular, have a negative view of schools and formal education systems as a result of residential schools" (Kavanagh, 2002, p. 13). As can be seen in the quotations below, several of the participants attributed the lack of parental participation to the intergenerational effects of residential schools:

> My mom never stepped in our school. I had talked to her about that, because even when it came time to register, we would have to register ourselves. She wouldn't come to the school to register us, whereas I always went to the school with my son. She said that, . . . well, back then there was a lot of alcohol abuse and drug abuse and lots of violence going on, so that was one of the reasons. The other reason my mom said was because, with the way she grew up, parents weren't allowed to be involved because of her residential school upbringing. Her parents weren't involved in any of her schooling. They just came to the school for how many minutes they were allowed to visit in a little tiny room at residential school, and that was it. (Suzanne)

> It could have been that my grandparents were products of residential school; it could have been that they didn't have a vehicle; and it could have been the oppression—the underlying oppression that was there. It could have been all those three combinations why they didn't get involved. (Marleen)

"Why can't you people just move on with your lives and quit blaming residential schools for their incompetence?" a non-Native person asked me one day. I gasped. Taken off guard by that remark, I did not even know how to respond. Later, as I was reflecting on this question, I thought, "I wish it was as easy as this woman suggested." If people grow up with consistent pain, feelings of powerlessness, apathy, sadness, anxiety, and anger, how are they supposed to turn that off, especially when they cannot fully comprehend where that pain comes from? That would be my question to her today: Show us how to do it, and we'll do just that.

The problem is that most non-Native educators are ignorant about residential school. Leah's story in Chapter 4 confirmed this ignorance: "I remember learning about residential school, and from my teacher's perspective it was a good thing that kids went to residential school." This teacher told his class that day that Native children were fortunate to have had the opportunity to be educated in these systems.

> He spoke about them as if they were things of the past, something that happened in another place at another time. I don't think he even realized that there was a residential school still standing only minutes away, a school that only ceased to be a residential school in the early 1980s.

It is obvious that the teacher knew nothing about the negative history of these schools. He could not have known anything about the atrocities that happened behind those doors or about the spiritual and physical deaths that occurred in those institutions while they were under the control of the Catholic church. It is unfortunate, but without knowing our history, teachers will continue to "convey the attitude that under-involved families do not care about education and have little to contribute when they do participate." (Kavanagh, 2002, p. 13).

Most of the discussion on challenges to parental involvement evolved around the topic of residential schools, but the parents also recognized that their own schooling experience had a significant impact on whether they were involved in in-school activities such as volunteering or sitting on parental advisory committees, or even whether they attended parent-teacher interviews. My cousin once told me that he let his wife take care of that because "she is White." I understood what he was saying, especially after hearing his heart-wrenching story. I cried as he told me the story, and I asked him whether I could use it in my work. He gave me permission, but because I have only my notes to rely on, his story is not verbatim. This heart-wrenching story might answer why some parents chose not to be involved.

> When I was in Grade 1, my teacher called me a dirty Indian. I didn't know what she meant by that, so in a casual conversation with my mother that evening I said, "Mom, what is a dirty Indian?" She asked why I wanted to know, and I responded, "My teacher called me that." She started to cry, and next thing I knew, I was in the big metal washtub, and my mom was scrubbing me with soap and a scrub brush. Tears were streaming down her face, and she kept repeating, "No one is going to call my boy a dirty Indian! No one is going to call my boy a dirty Indian!" She scrubbed and scrubbed, and she continued to cry. She was crying really hard, and I remember I started crying too. I can't remember if I was crying because the brush hurt or because my mom was in pain. When I look back now, I think I was probably crying for my mom. She appeared to be in so much pain.

Painful memories such as this prevent many parents from being involved in the education of their children, at least if it meant that they had to go to the school. It was not surprising when I read through the transcripts to find that everyone could recall numerous negative experiences that impacted how they viewed formal schooling. So why is it that we continue to send our children to off-reserve schools, where the negatives outweigh the positives?

Social and Familial Issues and Parental Involvement

Suzanne attributed her parents' lack of involvement in her schooling to their addictions, because "back then, there was a lot of alcohol abuse and lots of violence going on." Marleen confirmed, "There is no arguing that our community, like other First Nations communities in Canada, is feeling the effects of alcohol, drugs and other addictions." She explained that this prevents some parents from becoming actively involved in their children's education: "This does not mean these parents don't care though. Rather, what it means is that the addiction controls them and prevents them from doing the right thing."

Without concrete statistics on the extent to which these social issues affect our communities of Saddle Lake and Goodfish Lake, it is difficult to speculate on how many families are affected, but several parents suggested that these issues might affect parents' ability to be more involved in their children's education. Halee observed:

> But you know alcohol and drugs are an issue in your community when your own children fall into the drug scene. I didn't know about the drug problem, and I was caught. I was unaware, and before I knew it, my kids were in there.

Another parent reported, "My daughter got caught with marijuana, and I was just devastated because I wanted her to be drug free and finish school." Still another parent told me, "It is even to the point where I hear now that kids are . . . selling drugs right at the school." Drugs are obviously an issue in our communities, which impacts parental involvement in schools.

Social issues of course include more than the drug and alcohol addictions that are associated stereotypically with First Nations communities. Compared to statistics on mainstream Canadian communities, those on First Nations communities show lower levels of employment and economic viability; lower levels of educational attainment, with fewer numbers graduating from high school and postsecondary; and lower levels of health, with higher levels of medical and health needs and lower levels of health care access (Statistics Canada, 2001b). All of these factors must be considered in a discussion of Aboriginal parents' school involvement. These are not merely statistics; these numbers represent people such as those whom I interviewed in this study. These persons and their communities are the sources of these statistics; they are the numbers.

An extensive review of the literature revealed that Aboriginal parents are not involved for the reasons listed above, but most of the literature overlooked what I will refer to as the logistical reasons that hinder parents' participation in their children's schooling—reasons that are connected to the financial and other resources that are visibly absent from most Aboriginal communities. These logistical reasons include transportation, childcare, time, and money. Silver et al. (2002) alluded to this: "Many Aboriginal parents are simply struggling to survive, to make it from day-to-day economically. . . . Parents are stuck in survival mode" (p. 14). The participants agreed that many of our parents are, in fact, struggling to survive. Welfare payments and child tax benefits are often the main source of income, and when the family structure is built on the support of a single parent, it is hardly surprising that attending a parent-teacher interview at the school would be the last item on a parent's priority list. "Without a vehicle, many of these single parents cannot make it in for parent-teacher nights, even at the reserve school. Even if they did own a vehicle, they couldn't afford the gas and the babysitting that they would need," Marleen remarked. A ride to any one of the neighboring towns could easily cost a parent $40, and with childcare costs added, a parent-teacher interview would represent a good portion of the family budget for groceries that month. It could be a very expensive outing. In a discussion with a school counselor, she revealed that many families struggle financially, and the school understands why many parents do not attend the parent-teacher nights at the reserve schools: They are barely surviving. This is evident in the following comment:

> A lot of kids depend on our hot lunch program here. They eat because they get breakfast and lunch. I know for a fact that when the after-school program happens at the Boys and Girls Club, they go and eat there, because on the weekends I don't know what they eat. . . . Oh yeah, it is just meeting the basic needs of food, shelter, and some don't even have this. Some don't even have shelter; they move from here to there to here. So it is, "Where are you now? Is it safe?" I do my best in helping and in resources, and there are times I leave school [and just] cry. (Marleen)

The reasons for the low parental involvement in Aboriginal communities are multiple and interconnected, and they are tied in complex ways to the institutions and practices of Canadian society. The reasons that the participants identified are only a few of many, but within their words are embedded the interconnections that need to be studied further. Yet I keep in my mind the words of a community member who recently said to me, "Learning what can be done to increase parental involvement is even more important than dwelling on why they don't come." In the newly released *Our Words, Our Ways: Teaching First Nations, Métis, and Inuit Learners*, Alberta Education (2005) suggested ways to welcome parents:

> A key to welcoming Aboriginal parents is to establish a positive relationship with them as soon as their children join the class. This will help ensure that a teacher in not contacting parents for the first time if and when a problem arises. Invite parents to:
> - Meet informally in the classroom or, if this is not practical, ask to visit them in their home or at a friendship centre, recreation centre or Métis/band office.
> - Attend student presentations, portfolio reviews and other activities throughout the school year.
> - Ask parents for their insight and suggestions on how to build a cultural continuity in the classroom and the school. Invite them to:
> - Contribute their knowledge about their cultures to curriculum related activities.
> - Contribute their talents to classroom and schoolwide activities such as organizational skills or carpentry, crafts and creative skills. (pp. 62-63)

It is embarrassing to admit, but as I was reading this prescriptive solution on welcoming parents, I laughed. The suggestions are so idealistic, and Alberta Education (2005) has made so many assumptions about both teachers and parents. First, how many teachers can take the time to meet parents when their schedules are already so busy? Most have families of their own, as well as other ongoing responsibilities. As Claire said, "Their plates are already full."

The suggestion that teachers invite parents to meet informally in the classroom, their homes, at a friendship center, or at a band office (Alberta Education, 2005) are just as unrealistic, which is evident in the current relationships between most non-Native educators and Native parents in the two communities in this study. I know from experience that many parents do not want teachers in their home, particularly if they are non-Native: "I sure wouldn't want a White teacher in my home, knowing what many of them think of us!" Halee exclaimed. Taylor (1995) agreed that, for most non-Native teachers, going to a Native person's home would likely serve primarily to "justify their reality or their concepts of the way things should be" (p. 228). If the homes do not fit the teachers' views of how a yard or home should look, the visit would only perpetuate the already-existing stereotypes about Aboriginal people. Taylor referred to this as *legitimation*:

> Legitimation is a process by which people justify their reality or their concepts of "the way things should be." Simply put, it is a method by which individuals convince themselves that their way is the right way. This process is necessary for people to protect their symbolic universe, which is a socially produced set of realities within which a group of people exist. (p. 228)

It is also uncommon for community parents to go to a friendship centre or a band office, except for formal business purposes; these are spaces in which they are not comfortable. It may be that in the large urban and metropolitan areas Friendship Centers are a more culturally friendly setting, but in the two communities in this study the parents would not ordinarily go there. For example, it has been years since I have gone to the local band office of the reserve of which I am a member, and I have been at the Friendship Centre only when I attended a wake. I am sure that it is the same for many parents.

Mackay and Myles (1995) reported, "The vast majority of teachers and non-Native education counsellors had never visited the reserves" (p. 166). I have no reason to believe that they are going to start doing this any time soon, no matter how friendly the environment of band offices or friendship centers is assumed to be. As an educator, I found this section of Alberta Education's (2005) document very presumptuous and dangerously misleading to anyone who might sincerely want to make such connections with Aboriginal parents. Another section of the document recommended "ask[ing] parents for their insight and suggestions on how to build cultural continuity in the classroom and the school" (p. 6). This is obviously unrealistic if we remember that schools have a problem encouraging Native parents attend parent-teacher nights. Therefore how can they expect parents to come in and make formal presentations on topics on which they have been ridiculed for years? How will the schools undo the parents' feelings that they helped to create that they have nothing to offer? Further to the impracticalities of Alberta Education's recommendations, very few parents, including those in my extended family as well as myself, know how to do crafts or have practical knowledge of the traditional skills of our own people, so how can we assist educators who assume that we do just because we are "Indians"? This whole section confirms what most Aboriginal parents already know: "Most Canadians know little about Native people" (Douglas, 1987, p. 180).

In response to the question on ways to increase parental involvement, the parents had no definitive answers, and most of them responded, "I don't know." However, one parent, Pamela, put it into perspective:

> Food. Food is a good thing. It is costly, but it is one of the best ways that I know of. I remember us having a barbeque for parent-teacher interviews. Everyone came to have their supper there, and then parents went to see teachers. Attendance went way up!

Pamela's response caught me off guard, and although we laughed, it made sense. Despite my reviewing the literature and "how-to" books to try to find the one magical answer, it was as simple as that: food. Morrisseau (1998) explained:

> In our culture, a feast is the appropriate way to follow up a ceremony, workshop, or meeting. Food to us is more than a substance enabling us to sustain life. Food is life itself. To share food with someone is to share life and to honour life itself. The sharing of food builds trust, and trust is significant in the building of healthy relationships. (p. 36)

All of this reminds me that as we search for answers to the issues that plague our communities, we must never forget who we are. We must always be cognizant of our ways of knowing, ways of being, and ways of doing. Food helps to build trust, and trust is significant in building healthy relationships. Florence told me:

> Once schools figure out how to develop relationships with parents, then everything else will follow.... If healthy relationships are developed, all else will fall into place. Establish a relationship with that child's caregivers. So once you have a relationship with them, then they feel okay about telling you or communicating with you about their child. And you know, you always say, "We are in this together, you and I"—

—because you want what is best for your child. I cannot imagine parents' not wanting what is best for their child, no matter where they come from. They love that child and they want what is best—the best that they can give.

Native Teachers for Native Students

> We want education to provide the setting in which our children can develop the fundamental attitudes and values which have an honored place in Indian tradition and culture. We want the behavior of our children to be shaped by those values which are most esteemed in our culture. It is important that Indian children have a chance to develop a value system which is compatible with Indian culture. (NIB, 1972, p. 2)

The participants in this study clearly expressed their demand for more Native teachers in both Saddle Lake and Goodfish Lake. The parents also wanted to see an increase in Native teaching staff in the public schools, particularly when the numbers of Aboriginal students are very high. This came out clearly in the interviews, with almost 100% of those interviewed calling for more Native teachers, which they all felt would make a huge difference in student success. The 1966 Hawthorn report, the NIB's 1972 *Indian Control of Indian Education*, and the 1996 RCAP report, *Residential Schools*, as well as many other policy-related documents, called for "extraordinary measures . . . to address the historical blocks which have discriminated against Aboriginal peoples in their attempts to educate their children" (Silver et al., 2002, p. 41). The training, hiring, and retention of Aboriginal teachers became a top priority, but even with the emergence of a variety of Native teacher education programs across the country, Aboriginal teacher numbers are not increasing fast enough. With the Native population growing at twice the rate of the non-Native populations, we need to find ways to retain Aboriginal teachers who succeed in the system. If we want our children to learn our cultural values, we need to find ways to keep Native teachers.

Native teachers in classrooms are positive role models for Native children, but, as Williams and Wyatt (1987) suggested:

> The rationale for preparing Native teachers extends beyond this. Native teachers are in a far better position than non-Natives to bring Native linguistic and cultural resources into the classroom. Incorporation of these is seen by Native people and educators across North America as critical in reducing Native students' alienation from school and in building a positive self-image and educational success. (p. 217)

My oldest daughter told me:

> There is a certain level of comfort when you are being taught by a Native person. I remember when I was going to Saddle Lake, and Noella was my social studies teacher. We used to have so much fun because we talked about things that were of interest to us. Even when the concept was something foreign, she would find ways to bring it back home. We all seemed to click in that classroom.

Barnhardt (1982; as cited in Hampton, 1995) described Native teachers as "match[ing] student rhythms" (p. 25) when they were teaching, and I believe that this is exactly what was happening in my daughter's class: Noella was matching their rhythms and teaching accordingly. Hampton elaborated:

> Barnhardt (1982) in searching for reasons Native students succeed in Alaskan schools with more than 50% Native faculty studies videotapes of Native and non-native teachers of Native children. On first impression, the teachers seemed similar in their use of a variety of conventional teaching methods, but closer examinations of the tapes using a metronome disclosed a phenomenon she called "tuning in." Both students and teachers had a rhythm and tempo to both their body movements and to their talk. White teachers set the rhythms in their classroom while Indian teachers observed and then matched student rhythms. (p. 290)

Retention of Aboriginal Teachers

> It's hard to be a teacher. It's even harder to be an Indigenous teacher because you constantly have to work between two worlds. Many times you don't know if you are coming or going. But as an Indigenous teacher, you have a responsibility . . . to the children who are given to our care and to the information and knowledge that we convey. (Cajete, 2000a, p. 189)

The attrition rate for new Aboriginal teachers is very high. Grant (1995) explained that it is because

> they are mostly on the "front line" of educational issues; they see successes and failures daily and often the failures overshadow the successes. In locally controlled schools they may be hampered by a struggling, perhaps poorly trained, administration, which comes from within their own community, thus increasingly the stresses of the job. (p. 209)

One of the greatest sources of frustrations for new teachers is learning how to put their teacher-education classroom learning to useful practice in their own communities. I believe that this dilemma is even greater for new teachers who go directly to a First Nations community to work. Often the schools are administered in a way that is acceptable to the community, but this does not always align with what these teachers learned in university, particularly with regard to classroom management. At the university they may have been taught that if children cannot be controlled, they can be sent to the principal's office, whereas in a First Nations school the teacher may be expected and left to deal with the issue in the classroom without administrative support. In off-reserve schools the administrators usually deal with attendance and high absenteeism problems, whereas my interviews revealed that in First Nations schools teachers must often deal with these problems. Claire, a parent who is also a teacher, explained that all of these added responsibilities can be overwhelming to a classroom teacher:

> Usually when issues are brought up . . . at staff meetings, the administration throws it back at the teacher to do something—go on home visits or whatever—and a lot of times that is just too much because we are doing all this stuff. I don't know, . . . but I think it is too much. We are doing all this regular teacher work and maybe volunteering, coaching, and doing classroom management, and then to do this on top, . . . to do home visits—

There is a high rate of attrition among Aboriginal teachers, particularly within the public school system. Wotherspoon and Satzewich (2000) attributed this high turnover to the fact that Aboriginal teachers cannot seem to fit in. They are seen as being different from the rest of the teaching force, and this often places added pressure on them. These authors explained:

> School divisions commonly experience high rates of attrition among teachers of aboriginal origin. Between 1987 and 1990, for example, the Saskatoon Catholic Board of Education hired fifteen teachers of native ancestry but lost 9.5 native teachers over the same period. Typically, aboriginal teachers encounter problems over the issue of complete integration into school competence, their identity as teachers of aboriginal origin places them at risk of being singled out as different from the general teaching force.... Persons of aboriginal origin who are employed by school divisions are more likely to be in subordinate or teaching assistant roles, and are rarely found in administrative position. (p. 137)

"An Aboriginal student . . . seeing that almost none of the teaching and administrative staff is Aboriginal is likely to feel that the school is an alien institution (Silver et al., 2002). The four youths who participated in my study recognized that not ever having been instructed by Native teachers sent the message that "Aboriginal teachers are really not capable of teaching academic courses," according to Leah. All four of these youths pointed out that, although there might have been one or two Aboriginal teachers on staff, they never taught them because they were assigned to teach Cree or Native studies, and because of timetabling, they were unable to enroll in any Native studies classes. Simon explained that "[there is] only one [Native teacher], and he just teaches our Cree classes basically.... He doesn't teach math or English or any of the core subjects or anything like that." Dakota argued, "I am sure the Native teachers are capable of teaching other classes, there is no doubt about it, but why do they get pushed into teaching the classes that obviously have very little value to the school?" Pamela reasoned:

> When Native teachers are hired in the provincial schools, they know what courses they will be teaching, and it seems fitting that they teach the Native studies courses, but I don't think they realize just how insignificant those courses are to the administration.

Suzanne reported:

> The other thing that I noticed about Native teachers is that they have so little power.... The Aboriginal teachers that are there now [in the public school] are just treated like little tokens in the school system; ... they are not treated like equals. I've seen it in the school.

This was evident when her son was a student, and she also witnessed it when she was a student herself. She suggested that the only reason that public schools recruit Native teachers is because they are expected to do so. Suzanne claimed that they want to be able to say:

> "Look, we have a Native teacher on staff. We care about your children." But this is all for show. They don't care one bit about Native teachers, and this is evident in how little value, power and authority they are given.

When Suzanne was a student in high school, the one Native teacher on staff taught Cree, although she was fully certified, and "when [she] . . . would send me to the office, I wouldn't get talked to, but if another teacher sent me to the office, then the principal would talk to me. I didn't think they took [her] seriously" merely because she was Native. Bernice lamented, "It is a shame that still Native children (particularly in the public school system) may never have the opportunity to be taught by a Native teacher." In her view, Aboriginal teachers bring a different perspective into the classroom because of their lived experiences. "Receiving history lessons from a Native teacher can be very empowering," she added.

All of the participants agreed that being a Native teacher in the public school system can be very challenging, particularly for the new recruits, but "we need them there," insisted Suzanne. "We need them there because they would have a huge impact on the Native kids. They would listen more to that teacher because they would know that this teacher understood them." At least, that was her experience. Unlike the non-Native teachers, this teacher, who taught social studies, had very high expectations of the Native students in her classroom. "She was strict and demanded high quality work, but she was also gentle and compassionate at the same time. Learning about Native history like the Rebellion was empowering. I felt good being in her class." Bernice too had taken a class from this Native teacher: "Learning about the Louis Riel Rebellion and learning that from [the Native teacher] . . . was great! It was great having her take on it; it was a different take." Both participants were grateful to have had that Native perspective in a social studies class and understood that it could come from only a Native teacher, especially in a mainstream course such as social studies.

Dakota, who had always sent her kids off-reserve to school, wanted to see "more Aboriginal teachers" in her children's school, but she recognized that this might not happen unless Native parents took some drastic measures:

> I would like to see more Native teachers. I know of a guy who has had his teaching degree for more than 20 years that applied at [the school where my children attend], and he was told that he could possibly get a job as a liaison worker only. So if I don't see a change in the next couple of years, . . . I am going to ask them that question: How many [Native] teachers have applied here? And if I don't see a change, . . . I will pull my kids out of that school.

Native teachers are critical to the realization of quality education for Native children (Silver et al., 2002):

> Throughout the literature we witness the concepts of Indian identity, traditions, psychology, culture, language and history as being important in the education of Indians. It is appropriate to suggest that Indian teachers would be the most effective in transmitting these concepts. (p. 45)

In a qualitative research study that Bazylak (2002) conducted with five Aboriginal girls in a Saskatchewan high school, his participants clearly identified the need for Aboriginal teachers. One of his participants

> noticed a lack of Aboriginal teachers in the school, and among those present she noted that the Aboriginal teachers in the school hung around together and did not seem to associate with the other teachers. Zeara wondered whether this was a form of racism, a consequence of their being Aboriginal. (p. 145)

Bazylak added, "There is irony in her discussion regarding teacher groups and student clichés as both serve to marginalize a group. Transformation in Aboriginal education cannot take place while Aboriginal teachers are marginalized" (p. 145).

In a report on Aboriginal teachers, St. Denis, Bouvier, and Battiste (1998) elaborated on teacher marginalization in schools. They found that that "having more than one Aboriginal teacher on a staff is a valued experience for Aboriginal teachers. It enabled them to feel connected, relaxed and confirmed" (p. 49).

Bazylak (2002) concluded that, like Aboriginal students, Aboriginal teachers also have a need to feel comfortable in a school because "Aboriginal teachers experience racism from other teachers in their school" (p. 144).St. Dennis et al. (1998) expanded on this: "Despite the well meaning and the good-heartedness of some colleagues, teachers feel that racism remains invisible to them, manifested in their negative comments about Aboriginal students, families or other teachers" (p. 52).

Although the number of Aboriginal elementary school teachers has been growing steadily thanks to the many teacher education programs geared specifically at increasing the representation of Native people in the teaching profession, the majority of Aboriginal children are still not schooled in classrooms with Aboriginal teachers. This underrepresentation is acutely apparent in the provincial schools that serve Aboriginal children from Saddle Lake and Goodfish Lake, where I conducted my study. Even when the majority of students are Native, it is difficult to find even one Native teacher. One such school, which has a 99% Aboriginal population, had one certified Native teacher on staff at the time of these interviews, but that person has since left to take employment elsewhere.

Clare postulated:

> I know even with the Aboriginal teacher programs, such as the one that was at Blue Quills First Nations College, we are still going to have a Native teacher shortage. The majority of those will go to work in their communities, so it will be years before we see increases in public schools.

Consequently, the need to employ the services of non-Native teachers is likely to continue because the number of teachers of Native children far exceeds the number of graduates from Aboriginal teacher education programs. This would not be a problem if non-Native teachers could take the time to familiarize themselves with the communities and families from which these Native children come and if they increased their awareness of culturally appropriate content and teaching methods (Taylor, 1995). Barman et al. (1987) agreed:

> Some of the most successful patterns of classroom interaction have been pupil-centred, focused on the development of the potential of each child and so reinforcing the belief common to Indian cultures that the child is born with an identity and a spirit, with talents and character. . . . Successful teachers of Indian children, whether or not they are Indian are characterized by their ability to create a climate of emotional warmth and to demand a high quality of academic works. They often take the role of personal friend, rather than that of impersonal profession, and use many nonverbal messages, frequently maintaining close body distance, touching to communicate warmth, and engaging in gentle teasing. After establishing positive interpersonal relationships at the beginning of the year, these teachers become demanding, as an aspect of their personal concern in a reciprocal obligation to further learning. Highly supportive of any attempt students make, these

teachers avoid even minor forms of direct criticism. Thus, these teachers are effective because of their instructional and interactional style, and not because of their ethnic or racial group membership. (pp. 12-13)

The significance and presence of Native teachers in classrooms that serve Aboriginal students was of vital concern to all those who participated in this study; these participants contended that such teachers "affirm the validity of Indian cultures and definition of an Indian identity" (Barman et al., 1987, p. 14). I agree with these educators that Native teachers can serve as role models for our children, especially if they "embody the characteristics of cultural identity and lifestyle to which the young are being taught to aspire" (p. 14).

Concluding Reflections

Relationship building, parental involvement, and the significance of Native teachers in student success was the topic of discussion in this chapter. Parents and students alike considered these three factors prerequisites for Native students' success in school. Children need validation, and the parents were certain that each of these factors would support and provide it. Perhaps more relationship building between students and teachers and between parents and teachers and more Native teachers in the schools will make Native parents feel less intimidated and encourage them to become more active partners in their children's schooling. These factors are interconnected, and without one of them, a link is missing.

CHAPTER 7:
DISCUSSION, SUMMARY, AND CONCLUSION

Discussion of Findings

The last three chapters have shown that school-choice decisions are complicated by the many obstacles to which Native children are subjected as they journey through the education system. Although education is supposed to be an empowering experience, the interviews with parents revealed otherwise. The parents revealed that their children are often subjected to unfair treatment within the public school system, and they disclosed some of their fears about sending their children to the band-operated reserve schools. Schools choice decisions can be difficult for any parents, but for Aboriginal parents who live on a reserve, school-choice decision making can be even more complicated, knowing that the choices that they make can have long-term negative impacts on their children.

Despite the rhetoric of respect for diversity in the provincially accredited public school systems, the parents recognized that these school environments continue to emphasize ideas that reflect only Western knowledge and belief systems (Williams, 2000), which thus sends out the message that Native ways of knowing and being are not useful and should be abandoned.

Racism within schools continues to be a significant barrier for Native-student achievement. No one in this study was exempted from racism. Native children "are being denied access to knowledge bases that they need to sustain themselves. . . . To deny that tribal epistemology exists and serves a lasting purpose is to deprive Aboriginal children of their inheritance, as well as to perpetuate the belief that different cultures have nothing to offer" (Battiste, 2000, p. 202). Although all of the parents who participated in this study recognized the harmful and debilitating effects that the public school system had on them and continues to have on their children, the majority continue to send their children to these schools in the belief that Western knowledge systems are the ideal and must be closely adhered to if their children are going to compete successfully in contemporary Canadian society. Western forms of education have been promoted to and accepted by Aboriginal peoples as "a kind and necessary form of mind liberation that opens to the individual options and possibilities that ultimately have value for society as a whole" (Battiste, 2000, p. 194). Many First Nations parents, including some who shared their views with me in this work, believe in this promise of options and possibilities through the Western educational systems and believe further that these are more likely achieved in off-reserve public schools than they are in on-reserve schools.

School Choice Decisions and the Ideal School

Suzanne told me:

> I know that by sending my son off-reserve, he paid a price, we paid a price, but at the time I felt it was necessary. I wanted to give him what I thought was a better education, but I realize now I have robbed him of his cultural identity. He is not proud to be Indian at all.

With any school choice decision that they have made, the parents reported that they have also made significant tradeoffs, and they expressed their concern about it repeatedly. However, as

Marleen stated, "We do what we have to do, what we think is right for our kids." Dakota concurred: "I know we are hurting our children by sending them off-reserve, at least to some extent, but it is hard to send them on-reserve when we know that they are not getting the level of education they deserve." So what then are the choices available to First Nations parents? If they live on-reserve, parents have only two choices, neither of which they perceived or described as desirable or highly promising of school success for their child. Parents may choose to send their children to on-reserve schools, which they perceive as substandard in academic programming and suitable for only low achievers, or they may choose to send them to off-reserve public schools, where oppression, racism, marginalization, and Eurocentrism prevails. Neither choice offers much hope of success in academic achievement or personal development.

Within the context of this bleak picture of school choice for First Nations parents who live on reserves, I invited the parents to engage in a process of defining for themselves the ideal school that they envisioned for their children. I intended this exercise to bring appropriate closure to the process that I had initiated with the group and to allow us to synthesize the information from each of our respective contexts. The parents would be able to reveal their thoughts and emotions on a relevant and meaningful part of their daily lives through a visioning process of hope and to create a framework for their own ideal school. I, in turn, could listen to the participants organize their own data into a meaningful and useful analysis to arrive at an image of the ideal school—an image that would encompass within itself a positive response to the multiple issues that had been brought to consciousness in their articulation of an individual school-choice decision-making process.

The following section describes the ideal school in the words of the parent participants. It is perhaps the most integral part of the conclusion because it shows clearly that the parents in these communities are certain about the type of schooling that they want for their children and that they are willing to work towards building. The fact that the substance and content of this certainty are supported by solid contemporary educational research and scholarship merely highlights their strength and courage in persisting and enduring the ongoing ignorance and injustice represented by an imposed system of education.

Pamela yearned for "the ideal school for our children. But what is the ideal school?" Her children had had experiences in both on-reserve and off-reserve schools, and both systems involved a level of discomfort. As far as she was concerned, neither of these systems was ideal. Public schools' strict adherence to the curriculum meant that her children moved from one grade level to the next with relative ease, but the reserve school system provided her children with a sense of belonging and comfort. Here the children could forget that they were different, because racism was minimal because "a lot of the teachers are non-Native, and I know some have racist attitudes, but it doesn't seem to affect the children in the same way."

Many parents expressed this same concern about their school choice. They knew that the school system that they had chosen was not ideal, but it sufficed. Therefore, like Pamela, they all hoped that one day their children would have an ideal school that would transmit the values and knowledge of the Cree culture. They hoped that one day they would have a school that would "give our children the knowledge to understand and be proud of themselves and the knowledge to understand the world around them" (NIB, 1972, p. 1). All of the parents who participated in this study wanted the same thing: They wanted their children to be proud of their heritage. Therefore they wanted an ideal school that would "enhance Aboriginal consciousness of what it means to be an Indian, thus empowering and enriching the individual and collective lives of their children" (Battiste, 1995, p. xv). They wanted a new model of inclusive and participatory education.

Everyone who participated in the study recognized that the Western education that their children were receiving was "hostile in its structure, its curriculum, its context, and its personnel" (Hampton, 1995, p. 37). Like Hampton, they firmly believed that the current system "embodies and transmits the values, knowledge, and behaviors of white culture" (p. 37) only. Hookimaw-Witt (1998) agreed and insisted that the current school system continues to fail our children because "instead of developing our ways and adjusting them to the new environment, we have to give them up" (p. 160) by following the provincial curricula and conforming to the dominants group's social and cultural ideologies.

All of the participants were dissatisfied with the current education system and wanted a school system that would encompass all aspects of their children's development. They wanted a system in which their children "are viewed holistically without the separation between secular and sacred knowledge which characterizes schooling in the dominant Canadian society" (Barman et al., 1987, p. 5).

Kristine emphasized that "a holistic education must meet the mental, emotional, spiritual, and physical needs of a child." Mackay and Myles (1989) concurred that education must be holistic and cautioned that "those who work with children must never lose sight of the child's basic life components: physical, mental, social, emotional, and spiritual" (p. 64):

> These life components must be considered concomitantly, for when they interact with such environmental factors as socioeconomic status, the social structure of the child's community, the educational history of the parents, the fluctuating effect of the child's interactions with the teacher, and so one, the whole children concept is difficult to concentrate on. But one must consider the whole child, that is, all facets and phases of the child's life. It is this perception of the whole child that is needed if one is to unlock and unravel the learning difficulties of children. (p. 65)

Marleen asserted:

> We can say we want a holistic education, but saying it and doing it are two different things. We need to do it! Physical can be through physical education, and emotional and spiritual, that is where the Elders would come in. That would be our sweats and ceremonies. Perhaps teachers could begin teaching the whole child by incorporating the medicine wheel teachings in their lesson.

"But even before we do this, we need to get buy-in from the leadership and the community," Leah pointed out, and Bernice concurred:

> It has to be a whole community effort. There are too many things involved with creating an ideal school. Just getting people to realize where they are coming from, or why things are the way they are, is a job on its own.

Leah reported that

> when I was a student in school, I didn't see my community members getting involved, but it would have been great . . . because it would make the students feel important.

> Everything we do as students is for our community, and receiving validation from the leaders and community members is a reward in itself.

She emphasized the importance of community and did not see herself as separate from it. She alluded to *Mamokamatowin* (working together) throughout the interview and reiterated it when she shared her thoughts with me about what her ideal school would look like if she had the opportunity to be part of a design team. It would be more than just a physical space; it would also take into consideration the mental space. Although she affirmed that it would have to be holistic and exalt Aboriginal values, she admitted that it was beyond her to try to explain this concept any further. Every participant who chose to speak to the ideal school question said the same thing: Designing an ideal school was something that could not be done by just a few people; community involvement would be required, because, as Pamela stated, "Together we can create it; alone we can't." The "strength of the individual is the strength of the group," according to Hampton (1995, p. 21).

Others agreed and were confident that without this empowering structure of community involvement, a school that fully meets the needs of Native students would never be realized. Florence, the principal of the Saddle Lake Onchaminahos School, did not see any problem with organizing strategic planning sessions to consider concepts such as an ideal school because "there is no shortage of leaders in our schools." She elaborated:

> In terms of leadership, there are different kinds of leaders. We have educational leaders, we have instructional leaders, and social leaders in a school. I know one leader can't be all of it, so you have to focus on where you want to be a leader and what kinds of works you want to do and to realize. You have to see the leadership that is in teachers also. So you nurture that teacher to be a leader of this. It doesn't need to be a teacher; it could be a teacher assistant. . . . It can be anybody in that school that wants to have a leadership feeling, and you tell them, "It is okay; you can do it. I know you can do it; you have it in you." So you are empowering. You give them power and authority to do something, and they just blossom. And then you trust they know what they are doing; trust in the process. . . . So it is about empowerment and seeing leadership in people and giving them that permission to know what they can do.

A community member suggested at a recent school-community planning meeting, "We do have many good ideas in place, and in fact a strategic plan was made a few years back, . . . but the plans just have to be put into action." Louise acknowledged that

> the only way we will be able to achieve this holistic education we are after is if we go back to our teachings. This does not mean we go back to living in teepees and living off the land, but it does mean we have to honor the ways of our ancestors.

She suggested that our curriculum would have to reflect a cultural and historical balance, that it would need to be developed by educators who understand traditional transmission of Cree knowledge and heritage, and that the best place to start would be with our Cree Elders, because "they are the ones that are the keepers of that knowledge."

Kristine, a youth participant with two small children, visualized her ideal school:

> When I think of the ideal school, I think of a school where my children will thrive and be happy and secure in themselves. The school would have to be located on Native land, where children could develop the relationship with the land, where children would gain a respect for Mother Earth and all learn about all She has to offer us.

Battiste and Henderson (2000) concurred and explained that an ideal school would have to prepare children to live with our changing ecological system:

> An enhanced curriculum would teach Indigenous students in a holistic manner, offering them a way of living and learning in a changing ecology. It would teach them to believe that knowing requires a personal relationship between the knower and the knowledge. It would offer them an integral, interactive relationship based on trust in the face of unknowable risks in a realm where they are vulnerable. The task of adequate Indigenous education is to enhance students' awareness of their human capacities and of the dignities of Indigenous knowledge and heritage. Such education should develop, at a minimum the following capacities in Indigenous youth: (1) the ability to care and be responsible for the ecology, for others, and for oneself; (2) the ability to discern new and flexible images of meaning and patterns in these relationships; (3) the ability to hope and to have courage in an ecological realm filled with vitality and insight; and (4) the ability to develop a sense of "truthing" in all relationships. (p. 87)

Characteristics of the Ideal School for Aboriginal Children

All of the participants made suggestions and recommendations related to the characteristics of an ideal school. The next section of this chapter discusses and describes these characteristics within the context of the participants' sharing and carries with it the hope that these parents will move the work forward through their own thinking into the next phase of their own personal and their community's evolution. The recommendations (see Appendix) evolved from the discussions and were developed in response to requests from several members of the parent group that they also be written in a simplified but straightforward recommendations format. In this way the recommendations could serve as the basis of future community-wide discussions.

Strong Leadership

The participants from both Saddle Lake and Goodfish Lake agreed that ideal schools need strong leadership. Pamela maintained that "if you don't have effective leadership, you just can't have successful schools. I think you need good teachers, but you need somebody to hold them together, to create an environment to maximize their teaching opportunities." Many participants agreed, but most recognized that good schools require a shared form of leadership, "because the principal can't do it alone," according to George. Florence, the principal of the Saddle Lake Onchaminahos School, concurred and has encouraged all of her staff to take on leadership roles. She recognized the leadership potential in all staff members and suggested, "It doesn't have to be a teacher; it could be a teacher assistant; . . . it could be anybody in that school that wants to [be] a leader." Unfortunately, First Nations schools do not operate under the same governance structures that those in the public school systems do, and the principals do not hold the same authority even though they are expected to accept the same responsibility and accountability for the education of children. According to the participants, one solution would be to recommend to the Chief and Council that they keep their political interventions to a minimum and that the principal and the Board of Education be granted more authority in the decision making around schooling and education. The parents believed that if this were to happen, school principals would develop the strong administrative leadership that First Nations schools so desperately require.

Unity of Purpose

In both communities, Saddle Lake and Goodfish Lake, the participants spoke about the lack of unity that exists in the communities and schools. Pamela thought that "one of the biggest challenges on our reserves is that we can't seem to work with one another. Unless we address this, nothing is going to improve in our communities and our schools." Another parents stated, "We don't even have unity in the schools, . . . and the kids see it. They . . . play off of it, and they'll push the limits. Staff must cooperate if they are to achieve the desired unity." The parents noted that it is important that the school and community share a purpose and vision. Both Goodfish Lake and Saddle Lake Schools have their own mission and vision statements, "but I don't know if these are ever reviewed," Alexis remarked.

The mission statement for the Saddle Lake School (Saddle Lake Cree Nation, 2007) reads as follows: "The mission statement of Saddle Lake Onchaminahos School is to embrace all children in a loving and safe environment where culture is reflected and excellence is nurtured" (Onchaminahos Elementary section, ¶ 3). The Kihew Asiniy High School does not have a mission statement but does have a strategic plan with the following priorities:

1. *Nehiyaw pimatisiwin*—effective coordination of all available resources and involvement in the delivery of community-wide Cree language and cultural programming.
2. Holistic programming to nurture students' needs.
3. Create a safe and caring school environment.
4. Build healthy, strong, collaborative, and professional relationships.
5. Create a communicate plan to increase and improve school and community relationships. (Kihew Asiniy Education Centre section, ¶ 1)

The Goodfish Lake Pakan School mission statement reads, "Respecting, sharing, teaching and learning together with pride and success" (R. Hunter, personal communication, June 4, 2007), and the vision statement states:

1. We will achieve excellence in education at Pakan School.
2. We will educate the whole child toward good citizenship in the family, the community and society as a whole.
3. We will have a high enrolment in our junior Kindergarten (K4) to Grade 9 programs.
4. We will establish an integrated language and cultural program.

All of these statements reflect the importance of delivering holistic, culturally relevant programs in our communities. The value placed on relationships and communities is the foundation of our Cree culture, and this is also clearly evident. We are given substance, nurtured and sustained by the relationships we have with family, friends, colleagues, teachers, and the community as a whole. These relationships extend beyond family and friends and into the connection that we feel with the place and space that we call our community.

Mission statements should reflect the school's reason for being, but as Dakota suggested, "Not much attention is paid to them." The participants advised that mission statements reflect the school's intention, priorities, and values, but cautioned that, without a clearly visible mission statement that people both inside and outside know, it serves no purpose and has little value. "If these were followed, then we would have good schools," Halee suggested, "but they are not." If unity is to be created, then the core values that are identified in these mission statements must be made known to and shared by everyone, both inside and outside the school, adults and children alike. "If everyone is on the same page in the school, than people will begin to take pride in their schools" (Alexis). Therefore, a major responsibility of the school leadership has to be to find ways to keep the mission statements alive and to live up to them. If the mission is to find ways to keep our culture and language alive, then what we say must be more than symbolic. Marleen stressed that "everyone has to walk their talk."

A Caring, Nurturing, and Safe Environment

The participants pointed out that if the schools are going to achieve a caring and nurturing environment, then teachers and administrators must model behavior that treats children with warmth, love, affection, and validation. This would mean a drastic change, especially because teachers have been told that they must not touch a child or allow their relationship with them to become too personal. As the principal of Saddle Lake Onchaminahos School described it, hugging and telling children that you love them on a daily basis changes the school environment: Behavioral issues decease and attendance increases. Children thrive in environments of persistent caring and nurturing. Morefield (1996) concurred:

> We often hear the argument put forth, even in kindergarten, that life is tough so we must toughen up the children. The truth is, children do better in safe and nurturing environments. Children do not do as well in environments where adults are continually critical, constantly accentuating the negative, and not accepting children for who they are. Since we know this is true, then we are obligated to foster warm and caring environments where children will blossom. (p. 5)

Hampton (1995) recognized that an Aboriginal person "does not form an identity in opposition to the group but recognizes the group as relatives included in his or her own identity" (p. 21). Most Aboriginal people do not see themselves as separate from their communities. This is evident in Veronica's statement: "It does take community effort. We are all responsible for the children in our communities." To achieve this, however,

> we, us, the community have to be able to look within first and get rid of those issues we haven't dealt with and learn new ways to communicate—how to listen, how to show we care—and this will only happen if we have a vision of where we want to take that place [the school] for our children.

"What we really need . . . is for the whole community to become involved," Bernice recommended. "Making our schools safe will require everyone's help." The participants felt strongly that safety concerns in the school are a community issue, and Florence supported this view: "Our school is the centre of our community, and everyone has to learn to take pride in it." The parents suggested that an ideal reserve school would not have safety issues, but recognized, like Morefield (1996), that the "path to accomplishing a vision of schools for all children will require strong moral and sometimes physical courage" (p. 15). "Every student has the right to feel safe and be safe in school and on school grounds," Claire pointed out.

A Raised Bar

Research has shown that teachers, particularly non-Native teachers, often have very low expectations of Aboriginal children; as a result, they often "lower the bar" with regard to academic expectations (Bazylak, 2002; Goulet, 2001; Watt-Cloutier, 2000; Wilson, 1992). Watt-Cloutier went so far as to say that this perpetuates the cycle of racism:

> Many will agree that this rigor and challenge no longer exists in our schools and that we have gone from the extreme of a paternalistic system to the extreme of a system that challenges our youth so little that it undermines their intelligence.... The watering down of programs, the lowering of standards and expectations is a form of structural racism that we must make every attempt to stop.... What follows is the lowering of expectations of all involved, including students, teachers, and parents. The low self-esteem that we are living with today did not occur overnight, and we must work to rectify it in every possible way. (pp. 115-116)

"The problem is that teachers do not understand the children," Marleen complained. Teachers

> have to understand the level of our people, and it is not to say they are lower. [Native people] have a different understanding. You have two different things, of course. I'll give an example: skinning a deer.... Maybe this one knows,... but this one has actually done it.

With regard to behavior too, Brian Wildcat asserted that

> the school needs to raise the bar. You can't blame the kids because they didn't show up, because that's the message that the school has sent out. If children are not coming to school, it is because that behavior has been accepted in that school. So why should they even bother coming if the school isn't expecting them to be there? If you want good behavior, you have to build the expectations in your school.

Wildcat was adamant that children will rise to the level of expectations held for them, which research has confirmed (Morefield, 1996; Watt-Cloutier, 2000). Pamela warned, "When we treat the kids that come to the reserve school as bottom-of-the-barrel kids, that is what we are going to get. We reap what we sow."

"We must change the way we view our reserve schools, and Native children in general," Suzanne suggested, and everyone agreed. The parents knew that whether their children attend the reserve schools or public schools, they are just as capable of succeeding and flourishing when they have the same opportunities and exposure to the highest quality instruction and rigorous educational experiences that non-Native and more advantaged students have. Pamela asserted,

"If we have high expectations for our children, they will feel that, and they will perform to that level, I guarantee it." Youth want to be challenged, as Watt-Cloutier (2000) proposed:

> The hunger for challenge is so evident in our youth that, in or to see it, you only have to look at the popularity of arcade halls or the popularity of video games in people's living rooms. Our youth are not looking to exercise their fingers or hand-eye coordination as they play these games; they are looking for ways to challenge and build their character, the very thing that traditional skills offer but that is denied to them by most of what is offered in the schools or elsewhere.... Institutions such as schools are good at providing success, and they can often do that by simply reducing the challenge. Easy successes are not worth much in human development terms. (p. 117)

Suzanne suggested, "We need to change the perception that many teachers have about Native kids," but for educators to be able to do that, "many of them must unlearn some deeply held societal beliefs" (Morefield, 1996, p. 9). Florence reasoned that "teachers who sincerely believe that all children are capable of learning will have successful classrooms," which she has witnessed in her school: "Children will want to learn, they will want to come to school if this is what their teacher expects." Students are aware of their teachers' high expectations for them, as is revealed in the following story:

> Oh I had all kinds of teachers, but ... one teacher really had an influence on my education, and that had a real impact on me and really challenged me.... Boy, she just pushed me above where I wanted to go! I used to be so shy, extremely shy, and I used to think, "I can't do this." And then she'd make me go in front of the classroom. In those days prayer was allowed in school and the singing of *O Canada*. She would make me lead in that song [and] *The Lord's Prayer*. Then she would make me read this Bible storybook; I used to read that book every morning—one story. And then after school I would have the children sing *God Save the Queen*, and they all got up and sang when I said, "We are going to sing *God Save the Queen*." I don't know why she had that special interest in me, and I really believe in my mind now that the relationships that teachers have with their students can make a difference in their learning. I wanted to do work for her! I wanted to do my best! It was like I was doing it for her, and she would put my work on the bulletin board in the hallway. She would hang my handwriting in the hallway, so I tried even harder to write really well. I would take my time and make sure I did my best. She made a world of a difference for me.

A Native Teaching Staff

"As a child, I never had a Native teacher," Kristine revealed. "It wasn't until I went to high school on the reserve, that this changed." Unfortunately, Kristine's experience is not unique. As Taylor (1995) stated, "Ninety percent of Native children in this country will ... be taught by a non-Native teacher, and many of these children will have received most of their education from non-Native teachers" (p. 224).

All of the participants agreed that Native teachers should be teaching Native students, and although they saw more and more of their own teachers coming into the reserve schools, they were concerned that no Native teachers were seeking employment in the public school systems:

"They don't go to the provincial schools because they don't feel supported there," Nadine suggested. "I wouldn't want to go there either because of the racism that exists in these schools." Bernice reported, "The numbers of Aboriginal teachers is increasing now, because of Aboriginal teacher education programs like the one at Blue Quills First Nations College."

The participants were optimistic that within the next few years "our schools would be filled with Aboriginal teaching staff, thanks to the University of Alberta and the Aboriginal Teacher Education Program that is coming for the second time to Blue Quills First Nations College" according to Bernice. The participants were confident that more and more Native teachers will teach in the public schools as well, as Leah affirmed: "We will have more and more young people choosing to teach in provincial schools in the near future." Whether or not Leah's prediction will ever be realized in public schools is yet to be seen, but we are definitely seeing an increase in the Aboriginal teacher population in reserve schools.

The parents unanimously agreed that ideal schools would have to be situated within Native communities or at least on tribal lands. Although they recognized that public schools in Alberta are now attempting to incorporate Aboriginal cultures into their curricula, the parents also realized that this ideal school system that they were seeking would never be implemented within the public system. Dakota explained her thinking:

> Although I send my girls to the provincial schools, I realize that we will never be able to create an ideal school situation for them. Even if we have more Native teachers in these schools, we will still not achieve it fully because these teachers will not be allowed to move outside the box. They will have to do things the way the school thinks they need to do this, and I don't think that means incorporating our ways of doing.

In Dakota's view, the public school system will always cater to the White, middle-class child, so that "more Native teachers within that system is really not going to change too much. Therefore we shouldn't worry about that." Rather, she thought that the focus for Aboriginal parents should be on increasing the number of Aboriginal teachers in First Nations schools.

A Curriculum That Embraces a Native Epistemology

All parents hoped that they could find ways to reinforce a strong sense of pride and self-esteem in their children, but felt that this could be achieved only if their children learned about the value of their culture in a school setting. Most parents try their best to reinforce a positive self-image and self-identity in their children, but they find that this is often superseded by the negative messages that they receive about their culture as students within the school systems. "We need to make changes to our curriculum. Sure, we want the academics in there, but that can't be all. Our schools need to work with the whole child, not just with their minds" (Pamela).

The principal at Saddle Lake Onchaminahos School recognized that the "curriculum should speak to who we are." This is why she has asked the teachers, "How are you connecting this curriculum to that child's life? How are they going to feel connected to it? Does it mean anything to them?" She further explained:

> One of the questions in my teacher evaluation is, "How have you extended your curriculum so that it is extended to that student's life?" Teach something useful every day that they could use and for themselves to question, "How is this going to teach them?" So you start connecting spiritually, mentally, and socially with the different activities we

have in our school. We are trying to be really holistic by nurturing all the areas of the medicine wheel.

Pamela, a parent, concurred:

Our academics are number one in the school; they shouldn't be. As for Native people anyway, I think it should be us as human beings. I always think of our soul. Our souls need to be guided and nurtured; then we could focus on academics.

A youth participant suggested, "Right now children's mental needs are addressed for the most part, but not their physical, emotional, and spiritual needs." According to these participants, this system of working with only the child's intellect is not enough. Sheila contended:

Times have changed, and they [educators] now have to understand that there are different ways of learning, not just book and paper; there is a lot of kinesthetic, hands-on kind of stuff, and they have to get out of the box.

There were many suggestions about how to "get out of the box" in relation to curriculum:

1. We need to teach our children about their history:

   I think, they should already be teaching some Native history in high school. . . . I wish we had gotten . . . a little bit of that in school, because when I went to school, that is when you had these textbooks depicting the Native people as savages and killing and mutilating their enemies and raping women and all this BS. So I went off to school, but the confidence just wasn't there. I didn't feel up to par with everybody else, even though, in hindsight, I had a heck of a lot to offer to society too. (Halee)

2. We need to find ways to incorporate our cultural values into the curriculum:

   There are so many other ways that identify us as Native or give us our identity, I guess you can say. It doesn't necessarily have to be in that way [attending ceremony or practicing a religion]. It has to do with your morals, with your ways of being brought up, your values. Instead of getting values from outside and bringing them in, we need to bring our values and bring them back out. I guess I get that from my grandparents, from things like that. (George)

3. We need to put more focus on Cree language training:

   We are losing our language; we are losing a lot of our customs, morals, and things that our grandparents grew up with. We need to focus on ways of retaining these, especially our language. Our language is our survival tool. It connects us to the past, and it will hold us together in the future. (Sheila)

4. We need to incorporate an experiential learning environment:

For school programs and stuff like that, . . . we have the area for it. The science could be all outside, we have the lake right there, and these kids are intelligent; there's nothing stopping them. (Marleen)

5. We need to nurture the souls of our children:

We need to incorporate a spiritual component in our schools. Everything is about the soul and the spirit. Whatever our soul feels, that is how our actions are. If we have happy souls, then we have healthy behaviors. Our actions are healthier, and that's what for me an ideal school would be: for teachers to take into consideration that students have souls or spirits, and that is our foundation. (Pamela)

6. We need to find ways to increase Elder participation in our schools:

Elders have always held an important role in our communities. They were the leaders in ceremonies and were our main teachers. They taught us lessons through storytelling and shared information about our language, culture, and history. At one time they were the primary caregivers of their grandchildren and nonjudgmental advisers to those that came for help. They need to be utilized more now. . . . They should go into the school system and talk to the children about honesty, respect, caring, and sharing, all those core values. They need to go talk to these children about stuff like that. If we invited Elders to assist us in the school, than perhaps we wouldn't have the behavioral problems that we do. (Clarisse)

7. We need to believe in parents as educators. Nadine suggested that "the ideal school would be a community school where parents, relatives, friends, and community members would be welcome." The school always felt like an institution to her, and in an ideal school, this institution feel would not be there. The out-of-place feeling that parents often have when they enter their children's school would be replaced with a nurturing environment. Although Nadine did not know how this could be done, she felt that the school would have to become less formal and more inviting. Everyone agreed that the "feel in these schools had to change," as Pamela recommended, and that bridges have to be built, but several participants felt that this could not happen unless it was done with sincerity. Morefield (1996) agreed that bridges will not be built unless schools can prove that they truly value and appreciate parental involvement:

I am convinced that one of the reasons educators don't attempt to create new bridges is that they don't really believe that it takes educators and parents walking hand in hand together to accomplish the goal of effectively educating children. Many see parents as intrusive, invasive, and as impediments. (p. 12)

The ideal school has to be built on the premise that everyone has something to offer. The schools must find ways to make parents feel safe, valued, needed, and wanted within the school system. "Creating a more user friendly environment for parents requires educators putting themselves in the parents' perspective" (Morefield, 1996, p. 13).

8. We need to take an effective mental health approach. Repeatedly, the participants alluded to the social problems within First Nations communities. "This is reality," Louise suggested. Knowing that these communities suffer from suicide, alcohol and drug abuse, cultural confusion, sexual violence, and much more, the parents hoped to see more focus on the psychological and emotional needs of the children.

Social issues such as drug and gambling addictions, combined with socioeconomic problems, have a devastating impact on children and make it very difficult for teachers to do their jobs effectively. In addition to their full-time teaching loads, teachers are often required to be part-time counselors, social workers, and parents. The participants saw a need to hire respected Elders full-time and culturally sensitive mental and physical health workers to assist the teachers: "We need more Elders in our schools to assist the teachers and principals," Clarisse proposed.

Bernice recommended, "Elders could help with the discipline, and they could be counselors to our kids." Everyone agreed that Elders should be directly involved in the educational system, but they recognized the issues around funding, certification, and licensing, especially because they are largely controlled by INAC. "First Nations are involved in a continual exercise of going cap-in-hand to the federal government, but the economies of scale are such that few succeed" (Goddard, 2002, p. 165). The only way that full-time Elders can be hired is by using band-generated revenue, and, unfortunately, for most communities there is no economic base to support this. Nevertheless, all of the participants agreed that Elders are needed in the school system if the emotional, mental, and emotional needs of our children are going to be met. Suzanne cautioned, "The problems in our community have become too great, and we can't expect teachers to be everything to the kids any more. We need the Elders to come in and help." Deloria (2001) agreed:

[Elders] are the best living examples of what the end product of education and life experiences should be. We sometimes forget that life is exceedingly hard and that none of us accomplishes everything we could possibly do, or even many of the things we intended to do. The elder exemplifies both the good and the bad experiences of life, and in witnessing their failures as much as their successes we are cushioned in our despair of disappointment and bolstered in our exuberance of success. (p. 45)

9. We need to have a spiritual focus. "The Western secular system of education appears to be blind to the spirituality that infuses or underlies Aboriginal epistemology and thus culturally appropriate education for Aboriginal students" (Curwen Doige, 2003, p. 144). The participants wanted a school where the spiritual relationships, the interconnectedness of all things would be the primary focus. They wanted a place where their children would be free to pray every morning. Pamela thought that

the ideal school would need some foundation of spirituality. When the grounding is there, children will thrive. For sure you need a school that has morals and values taught, and this could only be effectively taught if children have spiritual foundation.

When the participants spoke of spirituality, I understood them to be referring to, as Curwen Doige identified it, the "immaterial aspect of one's personhood that connects with otherness, including for some a life force or immanence, especially the Creator, or God" (p. 144). They talked of spirituality as the "heart of values and morals and at the heart of education for Aboriginal students" (p. 149). Akan (1999) warned that

> to suffer from . . . spiritual poverty will invariably affect other areas of life that will prevent one from being functional. Not to have a solid spiritual foundation is not to have a good mind. Youth need to hear about their stories and myths, and the experiences of Elders and parents; and to learn about the importance of ceremony and ritual in life. (p. 214)

Conclusion

I have seen through this work that First Nations parents have had no opportunity for real school choice. Although for different reasons, both off-reserve and on-reserve school systems have failed and continue to fail their children. But I have also seen further, in that I have realized more deeply through this work and through the words of the parents that they have always held firmly to the ancient values and ways of being that have sustained them for thousands of years and that are reflected in the foregoing descriptions of their ideal school. Parental school choice for them is one small and very recent phenomenon in an ancient world of ancient knowledge and ancient being.

I leave this work with renewed hope and understanding that the ways of the spirit will not be destroyed and that the school that the participants have envisioned as ideal is based on exactly that spirit. School choice is a concept and practice that is based upon and derived from a Western system of schooling and thought. Issues around school choice will not be resolved except from within that system, and these First Nations parents were not speaking from the perspective of that system in their analyses and responses because they are not immersed and living within it. They spoke from the point of view of a more ancient system of knowledge and being and struggled to articulate their thinking on an issue that is not really their issue. In having moved the focus for the participants and the reader to a vision of the ideal school, I have stepped outside of the school choice question and outside of its particular context of thought. To do so, I believe, has offered perhaps the only possibility for these First Nations parents to begin to address the larger issues of schooling that have been shrouded under a superficial form of school choice.

It was my intention that the foregoing section on the ideal school would help us all to step outside of the standard or mainstream notion of school choice and to see more deeply into the larger issues that First Nations parents must face in making school choices for their children. In this study we have seen that school choice for First Nations parents who live on reserves is not about alternative philosophies, programs, and pedagogies that offer academic success equally; it is about one system of education that offers minimal academic success in two different environments. The parents in this case must make choices with the survival of their children in mind as members of a people, and they must make these decisions from within the context and social realities of contemporary Indian reserve life. I am honored with the trust that my own people and I have shared, and I am deeply grateful for the many teachings that were given to me this through this research.

In honor of my father and to appropriately bring closure to my own journey through this dissertation, I would like to share a letter that I wrote to my father the day that I finished writing this last chapter.

August 13, 2007

Dear Dad,

It will be 35 years on August 16, 2007, since you left us to return to our Heavenly Father, and yet today it seems like it was only yesterday. As the tears stream down my face, I feel like I am 12 years old again, crying because I realize you will not be coming home. We will not see you again until our time comes. . . .

Dad, today, I finished writing the final chapter of my doctoral dissertation! Although I should be feeling ecstatic about it, I feel an overwhelming sadness instead, not because I will miss the writing, but because I will miss you. I realized today just how big a role you played in this study. You were with me in my mind and in my heart throughout the writing process, and writing the final chapter feels as though I am closing a chapter in my own life.

My study was about parental school choice in First Nations communities. I wanted to know why First Nations parents living on a reserve chose the schools that they did when they had the option of choosing between on-reserve and off-reserve schools. Dad, I think I chose to study this topic because I needed to know why you made the decision to school us, your own children, off-reserve. For years, this question had plagued me.

I don't know if you know this, but going to school off-reserve was very difficult for me, to say the least. It was hard to be an "Indian" in that school. Children made fun of Indians all the time, so it didn't take long for me to conclude that being Indian wasn't worth much. Sometimes they would call me "squaw" or dance little "TV Indian" dances around me. They must have hated me. Did you know that, Dad? Did you know that I started hating being Indian from the first day I set foot in that school? Did you know that so many times during those years I wished I could be invisible, just so my peers wouldn't see the little Indian girl that they obviously didn't like very much?

But you know what, Dad? I did make it through school. Despite the fact that my self-esteem had dwindled to almost nil, I managed to graduate with my peers. I don't know how I did it, but I did. I was fortunate, Dad, because many of my Native peers had dropped out of school by that time, probably because they couldn't handle the racism and unfair treatment. Perhaps it was your words "Getting an education is important" that kept me in school.

I used to resent you sometimes for putting me through all that pain, but I don't feel that way any more. I understand now that the school-choice decision you made for us was made out of love. Like the parents who participated in this study, you knew that without an education, your children would struggle to survive. Today, I can honestly say I am grateful for having had the experiences, because I think it made me a stronger person. Because of my own experiences, I am better able to understand the many struggles that Aboriginal parents and students are confronted with on a daily basis. Without my public school experiences, I may not have ever had the desire to pursue graduate studies. I believe that your decision to send me off-reserve thus led me down the path of academia.

I learned from an Elder recently that in the 1960s you used to talk a lot about the concerns you had about the curriculum and the schooling system of those days, and he mentioned that you were often worried that the needs of the Native children were not being met. I didn't know that about you, but learning that has brought me closer to you. You used to say that, even before we were born, the Lord had plans for us. I believe that He knew, even before your passing, that I would continue the work that you had started. I hope I have made you proud, Dad, and I think I understand now why educating your children was so important to you.

At the beginning of my study I mentioned Henry Bird Steinhauer, for no other reason than to help explain my genealogy, but now as I think about it, I think I did it because you used to do the same, Dad, when you were sharing your ancestry with new acquaintances. Why does Henry Bird Steinhauer play such a significant role in our families and communities? To answer the question for myself, I think Henry Bird Steinhauer is significant to me because of his accomplishments. Despite the fact that he obviously had many obstacles to overcome as he went through the "Whiteman's" schooling system, he did it, and he never lost sight of who he was. He remained true to himself, to his people, and to his calling until the day he died—something you wanted for your own children as well.

Education was important to this man, just as it was so important to you, Dad. Doing this study and hearing the optimism in the voices of the participants have given me a renewed sense of hope. I feel better prepared to be of assistance to our people, and I want to thank you for helping me to get here.

Until we meet again, Dad, I love you.

Your daughter,

Evelyn

REFERENCES

Abele, F., Dittburner, C., & Graham, K. (2000). Towards a shared understanding in the policy discussions about Aboriginal education. In M. Brant Castellano, L. Davis, & L. Lahache (Eds.), *Aboriginal education: Fulfilling the promise* (pp. 3-4). Vancouver, BC: UBC Press.

Absolon, K., & Willett C. (2005). Putting ourselves forward: Location in Aboriginal research. In L. Brown & S. Strega (Eds.), *Researcher as resistance: Critical Indigenous and anti-oppressive approaches* (pp. 255-286). Toronto, ON: Canadian Scholars' Press.

Akan, L. (1999). *Pimosatamowin Sikaw Kakeequauwin*: Walking and talking: A Saulteaux Elder's view of Native education. *Canadian Journal of Native Education, 23,* 16-39.

Alberta Education. (2005). *Our words, our ways: Teaching First Nations, Métis, and Inuit learners.* Edmonton, AB: Author.

Alberta Learning. (2002). *First Nations, Métis, and Inuit policy education policy framework.* Edmonton, AB: Author.

Alberta Sweetgrass. (2002). *Top news: December 2002.* Retrieved January 13, 2007, from http://www.ammsa.com/sweetgrass/topnews-Dec-2002.html

Alberta's Commission on Learning. (2006). *Every child learns, every child succeeds: Report and recommendations, Alberta's Commission on Learning.* Retrieved July 16, 2007, from http://www.education.gov.ab.ca/commission/report.asp

Alfred, T. (1999). *Peace, power, righteousness: An Indigenous manifesto.* Don Mills, ON: Oxford University Press.

Ascher, C. (1988). *Improving the school-home connection for low-income urban parents.* New York: ERIC Clearinghouse on Urban Education.

Assembly of First Nations. (1994). *Breaking the silence: An interpretive study of residential school impact and healing as illustrated by the stories of First Nations individuals.* Ottawa, ON: First Nations Health Secretariat.

ATSIC. (2000). *Submission to the House of Representatives Standing Committee into the needs of urban dwelling Aboriginal and Torres Strait islander peoples.* Canberra, Australia: Commonwealth of Australia.

Auger, S. T. (2006). *Visions of Aboriginal education.* Unpublished master's thesis, University of Alberta, Edmonton, AB.

Baker, C. (2003). Education in small, remote and northern communities: Challenges to meet. *Education Canada, 43*(3), 13-14.

Balan, J. (1984). *Salt and braided bread: Ukrainian life in Canada.* Toronto, ON: Oxford University Press.

Barman, J., Hebert, Y., & McCaskill, D. (1987). The challenge of Indian education: An overview. In J. Barman, Y. Hebert, & D. McCaskill (Eds.), *Indian education in Canada: Vol. 2. The challenge* (pp. 1-21). Vancouver, BC: UBC Press.

Battiste, M. (1995). Introduction. In M. Battiste & J. Barman (Eds.), *The circle unfolds* (pp. i-xx). Vancouver, BC: UBC Press

Battiste, M. (2000). Maintaining Aboriginal identity, language, and culture in modern society. In M. Battiste (Ed.), *Reclaiming Indigenous voice and vision* (pp. 192-208). Vancouver, BC: UBC Press.

Battiste, M. (2002). *Indigenous knowledge and pedagogy in First Nations education: A literature review with recommendations.* Ottawa, ON: Department of Indian and Northern Affairs Canada.

Battiste M., & Henderson, J. Y. (Eds.). (2000). *Protecting Indigenous knowledge and heritage: A global challenge.* Saskatoon, SK: Purich.

Bazylak, D. (2002). Journeys to success: Perceptions of five female Aboriginal high school graduates. *Canadian Journal of Native Education, 26,* 134-150.

Berger, T. (1991). *A long and terrible shadow: White values, Native rights in the Americas.* Vancouver, BC: Douglas & McIntyre.

Binda, K., & Calliou, S. (2001). *Aboriginal education in Canada: A study in decolonization.* Mississauga, ON: Canadian Education Press.

Bivens, D. (1995). *Internalized racism: A definition.* Retrieved May 23, 2007, from http://www.thewtc.org/Internalized_Racism.pdf

Brady, P. (1995). Two policy approaches to Native education: Can reform be legislated? *Canadian Journal of Education, 20,* 349-366.

Breaker, R., & Kawaguchi, B. (2002). *Infrastructure and funding in First Nations education: Education renewal initiative* [Policy paper presented to the Minister of Indian and Northern Development]. Ottawa, ON: Author.

Breen, G. (2003). *Academic school performance of Native reserve students.* Unpublished doctoral thesis, University of Alberta, Edmonton, AB.

Britannica Online. (2007). *Egerton Ryerson.* Retrieved April 12, 2007, from http://www.britannica.com/eb/article-9064557

Bruno, S. (2003). *Aboriginal women: Journey towards a doctorate.* Unpublished master's thesis, University of Alberta, Edmonton, AB.

Buckley, H. (1992). *From wooden ploughs to welfare: Why Indian policy failed in the prairie provinces.* Montreal, QC: McGill-Queen's University Press.

Bull, L. (1991). Indian residential schooling: The Native perspective. *Canadian Journal of Native Education, 18,* 3-63.

Cajete, G. (2000a). Indigenous knowledge: The Pueblo metaphor of Indigenous education. In M. Battiste (Ed.), *Reclaiming Indigenous voice and vision* (pp. 181-191). Vancouver, BC: UBC Press.

Cajete, G. (2000b). *Native science: Natural laws of interdependence.* Santa Fe, NM: Clear Light.

Calliou, S. (1995). Peacekeeping actions at home: A medicine wheel model from a peacekeeping pedagogy. In M. Battiste & J. Barman (Eds.), *First Nations education in Canada: The circle unfolds* (pp. 47-72). Vancouver, BC: UBC Press.

Canadian Race Relations Foundation. (2007). *Combatting racism in Canadian schools.* Retrieved March 22, 2007, from http://www.crr.ca/Load.do?section=4&subSection=10&id=190&type=2

Cardinal, L. (2001). What is an Indigenous perspective? *Canadian Journal of Native Education, 25,* 180-182.

Castellano, M. B. (2000). Updating Aboriginal traditions of knowledge. In G. Sefa Dei, B. Hall, & D. Goldin Rosenberg (Eds.), *Indigenous knowledge in global contexts: Multiple reading of our world.* Toronto, ON: University of Toronto Press.

Castellano, M. B., Davis, L., & Lahache, L. (2000). Conclusion: Fulfilling the promise. In M. B. Castellano, L. Davis, & L. Lahache (Eds.), *Aboriginal education: Fulfilling the promise* (pp. 251-255). Vancouver, BC: UBC Press.

Chisan, S. (2001). *First Nations traditional teaching: Informing effective instructor/learner relationships in First Nations college environment.* Unpublished master's thesis, University of San Diego, San Diego, CA.

Chrisjohn, R., & Young, S. (1997). *The circle game: Shadows of substance in the Indian residential school experience in Canada*. Penticton, BC: Theytus Books.
Cohen, B. (2001). The spider's web: Creativity and survival in dynamic balance. *Canadian Journal of Native Education, 25*, 140-148.
Cowley, P. (2004). The good school. *Education Canada, 44*(3), 10-12.
Curwen Doige, L. (2003). A missing link: Between traditional Aboriginal education and the Western system of education. *Canadian Journal of Native Education, 27*, 144-160.
Daes, E. (2000). Prologue: The experience of colonization around the world. In M. Battiste (Ed.), *Reclaiming Indigenous voice and vision* (pp. 3-8). Vancouver, BC: UBC Press.
Deloria, V. (2001). Knowing and understanding. In V. Deloria, Jr., & R. Wildcat (Eds.), *Power and place: Indian education in America* (pp. 41-46). Golden, CO: Fulcrum Resources.
Denzin, N. K. & Lincoln, Y. S. (2000). The discipline and practice of qualitative research. In N. K. Denzin & Y. S. Lincoln (Eds.), *Handbook of qualitative research* (2nd ed., pp. 1-28). Thousand Oaks, CA: Sage.
Diamond, B. (1989). *The Cree experience*. In J. Barman, Y. Hebert, & D. McCaskill (Eds.), *Indian education in Canada: Vol. 2. The challenge* (pp. 86-106). Vancouver, BC: UBC Press.
Douglas, V. (1987). The education of urban Native children: The sacred circle project. In J. Barman, Y. Hebert, & D. McCaskill (Eds.), *Indian education in Canada: Vol. 2. The challenge* (pp. 1-13). Vancouver, BC: UBC Press.
Duran, B., & Duran, E. (2000). Applied postcolonial clinical and research strategies. In M. Battiste (Ed.), *Reclaiming Indigenous voice and vision* (pp. 86-100). Vancouver, BC: UBC Press.
Ellis, J. (1998). Introduction: The teacher as interpretive inquirer. In J. Ellis (Ed.), *Teaching for understanding: Teacher as interpretive inquirer* (pp. 5-13). New York: Garland.
Ermine, W. (1995). Aboriginal epistemology. In M. Battiste & J. Barman. (Eds.), *First Nations education in Canada: The circle unfolds* (pp. 101-112). Vancouver, BC: UBC Press.
Fettes, M., & Norton, R. (2000). Voices of winter: Aboriginal languages and public policy in Canada. In M. Brant Castellano, L. Davis, L., & L. Lahache (Eds.), *Aboriginal education: Fulfilling the promise* (pp. 29-54). Vancouver, BC: UBC Press.
Frideres, J. S. (1997). *Native peoples in Canada contemporary conflicts* (3rd ed.). Scarborough, ON: Prentice-Hall Canada.
Friedel, T. (1999). The role of Aboriginal parents in public education: Barriers to change in an urban setting. *Canadian Journal of Native Education, 23*, 139-158.
Friere, P. (2001). *Pedagogy of the oppressed: 30th anniversary edition*. New York: Continuum International.
Froese-Germain, B. (1998). What we know about school choice. *Education Canada, 38*(3), 22-25.
Goddard, T. (1993). Band controlled schools: Considerations for the future. *Canadian Journal of Nation Education, 20*, 163-167.
Goddard, T. (2002). Ethnoculturally relevant programming in northern schools. *Canadian Journal of Native Education, 26*(2),124-133.
Goulet, G. (2001). Two teachers of Aboriginal students: Effective practice in sociohistorical realities. *Canadian Journal of Native Education, 25*, 68-82.
Grant, A. (1995). The challenge for universities. In M. Battiste & J. Barman (Eds.), *The circle unfolds* (pp. 208-223). Vancouver, BC: UBC Press.

Graveline, F. J. (1998). *Circle works: Transforming Eurocentric consciousness.* Halifax, NS: Fernwood.
Haig-Brown, C. (1995). Taking control: Power and contradiction in First Nations adult education. In M. Battiste & J. Barman (Eds.), *The circle unfolds* (pp. 262-287). Vancouver, BC: UBC Press.
Hampton, E. (1993). Toward a redefinition of American Indian/Alaska Native education. *Canadian Journal of Native Education. 20*, 261-310.
Hampton, E. (1995). Towards a redefinition of Indian education. In M. Battiste & J. Barman (Eds.), *The circle unfolds* (pp. 262-287). Vancouver, BC: UBC Press.
Hanohano, P. (2001). *Restoring the sacred circle.* Unpublished doctoral dissertation, University of Alberta, Edmonton, AB.
Hawthorn, H. B. (Ed.). (1966-1967). *A survey of the contemporary Indians of Canada: A report on economic, political, educational needs and policies* (2 vols.). Ottawa, ON: Department of Indian Affairs and Northern Development.
Henderson, J. Y. (2000). Ayukpachi: Empowering Aboriginal thought. In M. Battiste (Ed.), *Reclaiming Indigenous voice and vision* (pp. 248-278). Vancouver, BC: UBC Press.
Hookimaw-Witt, J. (1998). Any changes since residential school? *The Canadian Journal of Native Education, 22*, 159-170.
Hoxby, C. (2001). Analyzing school choice reforms that use America's traditional forms of parental choice. In C. Hepburn (Ed.), *Can the market save our schools?* (pp. 75-99). Vancouver, BC: Fraser Institute.
Hurton, G. (2002). *A review of First Nation special education policies and funding directions within the Canadian context* [Policy paper presented to the Minister of Indian and Northern Development]. Ottawa, ON: Author.
Indian and Northern Affairs Canada. (2005). *Definitions.* Retrieved November 30, 2006, from http://www.ainc-inac.gc.ca/ps/mnl/alp/dfn_e.html
Indian and Northern Affairs Canada. (2006). *First Nations profiles.* Retrieved June 27, 2006, from http://sdiprod2.inac.gc/ca/FNProfiles_DETAILS.asp?BAND_NUMBER=462
Indian and Northern Affairs Canada. (2007). *Definitions.* Retrieved March 22, 2007, from http://www.ainc-inac.gc.ca/ps/mnl/alp/dfn_e.html
Indian Chiefs of Alberta. (1970). *Citizens plus: A presentation by the Indian Chiefs of Alberta to the Right Honorable P. E. Trudeau, Prime Minister, and the government of Canada.* Edmonton, AB: Indian Association of Alberta.
Ing, R. (1991). The effects of residential schools on Native child-rearing practices. *Canadian Journal of Native Education, 18*, 67-116.
Inger, M. (1992). *Increasing the school involvement in home literacy.* New York: ERIC Clearinghouse on Urban Education.
Jules, F. (1999). Native Indian leadership. *Canadian Journal of Native Education, 23*, 16-39.
Kavanagh, B. (2002). *The role of parental and community involvement in the success of First Nations learners: A review of the literature* [Policy paper presented to the Minister of Indian and Northern Development]. Ottawa, ON: Author.
King, T. (2003). *The truth about stories: A Native narrative.* Toronto, ON: House of Anansi Press.
Kirkness, V. (1998). Our peoples' education: Cut the shackles; cut the crap; cut the mustard. *Canadian Journal of Native Education, 22*, 10-15.

Kirkness, V. (1999). Aboriginal education in Canada: A retrospective and a prospective. *Journal of American Indian Education, 39,* 14-30.

Kirkness, V., & Bowman, S. (1992). *First Nations and schools: Triumphs and struggles.* Toronto, ON: Canadian Educational Association.

Kluczny, H. (1998). *The call to become an educator.* Unpublished doctoral candidacy proposal, University of Alberta, Edmonton, AB.

Kovach, M. (2005). Emerging from the margins: Indigenous methodologies. In L. Brown & S. Strega (Eds.), *Research as resistance: Critical, Indigenous, and anti-oppressive approaches* (pp. 255-286). Toronto, ON: Canadian Scholars' Press.

Lafrance, J. (2001). *Residential schools and Aboriginal parenting: Voices of parents.* Unpublished document, University of Calgary.

Lightning, W. (1992). Compassionate mind: Implications of a text written by Elder Louis Sunchild. *Canadian Journal of Native Education, 19,* 215-253.

Mackay, R., & Myles, L. (1989). *Native student dropouts in Ontario schools.* Toronto, ON: Queen's Printer for Ontario.

MacKay, R., & Myles, L. (1995). A major challenge for the education system: Aboriginal retention and dropout. In M. Battiste & J. Barman. (Eds.), *First Nations education in Canada: The circle unfolds* (pp. 157-178). Vancouver, BC: UBC Press.

Makokis, L. (2001). *Teachings from Cree Elders: A grounded theory study of Indigenous leadership.* Unpublished doctoral dissertation, University of San Diego, San Diego, CA.

Makokis, P. (2000). *An insider's perspective: The dropout challenge for Canada's First Nations.* Unpublished doctoral dissertation, University of San Diego, San Diego, CA.

Marshall, J. (2001). *The Lakota way: Stories and lessons for living.* New York: Penguin Group.

Martin, K. (2002). *Ways of knowing, ways of being, and ways of doing: Developing a theoretical framework and methods for Indigenous re-search and Indigenist research.* Unpublished manuscript.

McCaskill, D. (1987). Revitalization of Indian cultural survival schools. In J. Barman, Y. Hebert, & D. McCaskill (Eds.), *Indian education in Canada: Vol. 2. The challenge* (pp. 153-179). Vancouver, BC: UBC Press.

McInerney, D., McInerney, V., Ardington, A., & De Rachewiltz, C. (1997, March). *School success in cultural context: Conversations at Window Rock.* Paper presented at the annual meeting of the American Research Association, Chicago.

Melnechenko, L., & Horsman, H. (1998). *Factors that contribute to Aboriginal students' success in school in grades six to nine.* Regina, SK: Saskatchewan Education.

Meyer, M. (1998). *Native Hawaiian epistemology: Contemporary narratives.* Unpublished doctoral dissertation, Harvard University, Cambridge, MA.

Meyers Norris Penny LLP. (2006). *Saddle Lake Cree nation economic development strategic plan (2005 to 2030).* Unpublished manuscript.

Mihesuah, D. (1996). *American Indians: Stereotypes and realities.* Atlanta, GA: Clarity Press.

Miller, J. (1989). *Skyscrapers hide the heavens: A history of Indian-white relations in Canada.* Toronto, ON: University of Toronto Press.

Minister of Public Works and Government Services Canada. (2000). *Report of the Auditor General of Canada to the House of Commons: Chap. 4. Indian and Northern Affairs Canada: Elementary and secondary education.* Ottawa, ON: Author.

Morefield, J. (1996). *Recreating schools for all children.* Retrieved May 10, 2007, from http://www.newhorizons.org/trans/morefield.htm

Morgan, N. (2002). *If not now, then when? First Nations jurisdiction over education: A literature review* [Policy paper presented to the Minister of Indian and Northern Development]. Ottawa: Author.

Morrisseau, C. (1998). *Into the daylight: A wholistic approach to healing.* Toronto: ON: University of Toronto Press.

National Indian Brotherhood. (1972). *Indian control of Indian education* [Policy paper presented to the Minister of Indian and Northern Development]. Ottawa: Assembly of First Nations.

Pepler, D., Craig, W., Ziegler, S., & Charach, A. (1994). An evaluation of the anti-bullying intervention in Toronto schools. *Canadian Journal of Community Mental Health, 13*, 95-110.

Persson, D. (1986). The changing experience of Indian residential schooling: Blue Quills, 1931-1970. In J. Barman, D. McCaskill, & Y. Hebert (Eds.). *Indian education in Canada. Vol. 1. The legacy* (pp. 151-168). Vancouver, BC: UBC Press.

Potts, K., & Brown, L. (2005). Becoming an anti-oppressive researcher. In L. Brown & S. Strega (Eds.), *Research as resistance: Critical, Indigenous and anti-oppressive approaches* (pp. 255-286). Toronto, ON: Canadian Scholars' Press.

Rogers, B. (2001). A path of healing and wellness for Native families. *American Behavioral Scientist, 4*, 1512-1514.

Royal Commission on Aboriginal Peoples. (1996). *Residential schools (Vol. 10).* Ottawa, ON: Canada Communication Group.

Ryerson, E. (2007). *Egerton Ryerson.* Retrieved April 12, 2007, from http://www.britannica.com/eb/article-9064557

Saddle Lake Cree Nation. (2007). *Programs and services: Education authority: Primary and secondary schools.* Retrieved June 4, 2007, from http://www.saddlelake.ca/saddlelake1.html

Sefa Dei, G., Hall, B., & Goldin Rosenberg, D. (2000). Introduction. In G. Sefa Dei, B. Hall, & D. Goldin Rosenberg (Eds.), *Indigenous knowledge in global contexts: Multiple reading of our world* (pp. 3-17). Toronto, ON: University of Toronto Press.

Silver, J., Mallett, K., Greene, J., & Simard, F. (2002). *Aboriginal education in Winnipeg inner city high schools.* Winnipeg, MB: Canadian Centre for Policy Alternatives.

Sixkiller Clarke, A. (1994). *OERI Native American Youth at Risk Study.* Boseman, MT: Montana State University. (ERIC Document Reproduction Service No. ED373951)

Smith, L. (1999). *Decolonizing methodologies: Research and Indigenous peoples* London: Zed Books.

Snow, J. (1977). *These mountains are our sacred places.* Toronto, ON: Samuel Stevens.

St. Denis, V., Bouvier, R., & Battiste, M. (1998). *Okiskinahanmakewak: Aboriginal teachers in Saskatchewan's publicly funded schools: Responding to the flux.* Regina, SK: Saskatchewan Learning, Saskatchewan Education Research Networking Project.

St. Denis, V., & Hampton, E. (2002). *Literature review on racism and the effects on Aboriginal education* [Prepared for Minister's National Working Group on Education]. Ottawa, ON: Indian and Northern Affairs Canada.

Statistics Canada. (2001a). *2001 Alberta people's survey: Education and learning among Aboriginal children.* Retrieved November 15, 2003, from http://www.statcan.ca/english/freepub/89-597-XIE/2001001/education.htm

Statistics Canada. (2001b). *2001 census: Canada.* Retrieved November 13, 2006, from http://www12.statcan.ca/english/census01/products/analytic/companion/educ/canada.cfm

Stein, J. (2002). Choice and public education: A core civic challenge. *Education Canada, 42*(3), 4-7.

Steinhauer, E. (2002). Thoughts on an Indigenous research Methodology. *Canadian Journal of Native Education, 26*(2), 69-81.

Steinhauer, M. (2003). *The life of Henry Bird Steinhauer.* Unpublished manuscript.

Steinhauer, N. (1999). *Sohkastwawak, they are resilient: First Nations students and achievement.* Unpublished master's thesis, University of Alberta, Edmonton, AB.

Steinhauer, N. (2007). *Nâtwahtâw: Looking for a Cree model of education.* Unpublished doctoral thesis, University of Alberta, Edmonton, AB.

Steinhauer, P. (2001). *Finding a path to the Cree way.* Unpublished doctoral candidacy proposal, University of Alberta, Edmonton, AB.

Steinhauer, S. (2004). *The art of making candy out of fecal matter.* Unpublished document.

Strega, S. (2005). The view from the poststructural margins: Epistemology and methodology reconsidered. In L. Brown & S. Strega (Eds.), *Research as resistance: Critical, Indigenous, and anti-oppressive approaches* (pp. 199-236). Toronto, ON: Canadian Scholars' Press.

Tafoya, T. (1995). Finding harmony: Balancing traditional values with Western science in therapy. *Canadian Journal of Native Education, 21,* 55-60.

Taylor, A., & Woollard, L. (2003). The risky business of choosing a high school. *Journal of Education Policy, 18,* 617-635.

Taylor, J. (1995). Non-Native teachers teaching in Native communities. In M. Battiste & J. Barman. (Eds.), *First Nations education in Canada: The circle unfolds* (pp. 224-242). Vancouver, BC: UBC Press.

Tessier, D. (2003). *Developing a process for evaluation education.* Unpublished doctoral dissertation, University of Alberta, Edmonton, AB.

Titley, B. (1980). The education of the Canadian Indian: The struggle for local control. *Journal of American Indian Education, 20,* 18-24.

Tomlinson, S. (1997). Diversity, choice, and ethnicity: The effects of educational markets on ethnic minorities. *Oxford Review of Education, 23,* 1-13.

Ungerleider, C. (2004). Changing expectation, changing schools: The evolving concept of a good school. *Education Canada, 44,* 18-21.

United to End Racism Group. (2001). *Internalized racism.* Retrieved, May 16, 2007, from http://www.rc.org/uer/InternalizedRacism.html

Watt-Cloutier, S. (2000). Honouring our past, creating our future: Education in Northern and remote communities. In M. Brant Castellano, L. Davis, & L. Lahache (Eds.), *Aboriginal education: Fulfilling the promise* (pp. 114-128). Vancouver, BC: UBC Press.

Weber-Pillwax, C. (1999). Indigenous research methodology: Exploratory discussion of an elusive subject. *Journal of Educational Thought, 33,* 31-45.

Weber-Pillwax, C. (2001a). Coming to an understanding: A panel presentation: What is Indigenous research? *Canadian Journal of Native Education, 25,* 166-174.

Weber-Pillwax, C. (2001b). Orality in northern Cree Indigenous worlds. *Canadian Journal of Native Education, 25,* 149-165.

Weber-Pillwax, C. (2003). *Indigenous researchers and Indigenous research methods: Cultural determinants of research methods.* Unpublished manuscript.

Wells, A., & Crain, R. (1992). Do parents choose school quality or school status? A sociological theory of free market education. In P. Cookson, Jr. (Ed.), *The choice controversy* (pp. 65-99). Newbury Park, CA: Corwin Press.

Wijeyesinghe, C. L., Griffin, P., & Love, B. (1997). Racism curriculum design. In M. Adams, L. A. Bell, & P. Griffin (Eds.), *Teaching for diversity and social justice: A sourcebook* (pp. 82-109). New York: Routledge.

Wikipedia. (2007). *Cultural identity*. Retrieved May 23, 2007, from http://en.wikipedia.org/wiki/Cultural_identity

Wildcat, D. (2001). Understanding the crisis. In V. Deloria, Jr. & R. Wildcat (Eds.), *Power and place: Indian education in America* (pp. 30-44). Golden, CO: Fulcrum Resources.

Williams, L. (2000). Urban Aboriginal experience: The Vancouver experience. In M. B. Castellano, L. Davis, & L. Lahache (Eds.), *In Aboriginal education: Fulfilling the promise* (129-146). Vancouver, BC: UBC Press.

Williams, L. B., & Wyatt, J. (1987). Training Indian teachers in a community setting: The Mount Currie Lil'wat Programme. In J. Barman, Y. Hebert, & D. McCaskill (Eds.), *Indian education in Canada: Vol. 2. The challenge* (pp. 210-227). Vancouver, BC: UBC Press.

Wilson, P. (1992). Trauma in transition. *Canadian Journal of Native Education, 19*, 46-56.

Wilson, P., & Wilson S. (2002). Editorial: First Nations education in mainstream systems. *Canadian Journal of Native Education, 26*, 67-68.

Wilson, S. (1995). Honoring spiritual knowledge. *Canadian Journal of Native Education, 21*, 6-69.

Wilson, S. (2001). What is an Indigenous research methodology? *Canadian Journal of Native Education, 25*, 175-179.

Wilson, S. (2003). *Research is a ceremony: Articulating an Indigenous research paradigm.* Unpublished doctoral dissertation, Monash University, Victoria, Australia.

Wilson, S., & Wilson, P. (1999). Taking responsibility: What follows relational accountability? *Canadian Journal of Native Education, 23*, 137-138.

Wotherspoon, T., & Satzewich, V. (2000). *First Nations: Race, class, and gender relations.* Saskatoon, SK: Houghton Boston Press.

APPENDIX:
PARTICIPANTS' RECOMMENDATIONS FOR THE IDEAL SCHOOL

The following recommendations are based on the discussion on ideal schools:

1. That a recommendation be made to the Chief and Council of both Saddle Lake and Goodfish Lake communities that they support the creation of the ideal school for our children and that this work be left in the hands of the school administration and the Board of Education.

2. That a purpose and a vision statement be developed that includes a clearly articulated set of core values to serve as the foundation for decision-making on behalf of the children who attend these schools.

3. That educators and community members model behaviors that honor and respect children as needing love, affection, and affirmation in every aspect of their schooling.

4. That everyone, including Elders, parents, teachers, administrators and community members, be involved in the process of creating safe and comfortable schools for their children.

5. That a clear, culturally appropriate structure of discipline be developed and implemented immediately, in order for all children to feel safe and secure.

6. That academic standards and rigor, including teacher and parental expectations, be raised and maintained so that our children are challenged, encouraged and continuously validated towards their own success in school.

7. That preference in recruitment and hiring be given to Aboriginal teachers for our First Nations schools.

8. That school programs and curricula, as well as teaching styles and pedagogies, be holistic and culturally relevant to our First Nations students.

9. That bridges are built amongst schools, parents and community to ensure total and essential involvement in the education of all children.

10. That Elders be utilized to support our students in meaningful ways on a full-time basis in our schools, and that we find the resources to make this happen.

11. That the spiritual needs of our children be recognized as the basis of their identity development and that spirituality be incorporated into schools as essential for culturally appropriate education.